# WILSON
## AND
# CHINA

# WILSON AND CHINA

## A REVISED HISTORY OF THE SHANDONG QUESTION

Bruce A. Elleman

M.E. Sharpe
Armonk, New York
London, England

Copyright © 2002 by M. E. Sharpe, Inc.

All rights reserved. No part of this book may be reproduced in any form without written permission from the publisher, M. E. Sharpe, Inc., 80 Business Park Drive, Armonk, New York 10504.

**Library of Congress Cataloging-in-Publication Data**

Elleman, Bruce A., 1959–
    Wilson and China : a revised history of the Shandong question / by Bruce A. Elleman.
    p. cm.
    Includes bibliographical references and index.
    ISBN 0-7656-1050-7 (alk. paper)
    1. China—Foreign relations—Japan. 2. Japan—Foreign relations—China.
3. China—Foreign relations—1912–1949. 4. Shandong Sheng (China)—History.
I. Title: Revised history of the Shandong question. II. Title.

DS740.5.J3 E44 2002
327.51052–dc21

                                                           2002024699


Printed in the United States of America

The paper used in this publication meets the minimum requirements of
American National Standard for Information Sciences
Permanence of Paper for Printed Library Materials,
ANSI Z 39.48-1984.

BM (c)   10   9   8   7   6   5   4   3   2   1

To S.C.M. Paine

# Contents

| | |
|---|---|
| List of Maps | x |
| List of Documents | xi |
| Acknowledgments | xiii |
| Technical Note | xv |
| List of Abbreviations | xvii |

| | |
|---|---|
| **Introduction** | 1 |
| | |
| **1. The Diplomatic Situation Prior to the Paris Peace Conference** | 7 |
| The German Diplomatic Position in Shandong | 8 |
| Japan Declares War on Germany | 11 |
| Strategic and Military Importance of the Shandong Concession | 13 |
| Foreign Policy Issues Regarding the Shandong Concession | 14 |
| Japan Presents the Twenty-one Demands | 15 |
| The Japanese Ultimatum | 18 |
| China Joins the War Against Germany | 21 |
| The 1918 Secret Sino-Japanese Agreements | 24 |
| Conclusions | 27 |
| Notes | 29 |
| | |
| **2. The Chinese Delegation's Proposals to the Paris Peace Conference** | 33 |
| The Members of the Chinese Delegation | 34 |
| Wellington Koo and President Woodrow Wilson | 36 |
| The Chinese Delegation's Proposals to Paris | 39 |
| Wellington Koo and the Shandong Question | 41 |
| The Chinese Delegation's March and April Declarations | 44 |
| Direct or Indirect Restitution of Shandong | 46 |
| Conclusions | 49 |
| Notes | 50 |
| | |
| **3. The Japanese Delegation's Proposals to the Paris Peace Conference** | 53 |
| The Japanese Delegation and its Proposals | 54 |
| The American Delegation's Opening Position on Shandong | 56 |
| Who Wanted the Secret Agreements Kept Secret? | 60 |
| The Impact of the Secret Agreements on America's Proposals | 64 |
| The Japanese Delegation's April 1919 Proposals | 66 |
| Conclusions | 69 |
| Notes | 70 |

### 4. President Wilson's Compromise Proposal — 73
- The American Delegation and its Proposals — 75
- The Big Three's Negotiations with the Chinese Delegation — 77
- The Big Three's Negotiations with the Japanese Delegation — 80
- Wilson's Rationale Behind this Compromise Solution — 84
- The Impact of Wilson's Compromise — 86
- Conclusions — 89
- Notes — 90

### 5. The Myth of Woodrow Wilson's Betrayal — 93
- The Importance of "Face" in China — 94
- The Chinese Diplomatic Reaction to the Shandong Resolutions — 97
- The Japanese Diplomatic Reaction to the Shandong Resolutions — 98
- The Shandong Resolutions, the May Fourth Movement, and Wilson — 103
- Liang Qichao's Interpretation of the Shandong Resolutions — 105
- Conclusions — 107
- Notes — 108

### 6. Wilson's Failed Attempts to Secure a Japanese Statement of Intent — 111
- America Decides to Obtain a Japanese Statement of Intent — 112
- The Chinese Delegation Fails to Sign on a Provisional Basis — 114
- The Creation of a Draft Statement of Intent — 118
- Plans to Issue a Big Three Statement of Intent — 122
- Shandong and the League of Nations — 124
- Conclusions — 128
- Notes — 131

### 7. Shandong and the Origins of the Chinese Communist Party — 135
- The May Fourth Movement and Chinese Radicalization — 136
- The Karakhan Manifesto and the Birth of Chinese Communism — 138
- The Shandong Resolution's Impact on Li Dazhao and Chen Duxiu — 140
- Shandong and the Founding of the Chinese Communist Party — 145
- Shandong and the United Front Strategy — 148
- Conclusions — 149
- Notes — 151

### 8. The Myth of Soviet Equal Treatment of China — 155
- Shandong and the Diplomatic Legacy of Versailles — 156
- The 1921-1922 Washington Conference — 160
- Soviet Diplomacy and the United Front Strategy — 162
- Lev Karakhan's Secret Diplomacy and the CER — 164
- The 1925 Restoration of Soviet-Japanese Diplomatic Relations — 165
- Lev Karakhan and the Twenty-one Demands — 168
- Conclusions — 170
- Notes — 171

**Epilogue: The Impact of the Shandong Question** 175
   Notes 181

**Appendix A: 27 January 1919 Notes** 183

**Appendix B: 28 January 1919 Notes** 187

**Appendix C: 22 April 1919 Notes** 195

**Bibliography** 211

**Index** 221

# List of Maps

**Map 1.** Russian and Japanese Spheres of Influence in Manchuria and Mongolia as Delimited by the Secret Treaties of 1907, 1910, and 1912     xviii

**Map 2.** Shandong Province     9

**Map 3.** Japanese Map of USSR's "Red Influence" in China     174

# List of Documents

| | | |
|---|---|---|
| Doc. 1 | Ambassador W. G. Sharp's Letter to President Wilson, Proving that China Accepted the Twenty-one Demands in Advance | 19 |
| Doc. 2 | "Confidential Memorandum" of the Lansing-Ishii Notes, in which Japan Agrees to Adhere to the Open Door Policy in China | 23 |
| Doc. 3 | 24 September 1918 Secret Sino-Japanese Railway Agreement, Proving Chinese Acceptance of a Japanese Sphere in Shandong | 25 |
| Doc. 4 | Excerpt from 26 November 1918 Meeting between Minister V. K. Wellington Koo and President Woodrow Wilson | 37 |
| Doc. 5 | Excerpt from the 28 January 1919 Paris Discussion of Shandong | 45 |
| Doc. 6 | Excerpt from the 28 January 1919 Paris Discussion of Shandong | 57 |
| Doc. 7 | Excerpt from the 20 January 1919 "Disposal of Shandong Province" | 61 |
| Doc. 8 | Excerpt from the 24 April 1919 Memorandum from Stanley K. Hornbeck to E. T. Williams | 67 |
| Doc. 9 | Excerpt from the 22 April 1919 Big Three Discussions on Shandong | 79 |
| Doc. 10 | Woodrow Wilson's 30 April 1919 Note to Balfour | 83 |
| Doc. 11 | Tumulty's 1 May 1919 Cable to Woodrow Wilson | 87 |
| Doc. 12 | 7 May 1919 "Summary of the Conditions of Peace" | 95 |
| Doc. 13 | Excerpts from Lu Zhengxiang's 4 May 1919 Letter to President Wilson | 99 |
| Doc. 14 | 6 May 1919 *The London Times* reprint of Japan's 4 May 1919 Statement | 101 |
| Doc. 15 | 3 June 1919 Letter from Robert Lansing to Woodrow Wilson | 115 |
| Doc. 16 | 28 June 1919 Chinese Reservations to the Versailles Peace Treaty | 117 |
| Doc. 17 | 5 July 1919 Entry from the Unpublished Diary of Vance McCormick, Quoting Woodrow Wilson | 129 |
| Doc. 18 | 7 August 1919 Letter from Secretary of State Robert Lansing to President Woodrow Wilson | 141 |
| Doc. 19 | "China and the Lesson of Versailles" from the Vilenskii Pamphlet, which also included the 25 July 1919 Karakhan Manifesto | 159 |
| Doc. 20 | Excerpts from Ambassador Lev Karakhan's 26 February 1925 Letter to Minister of Foreign Affairs Shen Ruilin | 169 |

# *Acknowledgments*

This book has been an outgrowth of my first book, entitled *Diplomacy and Deception: The Secret History of Sino-Soviet Diplomatic Relations, 1917–1927* (Armonk, NY: M.E. Sharpe, 1997). I would like to thank in particular Sarah C. M. Paine and our two children, Anna Virginia Elleman and Steven Moyers Elleman. At the U.S. Naval War College, I am grateful for the support of Alberto Coll, Jonathan Pollack, George Baer, Andrew Ross, Peter Dombrowski, Lyle Goldstein, Christopher Bell, John Maurer, Andrew (Dex) Wilson, Steven Kenny, Bill Murray and, of course, Shirley Wilkins and Cheryl Rielly. Special thanks go to Paul Aswell for his help with the maps. For library assistance above and beyond the call of duty, I would like to thank in particular Alice Juda and Bob Schnare. At International Christian University, I would like to thank Bill Steele, Trish Sippel, and Roger Buckley. At Texas Christian University, I am especially grateful to my first department chairman, Spencer Tucker, and to the many faculty members who helped me with my research and writing, in particular Don Coerver, Don Worcester, Paul Boller, Gene Smith, Steve Woodworth, and Todd Kerstetter. Noriko Kamachi ceaselessly gave advice on how to rework the manuscript. And, last but not least, a great big "thanks" to Pat, Irina, and Ana at M.E. Sharpe.

I was fortunate to receive financial assistance from the following organizations: the Committee on Scholarly Communication with the People's Republic of China, with support from the United States Department of Education, funded twelve months of research in Beijing and Nanjing in 1990; the Pacific Cultural Foundation funded research in Taipei during ten months in Taiwan during the 1991-92 academic year; the Hoover Institution on War, Revolution and Peace funded the writing and initial publication of this research during the 1993-94 academic year under the Discretionary Grant Program, U.S. Department of State, Soviet-Eastern European Research and Training Act of 1983 (Public Law 98-164, Title VIII, 97 Stat. 1047-50), and during the 1994-95 academic year under the National Fellowship program; and the Institute of Asian Cultural Studies, International Christian University, Mitaka, Japan, provided generous support during my stay as a research fellow in 1998. At Texas Christian University, I received yearly research grants through the auspices of the Research and Creative Activities Fund. At the U.S. Naval War College, I received crucial funding and support through the Strategic Research Department, Center for Naval Warfare Studies.

I would also like to express my gratitude to the librarians and staff at the Academia Sinica and the Guomindang Archives (both in Taipei, Taiwan); the former Lenin Library in Moscow, Russia; the Number Two Historical Archives in Nanjing, People's Republic of China; the Foreign Ministry Archives in Tokyo, Japan; the Hoover Institution Archives at Stanford; the Bancroft Library at University of California, Berkeley; the Manuscript Division of the Library of Congress; the Seeley Mudd Archives at Princeton; the Houghton Library at Harvard; and the Rare Book and Manuscript Library at Columbia, all of which so generously shared their extensive collections of documents on foreign relations.

Permission was kindly granted by *Asian Cultural Studies, The American Asian Review,* and *Modern China* to reprint material that first appeared in article form. I alone am responsible for the interpretations in this work and for all shortcomings contained therein.

# *Technical Note*

The transliteration system used for Russian is the Library of Congress system minus the diacritical marks. For Chinese, the Pinyin system has been used, except for those names which have entered into common usage by another romanization, for example: Sun Yat-sen, Chiang Kai-shek, etc. Citations in the end notes, however, have retained the original transliterations throughout.

*Beijing government* refers to the internationally recognized central government in Beijing, while the *Guangzhou government* refers to Sun Yat-sen's opposition government in the southern Chinese city of Guangzhou (Canton). Similarly, the *Guomindang* refers to Sun Yat-sen's political party, also referred to as the Nationalist party. Although located in Beijing, Peking University retains the older spelling. The term *Outer Mongolia* refers to the northern portion of Greater Mongolia that roughly corresponds to modern-day Mongolia. *White Russians* refers generally to all Russians who fled to China in the aftermath of the 1917 revolutions, irrespective of whether they supported the Tsarist government, the provisional government, or some other faction. Finally, *Soviet Russia* is used to refer to the Bolshevik state prior to 1922, while *Soviet Union* or *USSR* is used after 1922.

All Chinese personal names are written with surname first, then given name, with the exception of Chinese who adopted Western usage, such as Wellington Koo (Gu Weijun) and C.T. Wang (Wang Zhengting). The Japanese, in line with their adoption of westernized usage at the Paris Peace Conference, are listed in the text with their given name first, followed by their surname. The reverse, however, often appears in footnotes, especially of modern Japanese sources. Underlined and italicized words are as in the original documents.

# List of Abbreviations

CCP         Chinese Communist Party

CER         Chinese Eastern Railway

Comintern   Communist International

Gaimushō    Japanese Foreign Ministry Archives, Tokyo, Japan

GMD         Guomindang

WJDA        Waijiao Dangan (Beijing government's foreign ministry archives, Academia Sinica, Taipei, Taiwan)

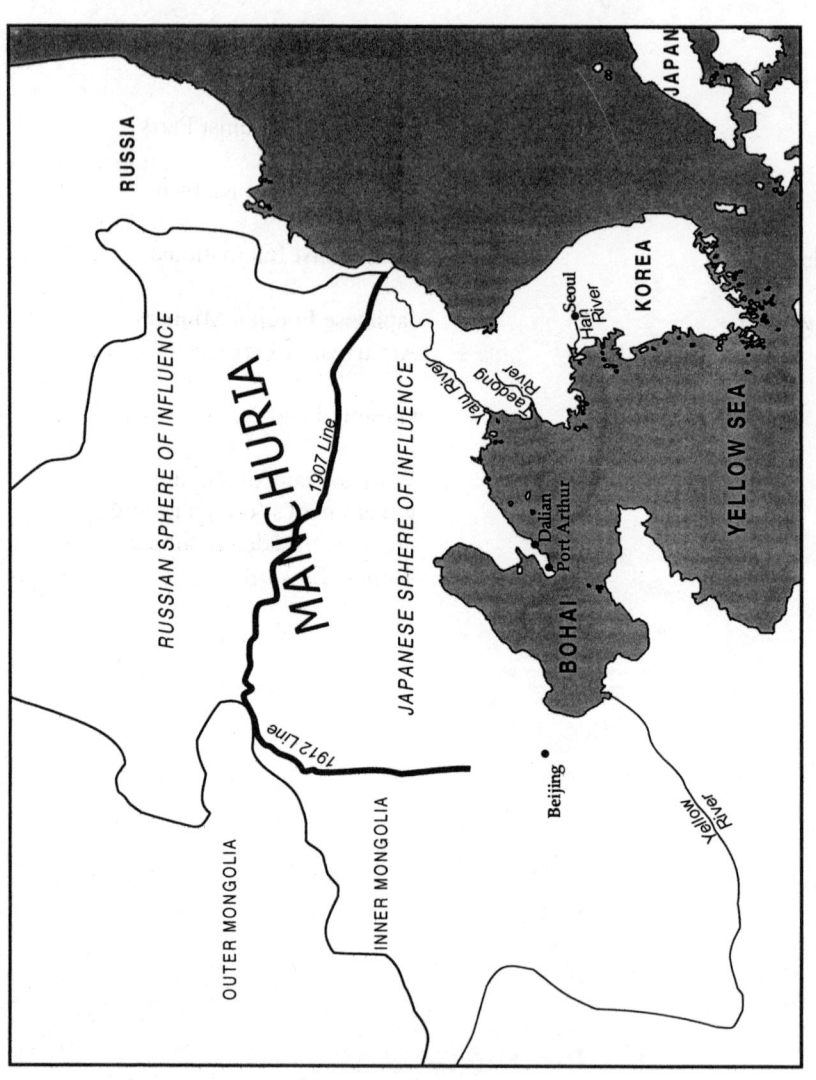

**Map 1:** Russian and Japanese Spheres of Influence in Manchuria and Mongolia as Delimited by the Secret Treaties of 1907, 1910, and 1912 (Ernest Batson Price, *The Russo-Japanese Treaties of 1907-1916 Concerning Manchuria and Mongolia*. Baltimore, MD: The Johns Hopkins Press, 1933, 124)

# WILSON AND CHINA

# *Introduction*

> Few people in Europe realize how momentous was the decision taken by the Council of Three in favor of Japan on the Shandong question. Without exaggeration, we say that it exceeds in importance all the other territorial adjustments made by the Conference because of the area and population affected. No well-informed man can have any doubt that it will profoundly modify the history of the Asiatic continent, if not that of the whole world.[1]
>
> Liang Qichao, journalist and reformer (Paris, June 1919)

Westerners and Chinese alike have blamed the United States government in general, and President Woodrow Wilson in particular, for betraying Chinese interests at the 1919 Paris Peace Conference terminating World War I. Specifically, they have criticized the terms for Japan's return to China of the Jiaozhou (Kiaochow) concession on Shandong peninsula, a German sphere of interest before the war. From the 1920s onward, Soviet and Chinese communists used this alleged betrayal to spur China to reject a Western democratic-capitalist model for political and economic development. In contrast to this Western betrayal, Soviet communists have pointed to their own country's allegedly "equal" treatment of China and used this difference to spread their own authoritarian command-economy model to China.

This book will demonstrate that both allegations are false. The United States did not betray China nor did the USSR treat China equally. The diplomatic paper trail is complex, scattered, and based on sources in a multitude of languages, but well worth examining since the consequences of the Shandong question were enormous. The widespread credence given to both myths by the Chinese public fueled the May Fourth Movement and the subsequent growth of the Chinese Communist Party. To this day the vocabulary routinely used to describe the Western diplomacy of this period continues to poison the waters of both Western and Chinese scholarship. For example, the Western powers were "imperialistic," a word used with a pejorative connotation, whereas the Soviet Union was "revolutionary," a word used without such negative stereotypes.

The Chinese and Soviet portrayal of the Shandong question was as persuasive and widely accepted as it was wrong. Their *ad hominem* attacks on Western activities in China paved the way for China's choice of the communist road to modernity, a road ultimately paved with the corpses of tens if not hundreds of millions of Chinese. Therefore, the Shandong question constitutes a very portentous and yet inadequately studied crossroads in Chinese history.

This work attempts to set the record straight by examining the available diplomatic records in English, Chinese, Japanese, and Russian, and in doing so to substitute for the propaganda that has heretofore stunted the Western and Chinese understanding of the late 1910s and early 1920s, arguably a key period in twentieth-century Chinese history.

\*       \*       \*

This book begins by examining President Woodrow Wilson's China policy at the 1919 Paris Peace Conference. During World War I Japan attacked and occupied Germany's 200-square-mile concession at Jiaozhou harbor. Wilson, as one of the so-called Big Three leaders at Paris, had to weigh Japan's and China's conflicting demands: the Japanese delegation claimed that Germany should first officially cede the concession to Japan and only afterward would Japan formally return it to China; the Chinese delegation insisted that Germany hand over the concession directly to China, thereby cutting Japan out of the transfer. In the end Wilson backed Japan's "indirect" over China's "direct" approach.

Wilson's decision to support Japan over China has led to seething judgments of Wilson's treatment of China, with the common usage of such terms as "betrayal,"[2] "wavering,"[3] "sacrifice,"[4] and "the failure of Wilsonian idealism."[5] Wilson's actions were fated to have an enormous impact in the Far East: in particular, they gave the newly-established Soviet government an unexpected opportunity to exert political and ideological influence over China.[6] As summarized by one Chinese scholar in 1959, the "mischief" that resulted from the Shandong question included the "intensification of the national sentiments of the Chinese people," the "awareness of the need for some drastic political-social reforms," and, finally, the "emergence of the Chinese Communists and the submergence of the mainland by the Red deluge."[7]

It has often been said that the United States lost China to communism after World War II. While granting that the very idea of one country losing another country verges on the absurd, this work will suggest that if one wants to posit when the United States government lost the support of the Chinese people, the turning point took place not after World War II, but after World War I, during 1919 as a result of the Shandong question.

This book will address five key issues of international history. First, as a contribution to the history of American foreign relations, it will present new archival documents that will rectify the largely negative press accounts of the Paris Peace Conference's handling of the Shandong question. One of the most important American journalists to write about the conference, Ray Stannard Baker, acknowledged the practical limitations of the press reports:[8]

Perhaps the greatest shortcoming of the Peace Conference was the inability or unwillingness—it was both—of the chief conferees to dramatize their day's work; to take the publics of the world along with them as they met their problems, and to explain clearly why they were forced to make the decisions they did. No one person can be blamed for this condition, and no one person, at this stage of development in world relations, could have much changed it; but the fact remains that each important decision made by the conferees, and presented baldly, without its background or proper setting, came to the world with a kind of shock.

In order to correct the failings of the contemporary world press coverage, this book will discuss in great detail the background to the Shandong question, the widely disparate goals of the Chinese and Japanese delegations at the conference, and President Wilson's efforts to resolve these differences and negotiate an acceptable compromise. This account will make full use not only of documents and information easily available to the press corps at that time, but also of formerly classified and hard-to-locate documents that surfaced only many years later.

Second, a reappraisal of the Shandong question overturns the widely accepted Chinese version of events, a version that ultimately became a justification for the growing anti-Western movement in China. Because of the misrepresentations by the press, as well as misinformation put forth by members of China's own delegation at the time, the myth that Wilson betrayed China is still widely accepted by Chinese and Western historians alike. To set the record straight it is necessary to take a critical look at the members of China's delegation, and in particular at the Columbia-trained V. K. Wellington Koo and Yale-trained C. T. Wang, in order to determine: a) what information they had available to them at the beginning of the Paris Conference; b) what tactics they used during their meetings with the Japanese delegates and with President Wilson; and finally c) what "spin" they tried to put on the proceedings once they failed to achieve their objectives. This study will cast a new and not altogether flattering light on the responsibility that China's own delegates must bear for the less than ideal outcome of the Shandong talks.

Third, this work shows how the Shandong controversy opened China to Bolshevik influence, both in terms of the growing interest among the Chinese people in the unfolding socialist experiment in Soviet Russia and in terms of government-to-government negotiations between Russia and China. Indeed, the Bolsheviks' greatest and most lasting impact abroad was not in Europe but in Asia, and the origins of the USSR's extraordinary influence in China were directly due to the Chinese peoples' disappointment with Wilson's resolution of the Shandong question. The secret to the Bolsheviks' success in China was not so much related to their efforts to disseminate their revolutionary philosophy, as to a general post-Paris revulsion with the West—and with the United States in particular—among Chinese intellectuals, reformers, and diplomats. The commonly accepted myth that Woodrow Wilson betrayed China was instrumental in leading Chinese intellectuals and diplomats to spurn American-style democracy and turn instead to Russian-style communism in order to address China's domestic and international problems. Thus the Paris Peace Conference's resolution on the Shandong question was an important turning point in twentieth-century Chinese history since this misunderstanding helped set China down the Soviet road of development.

Fourth, Japanese historians have long misunderstood their own diplomatic history with China and the Soviet Union. Prior to World War I, the Chinese government had managed to play Russia and Japan off each other, but with the October 1917 Revolution and the eventual collapse of eastern Russia into civil war, a political vacuum opened that Japan was eager to fill. Faced with this threat, Beijing government officials tried to use Soviet offers of equal treatment as a counterweight to rising Japanese imperialism. Soviet diplomats, after resorting to secret diplomacy with the Beijing government, the Manchurian warlord Zhang Zuolin, and the Japanese government, soon regained control over the former Tsarist concessions in northern China, including the Chinese Eastern Railway. This diplomatic success ushered in a new era of Soviet-Japanese competition, which ultimately exacerbated China's domestic chaos and led to the division of much of China into Soviet and Japanese spheres of influence. It was this division, and the international and domestic friction that it caused, that ultimately resulted in the 1937-45 Sino-Japanese War, the Chinese civil war, and the 1949 victory of the Chinese Communist Party.

Fifth, this book will describe not only the origins of China's tumultuous antiforeign movement during the 1920s and the Sino-Japanese War of 1937-45, but also the beginnings of the cold war in the Far East. In particular, it will outline the geopolitical importance of the Shandong concession, both as a Japanese military outpost only one day's drive from China's northern capital and as one half of a pincer movement—the other half being Japan's extensive concessions in Manchuria—which allowed Tokyo to exert extraordinary political and diplomatic pressure on Beijing. Following the end of World War II, the Soviet Union was able to move into the power vacuum created by Japan's surrender. These territorial assets then greatly assisted the Chinese Communist Party's efforts to consolidate power throughout China. Thus the Shandong question played a truly seminal role in twentieth-century Chinese history.

*　　　　*　　　　*

The diplomatic paper trail explaining these events is scattered across numerous archives. This book relies on primary documents from the Japanese and Chinese Foreign Ministry archives, the Stanley K. Hornbeck and Vance McCormick collections at the Hoover Institution Archives, the Edward T. Williams collection at University of California Berkeley's Bancroft Library, the V. K. Wellington Koo collection at Columbia University's Rare Book and Manuscript Library, the Leon Trotsky papers at Harvard University's Houghton Library, and from a wide range of other archival sources, such as the Woodrow Wilson, the Robert Lansing, the Ray Stannard Baker, and the John V. A. MacMurray papers at the Seeley Mudd Archives at Princeton University, the Tasker Bliss and the Henry White papers at the Library of Congress, and the State Department's records from the Paris Peace Conference.

Taken together, these records prove that the United States government did not sacrifice China or betray Chinese national interests. In sharp contrast to most previous accounts of the Shandong question, this book will show that it was the Chinese delegation at Paris that refused to compromise. In fact, these Chinese officials deemed it beneath China's dignity to receive the Shandong concession indirectly from what they claimed was a minor country—Japan—instead of directly from a major country—Germany. When the Chinese were forced to accept the former, they then put the onus on Wilson and the Paris peace process; it is this biased view that has been passed down as the accepted historical record. In the end, Wilson's negotiations with Japan failed to release China completely from its international obligations under these treaties and the Shandong concession was returned to China via Japan, the so-called "indirect" method of restoring Shandong. Perceiving this method as an enormous loss of "face," the Chinese delegates turned on their staunchest defender and blamed Wilson for their own failed diplomacy.

As this work will show, President Woodrow Wilson worked diligently at Paris to negotiate terms leading to the transfer of the Shandong concession to China in 1922, more than seventy-five years before the date stipulated by China's own treaty with Germany. In the process Wilson induced the Japanese delegation to set aside all of Japan's political rights in Shandong, rights that the Japanese government had gained by means of no fewer than six international treaties, including the 1915 Twenty-one Demands and a second group of secret agreements signed with China in 1918. In fact, against enormous odds Wilson succeeded in upholding and protecting China's political rights over the Shandong concession.

If there was one single point during the twentieth century that can truly be identified as the crossroads for China, it was the Paris Peace Conference's 1919 decision to transfer Shandong to Japan before it was returned to China, a decision Woodrow Wilson helped to negotiate. It is quite possible that if Wilson had satisfied the Chinese people at the expense of Japan, then the USSR would have experienced greater difficulties in cultivating close intellectual and diplomatic ties with China. This, in turn, might have later kept the Chinese theater out of the cold war.

This book will argue, however, that for Wilson to have unconditionally backed China would have meant overlooking no fewer than six internationally recognized treaties. But by doing so, Wilson would have called into question the sanctity of treaties. This would have undermined the very legal tradition on which Western democracy was founded. Wilson refused to do this. But when Wilson decided to back Japan's plan for "indirect" restitution over China's "direct" restitution, he perhaps unwittingly contributed to China's decision to take the Soviet path, a path that led it ever farther from the very goals and values that Wilson had championed at the Paris Peace Conference.

With the USSR's 1991 dissolution and China's gradual transition toward capitalism and possibly to democracy, a reevaluation of Wilson's true relations with China is long overdue. This work is especially relevant given that there may soon be a renewed struggle in China between advocates of democracy and communism, at a time when China's old leaders must pass the mantle of power down to the next generation. It is important to recognize, therefore, that the current intellectual and philosophical struggles in China to a large degree have their roots in the 1919 resolution of the Shandong question, which is when many Chinese leaders first considered turning away from Western democracy and capitalism.

**Notes**

1. Liang Qichao, "China and the Shantung Settlement," *Manchester Guardian*, 16 June 1919.
2. Maurice Meisner, *Li Ta-chao and the Origins of Chinese Marxism* (Cambridge, MA: Harvard University Press, 1967), 58.
3. Chow Tse-Tsung, *The May 4th Movement—Intellectual Revolution in Modern China*, (Cambridge, MA: Harvard University Press, 1980), 89.
4. Immanuel C. Y. Hsü, *The Rise of Modern China* (New York: Oxford University Press, 2000), 505.
5. Zhang Yongjin, *China in the International System, 1918-20: The Middle Kingdom at the Periphery* (London: Macmillan Press, 1991), 196.
6. Robert C. North, *Moscow and the Chinese Communists* (Stanford, CA: Stanford University Press, 1963), 41.
7. Wunsz King, "Woodrow Wilson, Wellington Koo and the China Question at the Paris Peace Conference," unpublished manuscript (dated 13 March 1959), V. K. Wellington Koo collection, Rare Book and Manuscript Library, Columbia University.
8. Ray Stannard Baker, "How Japan Forced Shantung Clause," *New York Times*, 17 August 1919.

# 1
# The Diplomatic Situation Prior to the Paris Peace Conference

> In the history of international politics there are but few, if any, incidents, the magnitude and significance of which can at all be compared to the magnitude and significance of what has been known as the Shandong question. In fact, it may safely be said that there is no single instance in modern history–not excepting the ruthless dismemberment of Poland, the gradual subjugation of India, and the shameless annexation of Alsace-Lorraine and of Korea–which has stood out so conspicuously as a case of imperialism and international immorality, or which has aroused so much moral indignation throughout the world as has this so-called Shandong question.[1]
>
> G. Zay Wood, publicist and historian (New York, 1922)

With these words G. Zay Wood opened one of the first comprehensive histories of the Shandong question, written in the immediate aftermath of the 1921-22 Washington Conference's final action on the Shandong question. The author himself admitted, however, that the material in his volume was "originally prepared by the author and used for publicity purpose by the Press Department of the Chinese delegation at the Washington Conference."[2]

This chapter will attempt to present a more even-handed account of the early history of the Shandong question. The first step is to review the multitude of agreements and treaties that were brought before the delegates to the 1919 Paris Peace Conference. It is difficult if not impossible to understand the final resolution on the Shandong question without first obtaining a feel for the diplomatic complexity that surrounded this issue.

Although Germany in 1897 occupied Jiaozhou harbor in China's Shandong province, this two-hundred-square-mile German concession remained a part of China and so was technically subject to Chinese sovereignty. But China, in fact, had ceded many political rights, certain territory, and various economic privileges to Germany. When Japan declared war on Germany in 1914 and stormed the German fortifications in Shandong, as the rightful victor Japan assumed most of Germany's rights, property, and privileges.

8   THE DIPLOMATIC SITUATION

Japan and China acknowledged this situation in 1915 when they signed the so-called Twenty-one Demands; moreover, in 1918 the two countries signed other agreements, this time secretly, which confirmed many of Japan's political and economic rights over the Shandong concession. Japan also signed secret agreements with Great Britain, Russia, France, and Italy as well as a public agreement with the United States in order to back up its position; of these only the U.S.-Japanese agreement did not specifically refer to the Shandong concession. The cumulative effect of these six Japanese treaties—the two with China and four with Great Britain, Russia, France, and Italy—put the Japanese delegation in an almost unassailable legal position at Paris.

When the conferees at Paris first raised the Shandong question in January 1919, most participants were surprised to discover that there were actually eight countries involved in the controversy: China, Germany, Japan, Great Britain, Russia, France, Italy, and the United States. Russia, wracked by civil war, was not represented at Paris, while Italy withdrew temporarily from the conference right when the Shandong question was discussed. This left the "Big Three"—the leaders of Great Britain, France, and the United States—to hear the arguments of the Japanese and Chinese delegations over how the former German concession in Shandong should be treated.

Of the six countries represented at Paris, the United States was arguably the only participant that retained even a modicum of objectivity. Easily outvoted on this issue by Great Britain and France, which had secretly pledged their support to Japan years before, President Wilson faced an almost insurmountable task of devising a diplomatic settlement that would on the one hand conform to China's own treaties with Japan and on the other hand grant firm guarantees respecting China's sovereignty and territorial integrity.

**The German Diplomatic Position in Shandong**

The starting point for an understanding of the Shandong question is the 1897 German seizure of Jiaozhou harbor. This took place during the period in Chinese history known as the "scramble for concessions," when the major foreign powers—with the notable exception of the United States government—attempted to divide control of China by carving out foreign concessions. The German government, after first receiving assurances from the other major powers that they would not interfere, responded to the 1 November 1897 murder of two German missionaries in Shandong by occupying Jiaozhou harbor. With its troops in a position to threaten Beijing, Germany forced China to agree to a long-term lease of Jiaozhou.

The resulting Convention for the Lease of Jiaozhou Bay was signed on 6 March 1898.[3] Qingdao was the major port in Shandong province (see Map 2).[4] The Qing government and Germany divided their negotiations into three parts. The first section contained five articles relating to the Jiaozhou concession itself. Articles One through Four outlined the general boundary of the concession area

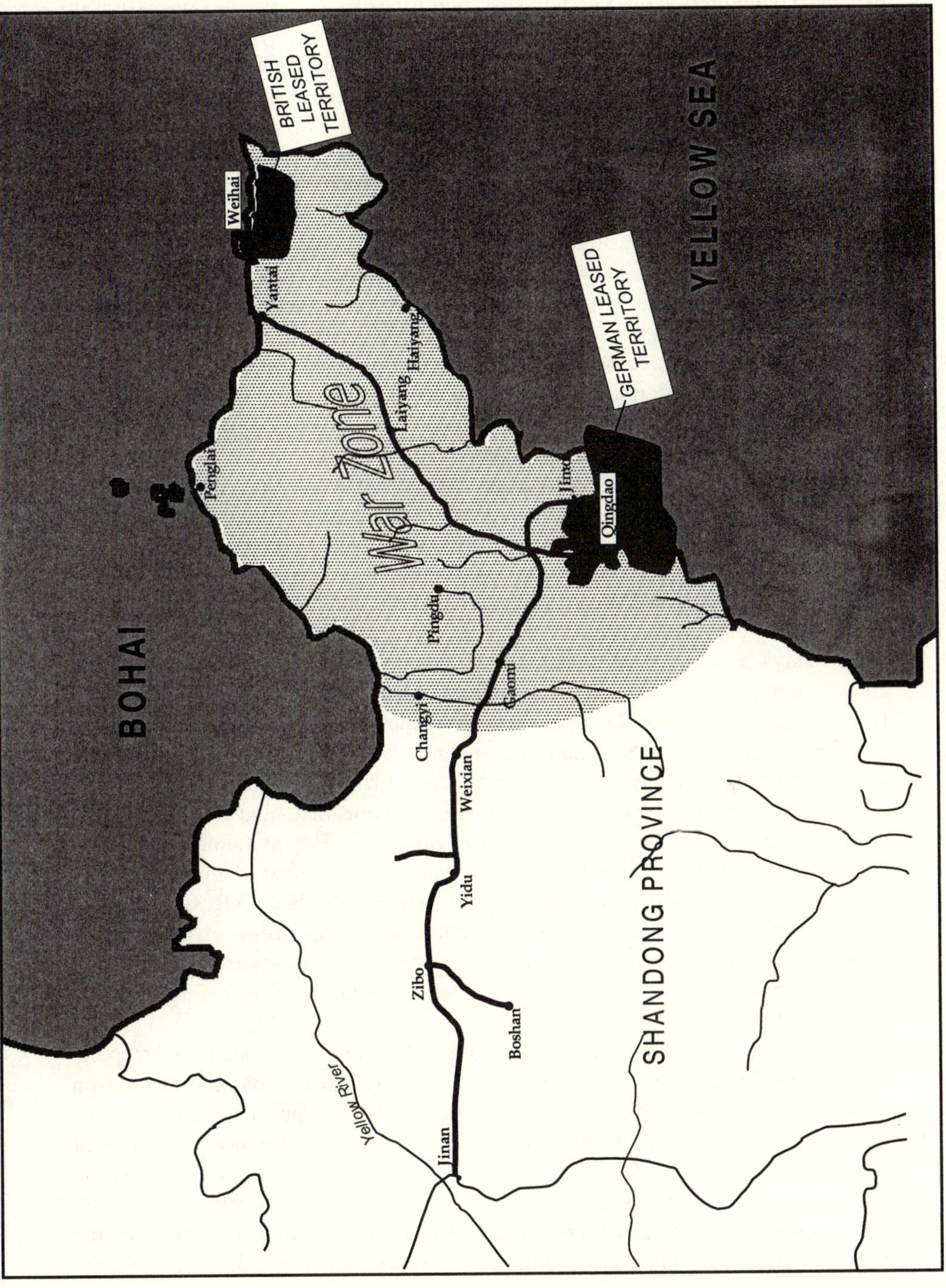

THE DIPLOMATIC SITUATION 9

**Map 2**: Shandong Province

and set the lease at 99 years. In Article Five it was agreed that Germany could exercise sovereignty within certain specified limits throughout the concession in return for Germany's promise "never to sublet the territory [leased from China] to another power."[5] This article would provide the basis for the Chinese delegation's claim some twenty years later at Paris that Germany had no legal right to transfer the Shandong concession to Japan.

The second section was concerned with the economic exploitation of Shandong province in general. In addition to ceding to Germany land around Jiaozhou harbor for its concession at Qingdao, the port city, Germany's economic interests were furthered by permitting German companies to develop several railway lines in Shandong. China also ceded mining rights on all land within 30 *li* (approximately ten miles) of these railway lines to the German companies. In return, the German government promised to use these railway lines solely to develop commerce in Shandong: "Germany entertains no treacherous intention toward China, and undertakes not to unlawfully seize any land in the province."[6]

In the third section China agreed that during the future development of Shandong province it would rely only on German experts, capital, and technology. By stipulating that German businesses had to be approached first, this part of the Sino-German agreement arguably made all of Shandong province an exclusive German sphere of influence.[7] This section of the 1898 agreement was in some ways the most important, since it virtually guaranteed the continued expansion of German influence in China. Such an economic guarantee was later to prove quite attractive to Japan.

Germany's acquisition of Jiaozhou sparked similar actions by Russia and Great Britain in northern China. On 27 March 1898 China was forced to cede Lüshun (Port Arthur) and Dalian (Dairen, and with Lüshun called Lüda) on the Liaodong peninsula to Russia for 99 years. Later, on 1 July 1898, it ceded Weihaiwei, located north of Germany's concession, to Great Britain for twenty-five years.

The United States strongly opposed this division of China into competing spheres of influence. In 1899 Secretary of State John Hay announced the Open Door Policy, which promoted free trade with China instead of the creation of foreign concessions. But following Russia's defeat in the 1904-5 Russo-Japanese War, the division of China continued with Japan's acquisition of Lüshun and Dalian in the Portsmouth Peace Treaty. As a result Japan's standing in northern China became equal, if not superior, to any other foreign power including Germany and Great Britain.

Between 1898 and 1914 Germany's lease in Jiaozhou continued uninterrupted. During this sixteen-year period China and Germany signed more than two dozen new treaties, most of which granted Germany additional political and economic rights either in the port city of Qingdao or in Shandong province. In a few of these treaties, however, Germany agreed to return some rights and privileges to China. One, on 21 March 1900, was a railway agreement stating that Chinese, not German, troops would protect the German railway interests outside of the fifty-kilometer German zone in Jiaozhou. On 24 July 1911, they changed the

1898 provision granting Germany the right to manage coal mines within ten miles of the railway so that two coal mines and one iron mine founded by German companies would be managed by a joint Sino-German company.[8] Later, the Chinese delegates at Paris used these as proof that some political and economic rights granted to Germany in 1898 had been returned prior to World War I.

Other Sino-German treaties, however, were not as favorable to China. On 31 December 1913 Germany obtained China's permission to build two new railway lines: the first would stretch from Qingdao to the southwest to join with the Tianjin-Pukou railway, while the second would extend the Shandong railway to the west to join with the Beijing-Hankou railway.[9] Although intended to be built by German companies with German capital, both railway lines were to be eventually owned and managed by the Chinese government.

After Japan took control of the Shandong concession from Germany, the Japanese government used this preexisting treaty to gain similar terms for Japanese companies. As discussed below, the resulting Sino-Japanese railway agreement of 1918 proved to be of enormous importance at the Paris Peace Conference.

**Japan Declares War on Germany**

After the beginning of World War I, Japan fulfilled its East Asian obligations to Great Britain under their 1902 alliance by declaring war on Germany and by demanding that Germany vacate its Shandong concession. On 15 August 1914, Tokyo issued an ultimatum that Germany "unconditionally hand over the territory [of Jiaozhou] to Japan which she intended to restore to China."[10] This ultimatum mirrored the German, Russian, and French Triple Intervention of 1895, when Japan was forced to return Liaodong to China. When Germany ignored this ultimatum, Japan attacked Qingdao.

The United States had tried, and failed, to keep East Asia out of the war.[11] To reassure Washington of Japan's intentions, Japanese Minister of Foreign Affairs Takaaki Kato sent the following message to U.S. Secretary of State William J. Bryan on 20 August 1914: "The history of the seizure of the place (Jiaozhou) by Germany and her conduct preceding and including her intervention, in conjunction with Russia and France after the Sino-Japanese War, show that it is absolutely necessary to eliminate such possession[s] completely if Japan is to restore immediately complete peace in the Far East in accordance with the terms of the Anglo-Japanese alliance. If Japan is to look far enough into the future and adopt measures to insure an abiding peace in Eastern Asia she must realize that a strong military base in the hands of a hostile military power right in the heart of the country [of China] cannot in itself fail to be a menacing factor."[12] Since the United States had not yet joined in the war, Washington adopted a neutral policy with regard to Japan's intended action against Germany.

When Germany did not issue any response to this ultimatum, Japan declared war on 23 August 1914. In this declaration Tokyo pointed to the threat of German aggression in the Far East: "Germany is at Jiaozhou, its leased territory in China, busy with warlike preparations, while its armed vessels cruising the seas of Eastern Asia are threatening our commerce and that of our ally [Great Britain]. The peace of the Far East is thus in jeopardy. . . . It is with profound regret that we, in spite of our ardent devotion to the cause of peace, are thus compelled to declare war."[13] Soon afterward what became a force of 21,000 Japanese troops landed on the Shandong peninsula and, after joining forces with about 1,000 British troops, laid siege to the German fortress at Qingdao.

One day after declaring war on Germany, Japanese Premier Shigenobu Okuma sent a cable to the *New York Independent* newspaper bearing the title "Message to the American People." Okuma's statement was specifically intended to reassure the United States government and the American people that Japan's actions in Shandong would not violate the Open Door Policy: "As Premier of Japan, I have stated and now again state to the people of America and of the world that Japan has no ulterior motive, no desire to secure more territory, no thought of depriving China or other peoples of anything which they now possess. My Government and my people have given their word and their pledge, which will be as honorably kept as Japan always keeps her promises."[14]

China, instead of breaking diplomatic relations with Germany and joining Japan and Great Britain, tried to remain neutral. Even at this early date, however, China's official republican government in Beijing attempted to limit Japan's scope of operations in Shandong by turning to President Wilson. On 1 October 1914 Minister of Communications Liang Dunyan informed U.S. Minister to China Paul Reinsch that China planned to "request the good offices of President Wilson in conferring with the British Government upon the possibility of prevailing upon Japan to restrict her action . . . according to the original assurances given to the Chinese Government with respect to the extent of these operations." It is important to note that Reinsch advised Beijing against this action, pointing out that all reports indicated "that Japan was acting in good faith and would respect the rights and interests of China if treated with confidence."[15]

It soon became evident that the Beijing government considered the most sensitive problem to be control over the railway lines running through Shandong province. Tokyo claimed that the Shandong railways were vital to Germany's continued hold over Qingdao and early in the campaign stated its intention to occupy them. Intensive Sino-Japanese negotiations were opened on this issue.

On 5 October 1914 Reinsch reported to Washington that Beijing and Tokyo had reached an agreement whereby: "The Japanese are formally to occupy the railway by *force majeure*, but the administration is to remain in the hands of the Chinese; Japanese conductors are to be placed on the trains."[16] Japan also promised to pay for all necessary military supplies with special bank notes, which could later be redeemed for silver at the Yokohama Specie Bank.[17] Reinsch interpreted both actions as positive indicators of Japan's good will with regard to eventually returning the Shandong concession to China.

After a two-month siege costing Japan an estimated 2,000 dead and wounded, Japanese and British troops finally defeated the German forces at Qingdao and occupied Jiaozhou on 7 November 1914. The heavy Japanese losses induced Tokyo to retain control over the Shandong concession, at least until after the war. With this goal in mind Foreign Minister Kato declared to the Japanese Diet in December 1914 that Japan had made "no promise whatever with regard to the ultimate disposition of what she had acquired in Shandong."[18]

**Strategic and Military Importance of the Shandong Concession**

Japan's 1914 victory over Germany changed the delicate strategic and military balance of power throughout the Far East. With the sudden defeat of Germany and the wartime retreat of Great Britain and the United States from Asia, Japan and Russia almost overnight became the two strongest military powers in Asia. Beijing, given its traditional policy of playing one 'barbarian' off of another, could not help but perceive this rapid shift as a strategic disaster. This was especially the case in northern China and Shandong, since Beijing had previously been quite successful in balancing Russian and Japanese spheres of interest in Manchuria against the British and German interests in Shandong. Now, this delicate arrangement was threatening to collapse.

In 1905 Imperial Russia and Japan promised in the Portsmouth Peace Treaty to respect the United States' Open Door Policy. However, in an effort to extend their spheres of interest in Outer Mongolia and Manchuria in violation of the Open Door Policy, Russia and Japan had signed a series of secret agreements. In the first of these, signed on 30 July 1907, Russia and Japan had agreed to "obviate for the future all cause of friction or misunderstanding with respect to certain questions relating to Manchuria, Korea and Mongolia." This resulted in demarcating an east-west line running through Manchuria, with Russia promising not to obtain any concession south of this line and Japan promising not to interfere north of it. In return for a free hand in Korea, Japan had promised to recognize "the special interests of Russia in Outer Mongolia" and undertook "to refrain from any interference which might prejudice those interests."[19]

By means of this 1907, treaty Russia and Japan secretly divided northeast Asia, with Japan taking Korea and Russia taking Outer Mongolia. They went even farther in a second secret treaty of 4 July 1910, by promising to protect these spheres against outside interference. In a third secret treaty of 8 July 1912, the two powers lengthened their demarcation line. Based on the meridian of the city of Beijing, Inner Mongolia was cut into an eastern and a western section, with Japan acquiring the former and Russia the latter. Both parties also promised to "recognize and respect" the other party's "special interests."[20]

Immediately prior to World War I, Imperial Russia further consolidated its sphere of interest in Outer Mongolia. In the fall of 1914 Russian negotiators in Beijing presented China with twenty-one draft resolutions that appeared to grant Outer Mongolia its autonomy, but in fact indirectly placed the Chinese province under Russian control. This draft Sino-Russian treaty was crucial in pushing Japan into making not just economic but also strategic and military demands in the Shandong concession. Japan responded to Russia's diplomatic move by proposing twenty-one resolutions of its own, popularly called the Twenty-one Demands (to avoid the appearance of being matched by Japan, Russia later added one demand to its list, to make twenty-two total). It is all too often overlooked that Russian and Japanese diplomacy were working in tandem.

Tsarist Russia's secret negotiations to increase its political control over Outer Mongolia was an important factor in leading Tokyo to consolidate its military gains in China. Strategic considerations furthermore pushed Japan into trying to retain economic rights over the Shandong concession, especially the German-built railway that started in Qingdao and ended in Jinan, a major commercial and transportation center to the southeast of Beijing. From Jinan, Japanese troops were only one day's journey from Beijing. This meant that Japan could use this position to directly counterbalance the threat of Russian troops on the Sino-Mongolian border, just one day's ride to the northwest.

**Foreign Policy Issues Regarding the Shandong Concession**

Japan's 1914 victory over Germany also forced upon it new international responsibilities, as well as opening up new opportunities. According to Ambassador Reinsch, the primary foreign-policy decision facing Japan was not so much whether it would become the greatest power in the Far East, but how it would go about doing so. Specifically, would Tokyo's foreign policy promote only Japan's economic influence in the Shandong concession, in line with the philosophy of America's Open Door Policy, or would it attempt to gain political control as well, thus setting off a new "scramble for concessions"? Japan apparently chose the latter course when it forced China to accept the so-called Twenty-one Demands in 1915. Tokyo's foreign policy was in fact driven by two events: Imperial Russia's ongoing expansion into Outer Mongolia during fall 1914, discussed above, and pervasive Sino-Japanese antagonism, perhaps best shown by Beijing's insistence that Japan withdraw its troops immediately and pay for all damages incurred during the Qingdao siege.

On 28 November 1914 Reinsch wrote a lengthy memorandum to Washington describing in great detail how the Japanese occupation of the Shandong railway and Germany's mining properties adjacent to the railway lines had resulted in a series of Chinese protests that its neutrality was being violated. He stated that since it was clear that Japan was determined to play a leading role in China the sole question left unanswered was "what character will that leadership assume." Public discussion on this topic in Japan furthermore indicated "that the Japanese nation is fully aware of the extent of the opportunity and of the momentousness of the decision."[21]

Reinsch succinctly explained Japan's predicament in the following terms: "It is, however, evident that the Japanese are at present put before the decision as to what their continental policy is to be in general purpose and in detail. The unusual opportunity which has presented itself in the train of the European War, the elimination of Germany for the time being as a factor in the Far East, the fact that the other great European powers are the allies of Japan and are entirely preoccupied with the war in Europe, would seem to give to Japan an opportunity for exercising an influence in China the like of which could not have been hoped for even by the greatest optimists. Whether this opportunity is now to be exploited in order to extend political predominance over a part or all of China, or whether the advantageous situation is to be utilized merely to create a favorable basis for Japanese economic enterprise on the mainland: that is the decision which now has to be made."[22]

In general, during late 1914 Reinsch backed Tokyo's stated position that Japan was merely assuming Germany's economic responsibilities in Shandong, including the management of railways and mines. Reinsch repeatedly suggested to Beijing officials, therefore, that it would be in their best interest if they achieved "a frank understanding between China and Japan." But, according to Reinsch, they stubbornly refused his suggestions, insisting instead that Japan's former incursions in China indicated "a determined policy of political advance, veiled by reassuring declarations."[23] On 7 January 1915, Chinese officials publicly insisted that all Japanese troops be withdrawn immediately from Shandong. Beijing also demanded that Tokyo pay for all damages incurred during the recent fighting.

Russia's expansion into China's northern territories combined with Beijing's refusal to open negotiations with Tokyo to determine their mutual economic needs and responsibilities left Tokyo little room to maneuver. Although Japan's victory over Germany gave it *de facto* military control over the Shandong concession, Tokyo had yet to consolidate this control by signing an official treaty or agreement with China. Since the German government had refused to accept Japan's 1914 ultimatum, Foreign Minister Kato was technically correct when he reassured the Japanese Diet that Japan had not made any promise to China concerning the disposition of Shandong; even American Far Eastern experts admitted that "Japan is not bound technically by the phraseology of the ultimatum."[24]

China's implacable hostility toward Japan, when added to the threat of the rapid growth of the Russian sphere of influence in Outer Mongolia, appears to have driven Tokyo to demand that Beijing sign a new treaty. For a model, Japan fell back on the series of treaties and secret agreements signed with Russia in the years 1907, 1910, and 1912 to demand both a predominant economic and political position in the Shandong concession. The Sino-Japanese treaty that accomplished this task was negotiated and signed in 1915 and became known as the infamous Twenty-one Demands.

**Japan Presents the Twenty-one Demands**

On 18 January 1915 Tokyo presented Beijing its Twenty-one Demands. By this action Japan hoped to define its new position of strength throughout China, especially in Shandong province. According to the most widely accepted historical interpretation of these events, Japan forced China to agree to these demands. But at the time the Beijing government rationalized its decision to sign by accusing Sun Zhongshan (hereafter Sun Yat-sen), the leader of the opposition Guangzhou government in South China, of making even greater promises to Japan than those embodied in the Twenty-one Demands; at the same time Sun accused Yuan Shikai, president of the Republic of China, of secretly agreeing in advance to accept Russia's and Japan's terms in return for their support for his bid to revive the monarchy in China with Yuan as emperor. Interestingly, although both accusations diverge on content, both accounts agree that the Beijing officials were not forced to sign Japan's Twenty-one Demands—as the Chinese delegates to Paris were later to argue as the major reason why Shandong should be returned directly to China—but signed them willingly to gain Japan's support for a domestic agenda.

Divided into five groups, the Twenty-one Demands gave Japan the right to dispose of Germany's concession in Shandong as it saw fit, to increase its influence in Manchuria and Inner Mongolia, to receive special mining and commercial privileges along the Yangzi River, and to stop China from leasing additional bays or harbors to other powers. In the highly disputed fifth group, Japan sought a wide range of political rights in China proper, including exclusive rights to sell arms to China and to develop Fujian province across the strait from the Japanese colony of Taiwan. This last point was included because of rumors that the United States was planning to strengthen its own position in China by leasing a concession there.

Although Tokyo did present a partial list of these terms to Washington in advance, it was later reported that when the entire list became known the Japanese officials insisted that the most onerous points had been presented to Beijing only later as "additional desiderata." This made it appear that the Japanese government was trying to keep the most important terms secret from Washington. American Far Eastern experts later concluded that "no such distinction was made in the list given to the President of China," thus undermining the Japanese case.[25]

On 13 March 1915, the United States government protested Japan's actions, stating that it "could not regard with indifference the assumption of political, military, or economic domination over China by a foreign power." In defense of the Open Door Policy, Washington requested that Tokyo refrain from "pressing upon China an acceptance of proposals which would, if accepted, exclude Americans from equal participation in the economic and industrial development of China and would limit the political independence of that country."[26] On 30 March 1915 Secretary of State Bryan sent a protest specifically criticizing Tokyo for trying to force Japanese advisers on the Chinese government and for claiming exclusive rights to manage Japanese police forces in Manchuria and Inner Mongolia.[27]

As a result of America's protest Japan modified the resolution forcing China to accept Japanese police and retracted the demand to make Fujian province an exclusive zone for Japanese development. On 28 April 1915, in the midst of the ongoing negotiations with Beijing, Japan also publicly announced that it had offered to restore the Jiaozhou concession to China in return for three less stringent conditions: opening the port of Qingdao to foreigners; allowing a Japanese concession as well as an international settlement; and turning the German public buildings and property over to Japan.[28]

Japanese diplomats furthermore requested that Beijing grant Japanese companies permission to build three railway lines from Nanchang to Hangzhou, from Jiujiang to Nanchang, and from Nanchang to Qingdao. This corresponded with the Sino-German railway agreements signed in 1913. But Tokyo reported that to its "surprise and disappointment . . . the Chinese Government, instead of showing any disposition to listen to these fair and reasonable representations of the Japanese Minister, flatly refused to consider the proposal."[29]

One of the most important and intriguing questions about the controversy surrounding the Twenty-one Demands revolves around the contradictory accusations made by the Beijing government and the opposition government in Guangzhou. Beijing officials blamed Sun Yat-sen for forcing China to negotiate with Japan. They argued that as Sun had already promised Tokyo extensive military and political rights throughout China in return for Japan's support for the Guangzhou government, Beijing had no choice but to match these offers.[30]

Sun responded by insisting that the Twenty-one Demands were not originally drafted by Japan, but by Yuan Shikai himself in return for Japanese favors. These reportedly included an agreement to recognize Yuan as the emperor of a revived Chinese monarchy.[31] In a 1917 publication Sun accused Yuan: "In fact, the Twenty-one Demands were presented by Japan at his own instigation; Japan did not, at the beginning, press him to accept these Demands."[32]

Further evidence supporting this interpretation was provided by the Chinese intellectual leader and reformer Liang Qichao, who discussed his failed attempts to stop the Beijing government from signing this treaty with Japan: "When the Twenty-one Demands were presented, the whole Chinese nation felt humiliated and the spirit of the people was stirred to the very depths. I tried [but failed] to convince those then in power by my various articles in the *Beijing Gazette* and the *Da Zhong Hua* that it was better by far to let the Japanese employ force and occupy China's territory than to yield to the demand and sign any document."[33]

Such accusations have since been supported by archival documents. In November 1917 the U.S. Ambassador to France reported to President Wilson that China's minister in Paris, He Weide, privately admitted to him that Tokyo had promised Yuan Shikai that "Japan would see him promoted" to emperor. To appease the Japanese people and to give Yuan Shikai a face-saving way of signing the treaty, Tokyo delivered an ultimatum to China when, in fact, only those conditions that Beijing agreed to in advance were included in the Twenty-one Demands (see Document 1).[34]

In January 1915 Japan had to make the important decision whether to rely simply on economic control or whether also to demand political control of the Shandong concession. Ultimately, Japan felt obliged to match Russia's ongoing negotiations with China; during fall 1914 negotiations revolved around a twenty-one point draft Sino-Russian treaty placing Outer Mongolia under Russian control. Although Washington succeeded in forcing Tokyo to retract some of its harshest measures from its own twenty-one point treaty, it was not able to stop the treaty.

Based on the above-cited evidence, responsibility for signing the Twenty-one Demands must be shared equally by Beijing and Tokyo. Faced with Russia's relentless expansion into Outer Mongolia, China sought to use Japan as a counterbalance. This new *status quo* was undermined in 1917, however, following the February and October revolutions in Russia, which resulted in the virtual collapse of Russian power in Asia. This meant that there was no longer any need to counterbalance Russia, thereby undermining the Chinese rationale for agreeing to the Japanese treaty. The Chinese scrambled to disavow this treaty as having been forced on China when, in fact, Beijing had signed it willingly. This is the origin of the controversy over the Twenty-one Demands. China's acquiescence was destined to play an enormously important role at the Paris talks; as Liang Qichao later concluded, if China had openly resisted Japan in 1915, "how strong her case would have been at the [Paris] peace conference."[35]

**The Japanese Ultimatum**

On 7 May 1915, Japan reportedly forced China to accept the Twenty-one Demands. Tokyo reminded Beijing of Japan's "immense sacrifices in blood and money" in winning the Shandong concession from Germany. Japan's ultimatum also reiterated that the circumstances of Japan's victory over Germany had altered its original promise to return the Shandong concession to China: "Therefore, after taking the place [Shandong], there is not the least obligation on the Imperial Japanese Government's part to return the place to China."[36] Still, it became clear that Japan would agree to return Shandong to China if Beijing met three conditions: opening Jiaozhou to international trade, establishing a Japanese concession there, and ceding most of Germany's public buildings and property to Japan.

Once news of Japan's ultimatum was released, Washington quickly reacted. On 13 May 1915, an American note stated that "it cannot recognize any agreement or undertaking which has been entered into or which may be entered into between the Governments of Japan and China impairing the treaty rights of the United States and its citizens in China, the political or territorial integrity of the Republic of China, or the international policy relative to China commonly known as the 'Open Door Policy.' "[37] Instead of taking advantage of American offers by refusing to sign, Beijing claimed publicly that it was acting under duress. It signed a series of agreements with Tokyo on 25 May 1915. These agreements granted Japan political and economic rights in the Shandong concession.

The first subject of the Twenty-one Demands pertained directly to the Shandong concession. Most importantly, China pledged herself to agree to whatever terms Japan and Germany later arranged for the "disposition of all rights, interests and concessions which Germany, by virtue of treaties or otherwise, possesses in

THE DIPLOMATIC SITUATION    19

PARIS, November 12, 1917

My dear Mr. President:

In my letter of some little time ago, after having dwelt upon conditions then prevailing in France, I promised to write you giving my observations concerning some of the problems confronting the Allies, having to do with their relations toward each other.

Mr. Hoo Wei Teh said that he strongly believed it was Japanese intrigue that later fomented the disturbances in Southern China, with the object of furnishing an excuse for Japan to come in and establish order. He narrated in an amusing manner an interesting story of how, to appease the people of Japan, that Government had given out for home consumption the fact that an ultimatum had been given to China imposing certain conditions upon her which she would be compelled to accept. As a matter of fact, a considerable number of the original provisions of the ultimatum had been refused by China and others compatible to her dignity and security had been accepted. Those that had been accepted were proudly announced in Tokio as being the ultimatum to which Japan was soon going to force China to agree. A further phase of this international game lay in the fact that, while it had been solemnly enjoined upon the Chinese Government not to make known any of the rejected Articles of the so-called ultimatum which had been proposed, yet the British and other Governments at Pekin had been let into the "secret", that only the accepted provisions had been proposed to China.

As I am despatching this letter, I am reminded by its date that it should reach you on the eve of the day when the fine sentiments expressed in your Thanksgiving Day proclamation will be read from a number of the public places in Paris.

Believe me, dear Mr. President,
Very sincerely yours,

W. G. Sharp

**Document 1**: Ambassador W. G. Sharp's Letter to President Wilson, Proving that China Accepted the Twenty-one Demands in Advance relation to the Province of Shandong." In addition, if Germany gave up its options on railway loans, then Japanese capitalists would be approached to assume them. China also agreed to open up additional ports in Shandong province to international trade, an action that should be made after "consulting the Minister of Japan." Beijing further promised not to lease or cede any territory in Shandong or any island along its coast to any foreign power.[38]

Finally, in a separate exchange of notes Tokyo renewed its promise to restore the leased territory to China once Germany transferred its rights to Japan and "the leased territory of Jiaozhou Bay is completely left to the free disposal of Japan." These notes specified that the following conditions had to be met:[39]

> 1. The whole of Jiaozhou Bay to be opened as a commercial port.
>
> 2. A concession under the exclusive jurisdiction of Japan to be established at a place to be designated by the Japanese Government.
>
> 3. If the foreign powers desire it, an international concession may be established.
>
> 4. As regards the disposal to be made of the buildings and properties of Germany and the conditions and procedures relating thereto, the Japanese Government and the Chinese Government shall arrange the matter by mutual agreement before the restoration.

These conditions primarily concerned economic matters, not political control over the Shandong concession. This indicated that Japan was attempting to meet the conditions set by the United States in its Open Door Policy.

As a result of the U.S. protests the final Sino-Japanese treaty signed on 25 May 1915 was much weaker than previous versions. Japan agreed that China would herself build all new railways and would obtain financing from Japanese capitalists only if Germany abandoned its prior agreement with China. Furthermore, while the original version stated that Japan and China would jointly decide in a separate agreement which port cities in Shandong would be opened to foreign trade, the revised version agreed that China would make this decision and only afterward would consult with the Japanese minister.

In the public declaration protesting Japan's ultimatum Beijing stated that it agreed to sign the Twenty-one Demands only "to preserve the Chinese people, as well as the large number of foreign residents in China from unnecessary suffering, and also to prevent the interests of friendly Powers from being imperiled."[40] China appeared all too willing to sign this agreement with Japan, even though Washington repeatedly offered to help Beijing oppose it.

In fact, Beijing was negotiating a similar treaty with Imperial Russia concerning the status of Outer Mongolia. Because of differences between the Western calendar and the Russian calendar, which was thirteen days behind, the final twenty-two point Sino-Russian-Mongolian agreement outlining the status of Outer Mongolia was signed on 25 May 1915 by the Russian calendar, or 7 June 1915 by the Western calendar. Beijing clearly linked these two treaties since it waited to ratify the Sino-Japanese treaty until 8 June 1915, one day after it signed the so-called Tripartite Treaty with Russia and Outer Mongolia.

From Japan's point of view, Tokyo's new treaty with Beijing was necessary to counterbalance Imperial Russia's simultaneous efforts to expand into Outer Mongolia. Although Tokyo promised to return political control of the Shandong concession to China once Germany ceded Japan the rights, Tokyo would still retain important economic rights. On 16 December 1918, following the Bolshevik revolution, the American Chamber of Commerce in China stressed how the international situation had changed when it warned that if Japan was granted its four conditions for returning Shandong it would result in the "absolute control of Qingdao and its hinterland" and would be equal to the "outright annexation of the Port and to the virtual annexation of the Province by the Japanese Government." Some of the top American businessmen in China believed it was best either to internationalize completely the port of Qingdao or to restore it *in toto* to China.[41]

This fear was perhaps the root cause of the generally held belief that Japan intended to annex all of Shandong province. In fact, although Tokyo undoubtedly hoped to use negotiations with Beijing to provide a congenial atmosphere for Japanese economic investments both inside and outside of the Jiaozhou concession, its later actions proved that it did not intend to annex Shandong outright. Instead, Japan sought to retain a favorable balance of power. To this end Tokyo quickly signed secret agreements with most of the other Allied powers during 1917 to insure that even these more limited diplomatic gains would not be reversed.

**China Joins the War Against Germany**

The United States, perhaps because it had not yet joined World War I and so did not need Japanese cooperation in the war effort, was the only major power that refused to recognize Japan's Twenty-one Demands. As an important first step in reversing these provisions, Washington repeatedly urged Beijing to sever diplomatic relations with Germany and Austria and join the Allies, a course of action that China belatedly adopted in 1917. In response, Japan signed a series of secret agreements with Great Britain, Russia, France, and Italy to back up its claim to the Shandong concession. Tokyo also exchanged notes with Washington that recognized Japan's legitimate economic interests in China. This treaty, although a far cry from recognizing the Twenty-one Demands, helped block China's later attempts to undo the Twenty-one Demands once Yuan Shikai had died and his plans for a revived Chinese monarchy had collapsed.

On 14 March 1917, almost three years after World War I began and after repeated urging by the United States, China finally broke diplomatic relations with Germany and Austria. Many Chinese intellectuals and reformers, such as Liang Qichao, had long advocated that China join the Allies as a first step to international equality; even Chen Duxiu, future leader of the Chinese Communist Party, supported the war effort in the hope that this would enhance China's world standing.[42] But it would be another five months before China declared war against Germany and Austria on 14 August 1917.

China almost immediately benefited from its declaration of war. From that date Beijing no longer had to pay Germany's and Austria's combined 20.91 percent yearly share of the Boxer indemnity. Belgium, France, Great Britain, Italy, Japan, Portugal, and later Russia and the United States also agreed to allow China to defer their shares of the Boxer payments for five years, beginning on 1 December 1917.[43] Beijing, by formally becoming an ally, also hoped that the articles in the 25 May 1915 treaty dealing with Shandong would be null and void, especially since it now seemed probable that Germany would have to return the Shandong concession directly to China instead of ceding it to Japan.

Japan quickly foresaw the problems that China's declaration of war might cause for the claim to Shandong.[44] On 21 February 1917, Japan signed a secret agreement with Great Britain in which London promised to support Tokyo's claim to the Shandong concession at the upcoming peace conference in return for Japan's supporting British claims to all of Germany's South Pacific islands. On 5 March 1917 Russia agreed to recognize the Twenty-one Demands in return for Japan's recognition of Russia's preeminent position in Outer Mongolia. On 6 March 1917 Japan secretly agreed with France to work to persuade China to break off diplomatic relations with Germany and impound German ships. Finally, on 28 March 1917 Japan and Italy signed a similar secret agreement.[45]

On 2 November 1917, the United States and Japan exchanged what became known as the Lansing-Ishii notes. Although Secretary of State Robert Lansing did not support either the Twenty-one Demands or Japan's rights to Shandong, the United States did recognize Japan's "geographical propinquity" in China. A "Confidential Memorandum" that originally accompanied these notes (see Document 2) confirmed that Japan agreed not to take "advantage of present conditions to seek special rights and privileges in China."[46] This memorandum was later eliminated when the text of the Lansing-Ishii notes was rewritten to include a similar, albeit weaker, statement of intent. The notes were permanently cancelled on 14 April 1923 following the Washington Conference.[47] Tokyo chose to interpret the Lansing-Ishii notes as meaning that the United States supported Japan's legitimate economic interests in China, while Washington emphasized Tokyo's promise to uphold the Open Door Policy. Therefore, President Woodrow Wilson proclaimed these notes a "distinct gain for China."[48]

On 5 November 1917, Lansing informed Minister Reinsch in Beijing that Washington was pleased that these notes "not only contain a reaffirmation of the 'open door' policy but introduce a principle of non-interference with the sovereignty

Handed copy to Viscount Ishii
at Conference, Oct.22/17.   RL

CONFIDENTIAL MEMORANDUM To Accompany
the Reply of the Japanese Government.

In the preliminary draft note dealing with questions relating to the Republic of China, which are of mutual interest to Japan and the United States and which, on September 26, 1917, was submitted by the Government of the United States to the Government of Japan for their consideration, there appeared, following the declaration by the two Governments of their adherence to the so-called "Open Door" policy, a further declaration "that they will not take advantage of present conditions "to seek special rights and privileges in China which would abridge the "rights of the citizens or subjects of other friendly states."

For certain reasons of expediency, which have been orally explained to the Government of the United States, the Government of Japan considered it to be unwise to include the above-quoted declaration in the proposed note, and it was, therefore, stricken out by mutual consent.

In order, however, to avoid misconstruction being placed upon this amendment of the note, the Government of Japan desire to affirm that by doing so there was no purpose on their part to assert a contrary principle or policy, and that the elimination of the declaration has no significance whatsoever in determining the terms of the note as finally agreed upon by the two Governments.

**Document 2**: "Confidential Memorandum" of the Lansing-Ishii Notes, in which Japan Agrees to Adhere to the Open Door Policy in China and territorial integrity of China, which, generally applied, is essential to perpetual international peace, as has been so clearly declared by President Wilson."[49] Lansing repeated this argument on 12 November 1917 when he spoke with the Chinese Minister, emphasizing that these notes "restrained" Japan and that "such a bargain seemed to me decidedly in favor of China."[50]

Japan's 25 May 1915 treaty with China; its secret agreements with Great Britain, Russia, France, and Italy; and its public and private exchange of notes with the United States placed the Japanese delegation in a strong diplomatic position when it arrived at Paris in 1919. These treaties either gave legitimacy to Japan's economic interests in China outright or they indirectly recognized the Twenty-one Demands. Taken together, these treaties almost completely undermined China's attempts to regain control over the Shandong concession by declaring war on Germany and Austria. Moreover, Japan and China soon signed several bilateral agreements in 1918 that further undermined China's diplomatic standing at the Paris Peace Conference.

**The 1918 Secret Sino-Japanese Agreements**

The complex mosaic of treaties and agreements discussed above was made even more complicated on 24 September 1918 when Tokyo and Beijing exchanged confidential notes on the administration of Shandong and the construction of two new Japanese-financed railway lines in Shandong. On 28 September 1918, the two governments signed another secret treaty fixing the terms and repayment of these railway loans. By signing these agreements Beijing tacitly recognized the continued validity of the Twenty-one Demands as embodied in its 25 May 1915 treaty with Tokyo. These agreements also effectively counteracted Beijing's 14 August 1917 declaration of war against Germany and Austria. Now China could no longer argue that its declaration of war cancelled all earlier obligations to Japan, since the 1918 agreements followed the declaration of war and therefore superseded it. From a diplomatic standpoint these two secret Sino-Japanese agreements were to prove disastrous for the Chinese delegation at Paris.

Just three months prior to the formal beginning of the Paris Peace Conference, Chinese Minister to Japan Zhang Zongxiang and Japanese Minister of Foreign Affairs Baron Shimpei Goto met and agreed to end Japan's civil administration of Shandong. In another agreement, Zhang acknowledged that Japan could build two railway lines in China in exchange for Japanese loans (see Document 3).

Baron Goto, however, in his 24 September 1918 note to Zhang, stated that while Chinese troops would guard the Qingdao-Jinan railway, Japanese military experts would continue to work at the headquarters of the railway police force, at all major stations, and at the police training school. In return for the Japanese withdrawal of its civil administration from Shandong, Beijing agreed the railway line would become a joint Sino-Japanese company.[51]

Tokyo, September 24, 1918

Monsieur le Ministre,

The Chinese Government have decided to obtain loans from Japanese capitalists and to proceed speedily to build the railways connecting points as below set forth. Having received an authorisation from my Government, I have the honour herewith to communicate the same to your Government.

1. Between Tsinan and Shuntoh
2. Between Kaomi and Hsuchow

However in case the aforementioned two lines are deemed to be disadvantageous from the point of railway management, other suitable lines will be decided upon by consultation.

Should there be no objection to the above propositions; it is requested that your Government will lose no time in taking necessary steps to cause the capitalists of your country to agree to enter negotiations for loans on the same.

Reply to the above is awaited and will be appreciated.

I avail, etc., etc., etc.,

(signed) Tsung-hsiang Chang

His Excellency
 Baron Shimpei Goto
  Etc., etc., etc.

**Document 3**: 24 September 1918 Secret Sino-Japanese Railway Agreement, Proving Chinese Acceptance of a Japanese Sphere in Shandong

On 28 September 1918 the Vice-President of the Industrial Bank of Japan Yeiji Ono and Minister Zhang further agreed that two new railway extensions would be built in Shandong and financed by a syndicate of Japanese banks. As security for these loans Zhang promised the Japanese banks "all present and future property and revenues of the two railways." In return, Beijing was granted an immediate advance on the Japanese loans of 20 million yen (approximately $9,000,000 in 1918 dollars) at a yearly interest rate of 8 percent.[52]

Formerly, historians of the Shandong question have been unaware that on 13 October 1918 the Japanese Ambassador in Washington handed Secretary of State Lansing a confidential memorandum describing in detail the new Sino-Japanese agreement. Japan assured America that with regard to the projected railway construction in Shandong: "It may be noted that the projected lines in Shandong Province are within the scope contemplated in Article I of the Chino-Japanese treaty respecting Shandong Province of 1915, the particulars of which were made known to the American Government at the time of the conclusion."[53]

Washington did not immediately accept Tokyo's explanation, however, but replied instead:[54]

> The Government of the United States observes that as the question of succession by Japan to the rights formerly enjoyed by Germany in Shandong Province and the related matters may be the subject of consideration at the forthcoming peace conference and will doubtless be adjusted in connection with the terms of peace. This government, pending the outcome of deliberation of the peace conference and conclusion of peace, reserves the announcement made in His Excellency's note for future discussion in so far as it relates to Shandong and in so far as the interests of the United States are concerned. Certain reservations as above said of the Chino-Japanese agreement of 1915 were made at the time of their announcement.

Washington, in addition to clarifying that Tokyo told the United States in advance of the 1918 Sino-Japanese agreements, also stated its intentions to dispute them.

As a result of Japan's numerous secret agreements, when the Japanese delegation arrived at Paris in early 1919 its diplomatic position seemed secure. Not only had Japan signed agreements with all of the major Allied powers backing its claim to the Shandong concession, but it had concluded official treaties with China during 1915 and 1918 that did likewise. In particular, the 1918 agreements appeared to recognize the validity of those sections of the Twenty-one Demands pertaining to Shandong, since one of the main provisions of this 1915 treaty was that China would pay for all future Shandong railway construction by assuming loans from Japan. The linking of the 1915 and 1918 treaties was to make it much more difficult for the Chinese delegation to prove that Japan had used force to make China sign the Twenty-one Demands.

Finally, as for the 1918 secret agreements themselves, on 24 September 1918, at the conclusion of the Sino-Japanese talks, Minister Zhang wrote to Minister Goto: "I beg to acquaint you in reply that the Chinese Government gladly agree to the proposals of the Japanese Government above alluded to."[55] As Liang Qichao was to point out after the Paris Peace Conference was already over, the Chinese acknowledgment that it had "gladly agreed" to the 1918 secret agreements largely invalidated China's main argument that it had been forced to sign the 1915 treaty only because of Japan's ultimatum. Thus, this simple note rendered "China's trump card . . . at once ineffective."[56]

**Conclusions**

When the Paris Peace Conference convened in January 1919 and began to address the Shandong question, the participants were faced with the daunting task of not only untangling China's 1898 treaty with Germany but also China's 1915 and 1918 agreements with Japan, as well as Japan's treaties with Great Britain, Russia, France, Italy, and the United States. The total number of treaties and agreements was even greater: the appendices of the American peace commission's summary on Shandong included copies of no fewer than nineteen official treaties and agreements relating in one way or another to the Shandong question.[57]

The Japanese government and its people were understandably proud of their contribution to the Allied war effort and, in particular, of Japan's actions that had "destroyed at one stroke the German power in the Far East by the reduction of the fortress of Qingdao."[58] Tokyo thought it important to Japan's national honor that a concrete symbol of its military victory over Germany be preserved. Many Japanese favored retaining Shandong indefinitely to provide this symbol. Three reasons for this included: 1) Germany's mistreatment of Japan after the Sino-Japanese War; 2) the large number of Japanese casualties suffered at the siege of Qingdao; and 3) a lack of Chinese cooperation during Japan's military operations against Germany.

In particular, the Japanese were eager to exact revenge on Germany for its actions against Japan following the end of the 1894-95 Sino-Japanese War. On 23 April 1895 Germany had joined Russia and France in the so-called Triple Intervention whereby Germany was instrumental in forcing Japan to return the Liaodong peninsula, which a week before China had ceded to Japan in the peace treaty of Shimonoseki. This opposition by three of the world's strongest powers forced Tokyo to return the territory to China on 4 November 1895.

To add insult to injury, in 1898 Russia and Germany had come to an understanding by which Russia acquired the very same territorial rights from China, while Germany took the Shandong concession, leaving Japan looking on from the sidelines. Russian expansion in the Liaodong peninsula and Manchuria increased Russo-Japanese tensions and eventually led to war. To general surprise, Japan defeated Russia in the 1904-5 Russo-Japanese War. Japan's victory marked the first time in modern history that an Oriental country had defeated an Occidental country. In the subsequent peace negotiations Russia was then forced to cede the Liaodong concessions to Japan.

Therefore, the Shandong situation in 1914 undoubtedly was connected to Germany's humiliation of Japan twenty years earlier; Japan was eager to punish Germany for its role in the Triple Intervention. This may also help to explain why Japan's 15 August 1914 ultimatum to Germany specifically stated that Shandong would be returned to China: just as Japan had lost face in 1895 when Germany had forced it to return Liaodong to China, Germany could be similarly made to lose face by Japan's forcing it to hand over the Shandong concession to China. Germany's participation in the Triple Intervention would finally be avenged.

Another important factor was the high number of Japanese casualties in the siege of Qingdao, a number much greater than originally anticipated by Tokyo when it had declared war in August 1914. Tokyo needed something to show the Japanese people for these losses. Because of the relatively high number of killed and wounded it became extremely important to national pride, not to mention that of the Japanese military, to assume at least temporary legal control over all former German holdings that Japan's armed forces had taken in battle. This meant that Germany would officially cede the Shandong concession to Japan at Paris and only after this transfer was complete could Japan carry out its promise to return the concession to China. In this regard Tokyo's moral claim to Shandong did not differ greatly from those of Japan's European allies, most of whom made similar financial and territorial claims against Germany and Austria in an attempt to appease public opinion.

As a result the Japanese delegation would persuasively argue at Paris that "full justice" should be accorded to Japan based "upon her sacrifices and achievements and upon the fact of actual occupation, involving [a] sense of national honor."[59] President Wilson clearly understood the importance that the Japanese attached to national honor and dignity, and he insisted repeatedly that he "wanted to support the dignity of Japan."[60] Because of the Japanese casualties it was impossible for Tokyo to agree to any solution of the Shandong question that entailed a "loss of face" for those Japanese veterans who sought honor and international recognition for their military achievement.

Finally, many Japanese felt that China did not deserve to regain the Shandong concession because Beijing had not immediately broken diplomatic relations with Germany and had not assisted Japan in its military operations. In fact, to the contrary, Beijing insisted soon after Japan's victory that Tokyo agree to pay for all damages irrespective of whether they were caused by Japanese or German troops. Stung by China's apparent ingratitude, many Japanese thought that Shandong should be treated as spoils gained directly from Germany rather than from China since, in accordance with its 1898 treaty with Germany, China could not legally reclaim its right to the Shandong concession until 1997.

It was also widely assumed that Tokyo's promise to return Shandong to China was nullified by the fact that China had maintained diplomatic relations with Germany through early 1917. China did not actually declare war against Germany and Austria until 14 August 1917, almost three years to the day after Japan had presented its Shandong ultimatum to Germany. In the interim, however, Japan and China had signed official agreements pertaining to the disposition of the Shandong concession.

To many Japanese, it appeared that Tokyo's earlier promises to return Shandong to China had been invalidated by Beijing's own actions. To abide by Tokyo's original promises to transfer the Shandong concession to China, as the Japanese delegation would later agree to do at the Paris Peace Conference, meant ignoring these domestic views. In fact, Japan's decision to stand by its pledge and to return Germany's concessions to China actually required a great deal of political determination to overlook domestic opposition.

As this chapter has attempted to show, the Shandong question, which appeared deceptively simple to many outsiders—including, all too often, the international press corps—actually involved eight countries: China, Germany, Japan, Great Britain, Russia, France, Italy, and the United States. Of these the United States alone had not signed any agreements with Japan that specifically recognized its 1915 and 1918 treaties with China. This made President Woodrow Wilson the only relatively disinterested Big Three leader when discussion of the Shandong question was brought before the Paris Peace Conference in 1919. Considering the complexity and number of potential conflicts surrounding the Shandong question, it should come as no surprise that the final solution Wilson proposed did not completely satisfy anyone, least of all the Chinese delegates.

**Notes**

1. G. Zay Wood, *The Shantung Question: A Study in Diplomacy and World Politics* (New York: Fleming H. Revell Company, 1922), 13.

2. *Ibid.*, 7.

3. "Convention for the Lease of Kiaochow Bay," 6 March 1898, Hoover Archives, Stanley K. Hornbeck Papers (hereafter SKH Papers), Box 382.

4. Morinosuke Kajima, *The Diplomacy of Japan 1884-1922* (Tokyo: Kajima Institute of International Peace, 1980), Volume 3, 110.

5. 中外舊約章彙編 (*A Collection of Chinese-Foreign Treaties*), (Beijing: Xinhua Publishers, 1982), Volume 1, 738-740; the exact phrasing was: "德國應許永遠不轉租與別國."

6. "Convention for the Lease of Kiaochow Bay," 6 March 1898, SKH Papers, Box 382.

7. *Ibid.*

8. "Memorandum from Edward T. Williams to Henry White," 27 April 1919, SKH Papers, Box 387.

9. *A Collection* . . . , Volume 2, 981-982.

10. "Japanese Ultimatum to Germany," 15 August 1914, 外務省外交史料館 (Archives of the Gaikō Shiryōkan, hereafter Gaimushō), Tokyo, Japan. Gaimushō, File 2.3.1-3.1.

11. Ernest R. May, "American Policy and Japan's Entrance into World War I," *The Mississippi Valley Historical Review*, Vol. XL, No. 2 (Sept. 1953), 279-290.

12. "Baron Kato, Japanese Minister of Foreign Affairs, to Mr. Bryan, Secretary of State of the United States," 20 August 1914, in *Diplomatic Record: Japan in Shantung Province*, SKH Papers, Box 382.

13. "Japan Declaration of War on Germany," 23 August 1914, in *Diplomatic Record: Japan in Shantung Province*, SKH Papers, Box 382.

14. "Count Okuma, Cable to New York Independent, 'Message to the American People,'" 24 August 1914, in *Diplomatic Record: Japan in Shantung Province*, SKH Papers, Box 382.

15. "Memorandum: Conversation with His Excellency, Liang Tun-yen, Minister of Communications," 1 October 1914, SKH Papers, Box 382.

16. Note from Minister to China Paul Reinsch, dated 5 October 1914, and added to "Memorandum: Conversation with His Excellency, Liang Tun-yen, Minister of Communications," 1 October 1914, SKH Papers, Box 382.

17. "Memorandum from Edward T. Williams to Henry White," 27 April 1919, SKH Papers, Box 387.

18. "Baron Kato, Statement in the Japanese Diet," December 1914, in *Diplomatic Record: Japan in Shantung Province*, SKH Papers, Box 382.

19. Ernest Batson Price, *The Russo-Japanese Treaties of 1907-1916 Concerning Manchuria and Mongolia* (Baltimore: The Johns Hopkins Press, 1933), 107; Appendix B: Russia–Japan, Secret Convention of 17/30 July 1907.

20. *Ibid.*, 117; Appendix D: Russia–Japan, Secret Convention of June 25/July 8, 1912; Professor Kajima has discussed at some length how Japan and Russia later strengthened their cooperation in a fourth secret agreement that changed "special interests" to "vital interests." There has been much speculation that this fourth agreement was primarily directed against the United States, which was trying to use the Open Door Policy to limit Russian and Japanese expansion throughout China. See the Chapter entitled "Fourth Russo-Japanese Entente," in Kajima, *The Diplomacy of Japan 1884-1922*, Volume 3, 225-276.

21. "Memorandum from Minister to China Paul Reinsch to the State Department," 28 November 1914, SKH Papers, Box 382.

22. *Ibid.*

23. *Ibid.*

24. "Memorandum from Edward T. Williams and Stanley K. Hornbeck," January 1919, SKH Papers, Box 382.

25. "Memorandum from Edward T. Williams to Henry White," 27 April 1919, SKH Papers, Box 387.

26. "U.S. Protest to Japan," 13 March 1915, Gaimushō, File 2.1.1-32.2.

27. "Letter from Secretary of State Bryan to the Japanese Government," 30 March 1915, Gaimushō, File 2.1.1-32.3.

28. "Memorandum from the Japanese Government," 28 April 1915, Gaimushō, File 2.1.1-32.3.

29. *Ibid.*

30. Paul S. Reinsch, *An American Diplomat in China*, quoted by Henry Bond Restarick, *Sun Yat-sen: Liberator of China* (New Haven, CT: Yale University Press, 1931), 135.

31. Tokyo later decided to oppose Yuan's attempt to reinstate a monarchy. See Kwanha Yim, "Yuan Shih-k'ai and the Japanese," *The Journal of Asian Studies*, Vol. XXIV (1964-65), 63-73.

32. Sun Yat-sen, *The Vital Problem of China* (Taipei: China Cultural Service, 1953), 55.

33. Liang Qichao, "Causes of China's Defeat at the Peace Conference," *Millard's Review*, 19 July 1919, 262-265.

34. "Personal Letter from U.S. Ambassador to France Sharp to President Woodrow Wilson, November 1917," *The Woodrow Wilson Papers* (hereafter WWP), Microfilm Reel #384, 703-711.

35. *Ibid.*

36. "Japanese Ultimatum to China," 7 May 1915, SKH Papers, Box 382.

37. "U.S. Protest to the Japanese Government," 13 May 1915, Gaimushō, File 2.1.1-32.2.

38. "Japan's Twenty-one Demands," 25 May 1915, SKH Papers, Box 382.

39. "Memorandum on Policy from Stanley K. Hornbeck to Dr. I. Bowman," 20 January 1919, SKH Papers, Box 382.

40. "The Chinese-Japanese Agreement of 1915, China's Protest," *The Far Eastern Economic Review*, May 1915; SKH Papers, Box 383.

41. "Is Japan's Promise to Return Kiaochow Camouflage?" *Peking Leader*, 21 March 1919, Gaimushō, File 2.3.1-3.1. Japan's four points were also listed in a letter written by the American Chamber of Commerce in China to the United States government; the American Chamber of Commerce in China's president was J. Harold Dollar of the Robert Dollar Company, its vice-president was W. C. Sprague of the Standard Oil Company, and its treasurer was J. W. Gallagher of the U.S. Steel Products Company. It is important to recall that this letter was written after the Bolshevik revolution in October 1917, at which point Russia no longer played a counterbalancing role to Japanese expansion in China. Once Russian power diminished, the other powers were eager to move into the political and economic vacuum. Since Japan already had concessions bordering on the Russian sphere of interest in Manchuria and Inner Mongolia, other foreigners feared that Japan would reap the greatest bounty if it was allowed to retain Germany's former sphere of interest in Shandong.

42. Lee Feigon, *Chen Duxiu, Founder of the Chinese Communist Party* (Princeton, NJ: Princeton University Press, 1983), 105-110.

43. *The China Yearbook,* 1919-20, 348-349.

44. Ray Stannard Baker, *Woodrow Wilson and World Settlement* (Gloucester, MA: Peter Smith, 1960), Volume One, 59-62; Volume Two, 244.

45. "Letter marked 'Very Secret' from Secretary of State Lansing to President Wilson, 26 February 1919," WWP Microfilm Reel #394, 11121-11122; Hsü lists Japan's agreement with Russia as being signed on 20 February 1917, 502.

46. "Confidential Memorandum to Accompany the Reply of the Japanese Government," 22 October 1917, Box 2, Robert Lansing collection, Seeley G. Mudd Manuscript Library, Princeton University.

47. James Brown Scott, "The Cancellation of the Lansing-Ishii Agreement," *The American Journal of International Law*, Vol. 17 (1923), 510-512.

48. "Letter from President Woodrow Wilson to Secretary of State Robert Lansing," 7 November 1917, WWP Microfilm Reel #384, 691.

49. "Telegram from Secretary of State Robert Lansing to U.S. Minister to China Paul Reinsch," 5 November 1917, WWP Microfilm Reel #384, 695-6.

50. "The Lansing-Ishii Agreement 1917," Robert Lansing collection, Box 2.

51. "Exchange of Notes Embodying an arrangement concerning questions in Shantung, September 24, 1918," John V. A. MacMurray, ed., *Treaties and Agreements with and Concerning China, 1894-1919* (New York: Oxford University Press, 1921), Volume II, 1445-1446.

52. "Preliminary Agreement for a loan for the Tsinanfu-Shuntefu and Kaomi-Hsuchow extensions of the Shantung Railway, September 28, 1918," MacMurray, Volume II, 1450-1452.

53. "Japanese Memorandum Handed to Secretary of State Lansing," 13 October 1918, Gaimushō, File 2.3.1-22, pp. 116-119.

54. "American Reply to the Japanese Memorandum," 22 December 1918, Gaimushō, File 2.3.1-22, p. 109.

55. "Exchange of Notes Embodying an arrangement concerning questions in Shantung, September 24, 1918," MacMurray, Volume II, 1445-1446; also referred to in Chow, 187.

56. Liang Qichao, "Causes of China's Defeat at the Peace Conference," *Millard's Review*, 19 July 1919, 262-265.

57. "Precis of Memorandum and Appendices laid before the Peace Conference by the Chinese Delegates," 28 January 1919, SKH Papers, Box 328.

58. Toyokichi Iyenaga, "Iyenaga Decries Shantung Charge," *New York Times*, 1 August 1919.

59. "Transcript of Japanese Delegation's Meeting with President Woodrow Wilson," 23 April 1919, Gaimushō, File 2.3.1-3.1.

60. "Transcript of Japanese Delegation's Meeting with President Woodrow Wilson," 29 April 1919, Gaimushō, File 2.3.1-3.4.

# 2
# *The Chinese Delegation's Proposals to the Paris Peace Conference*

> Mr. Koo said that he could not lay too much emphasis on the fact that the Chinese people were now at the parting of the ways. The policy of the Chinese Government was cooperation with Europe and the United States as well as Japan. . . . The position of the Government was that they believed in the justice of the West and that their future lay there. If they failed to get justice there, the consequential reaction might be very great.[1]

> V. K. Wellington Koo, Chinese delegate (Paris, 22 April 1919)

The expectations of the Chinese public as the Paris Peace Conference opened were extraordinarily high. When China joined the Allies in 1917 many Chinese assumed that Germany would have to return the Shandong concession directly to China. On 4 March 1919, China's parliament even cabled the following petition to Woodrow Wilson: "Since the declaration of war against Germany, all treaties concluded between China and Germany have become null and void. We therefore venture in the most earnest manner possible to get you to support the demand of this country at the Peace Conference that the leased territory of Jiaozhou be handed back to China direct[ly] by Germany."[2]

The implied assumption that all of China's international obligations connected with the Shandong concession were also "null and void" ignored the continuing impact of China's 1915 treaty with Japan, not to mention the recently signed 1918 secret agreements. Under international law China could not unilaterally rescind these treaties. China's international obligations could in fact be altered only by the mutual consent of all parties involved. It became evident at Paris that the Chinese delegates were not willing to participate in this kind of dialogue with the Japanese delegation.

China's position at Paris was actually quite weak compared to that of Japan. It must be recalled that China declared war against Germany and Austria three years into the war, whereas Japan joined the Allied side in 1914. China also never sent troops into action or took part in the fighting. While approximately 135,000 Chinese workers did assist the Allies in Europe by working on the docks, in construction, and trench digging, many of them were recruited before China had declared war.[3] Chinese workers were lured to France by the free food and clothing, the generous wages, and the opportunity for a free trip to Europe. And although China organized a "War Participation Bureau" in 1917, it existed mainly on paper and contributed little to the war effort. By contrast Japanese troops fought and died in World War I and the Japanese government expended huge sums neutralizing the German threat in Asia.

Finally, as soon as Beijing announced that it had joined the Allies, China was rewarded by the outright cancellation of the German and Austrian shares of the Boxer indemnity. The majority of the other Allies also agreed to defer payments on their shares of the indemnity for five years. By contrast, Tokyo did not receive any monetary compensation for defeating Germany, while Japan's offer to return the Shandong concession to China stripped it of what little territory it had won by force of arms.

Many of the Allied countries considered the cancellation and deferment of the bulk of the Boxer indemnity to be more than sufficient recompense for China's minimal contribution to the war effort. But this did not stop China's delegation from demanding that the participating nations at Paris agree to discard almost a century of international treaties that China had signed under duress with the various foreign powers—treaties that the Chinese delegation now claimed were to China's disadvantage. Chief among these was Japan's Twenty-one Demands. Unfortunately for China's delegates, Beijing's decision not to inform them about its most recent secret agreements with Tokyo undermined the logic of this argument; none was more surprised than those in the Chinese delegation when Japan made public the existence of these secret agreements on the floor of the conference.

**The Members of the Chinese Delegation**

Lu Zhengxiang headed China's six-member delegation to the Paris Peace Conference. He was one of China's best known and experienced diplomats. The remaining delegates were C. T. Wang, representing Sun Yat-sen's opposition party in Canton; Minister to Great Britain Alfred Sze; Minister to the United States V. K. Wellington Koo; Minister to Holland Wei Chenzu; and Minister to France He Weide. Never before, and it could be argued very rarely afterward, was China able to assemble such a distinguished delegation of experienced diplomats to represent its interests abroad. These delegates were also, at least at the beginning of the Paris Peace Conference, quite pro-American in their outlook and interests.

Lu Zhengxiang had gained notoriety during the 1911 Revolution when he became the first overseas Chinese minister to telegraph and advise the Manchu government to abdicate. At that time Lu had been China's minister to Russia. Shortly afterward he became the Republic of China's first minister of foreign affairs. After temporarily taking upon himself the duties of premier, he became

## CHINA'S PROPOSALS    35

the acting secretary of state and minister of foreign affairs in 1915 and was thereafter reappointed minister of foreign affairs in November 1917. Married to a Belgian woman, he spoke French and English and was reportedly a Roman Catholic. According to the U.S. State Department's biographies of the Chinese delegates, Lu was "friendly to the United States."[4]

Wang Zhengting, better known as C. T. Wang, owed his appointment to President Xu Shizhang as proof of Beijing's desire to reunite with the opposition government in Guangzhou. Trained in law at Yale University, Wang spoke fluent English, was for a time International Secretary of the Y.M.C.A. in China, and rose to vice-president of China's Senate during the early Republican government. A member of Sun Yat-sen's Guomindang—Nationalist—party, Wang became president of the Guangzhou Senate once it split away from Beijing. In Washington's judgment, Wang "places great confidence in the United States."[5]

Sao-ke Alfred Sze, whose Chinese name was Shi Shaoji, was educated at Cornell University, spoke English fluently, and had a long career representing China's interests abroad. Sze was related by marriage to Dang Shaoyi, former premier of China. Prior to his participation at the Paris Peace Conference he had been China's commissioner to the International Plague Conference in Mukden, Manchuria, in April 1911. Sze had been China's minister to Great Britain since June 1914 and had many acquaintances both there and in the United States. The State Department concluded that Sze was "very friendly to the United States," and that he was "amiable, has considerable influence, but cannot be called a man of initiative."[6]

Arguably the second most important member of the Chinese delegation after Lu Zhengxiang was Gu Weijun, better known as V. K. Wellington Koo. Koo had received his M.A. and Ph.D. from Columbia University, where he excelled as a student. He worked as secretary to the minister of foreign affairs and became China's minister to the United States in 1915. Married to former premier Dang Shaoyi's daughter, which also made him related by marriage to Alfred Sze, Koo was described as a "protégé and close friend of Lu Zhengxiang." He was a leading member of the debate club during his years at Columbia and he was perhaps the most fluent in English of any member of China's delegation. Considered friendly to the United States, Koo was described by Washington as "highly polished, diplomatic, tactful, amiable, and of keen intelligence." Koo's only apparent fault was that he was "looked upon in some quarters as lacking in strong convictions."[7]

He Weide, minister to France, had a long and distinguished career. He served as minister to Russia from 1904-8 and minister to Japan from 1908-12 before being reassigned as minister to France in November 1912. His father-in-law was one of the earliest Chinese students to study in the United States, while his wife was a graduate of Vassar College.[8] Although He Weide was not destined to play a major role at Paris, it should be recalled that he told Ambassador William Graves Sharp in Paris how Japan induced Beijing to accept the Twenty-one Demands by promising to help make Yuan Shikai the next emperor of China.

His presence at Paris is strong proof that China's delegation knew quite well that Japan's 1915 so-called ultimatum was actually nothing of the sort, a fact that seriously undermined China's oft-repeated claim that it had signed the 1915 agreement only under duress.

By all accounts the members of the Chinese delegation to the Paris Peace Conference were accomplished diplomats and statesmen. Records and transcripts from the early sessions reveal that they were also self-confident in their belief that they could succeed in their mission to reclaim the Shandong concession directly from Germany. But the Beijing government had neglected to inform them about the complete range of Chinese agreements affecting Shandong. Therefore, the delegates' ignorance concerning the 1918 Sino-Japanese agreements was to wreak havoc with the delegates' chances of success. Wellington Koo's private meetings with Woodrow Wilson in the months preceding the opening of the Paris Peace Conference show that China's own delegates, and as a result Wilson himself, were not privy to this important information.

**Wellington Koo and President Woodrow Wilson**

Immediately prior to the convening of the Paris Peace Conference, Minister Wellington Koo met with Wilson in Washington. The first such meeting took place in November 1918. During their discussion Koo informed Wilson of China's planned proposals, which included the elimination or revision of virtually all of China's treaties with the foreign powers. It should be noted that even before the Paris Conference convened, and long before President Wilson became fully cognizant of the 1918 Sino-Japanese secret agreements, he warned Koo that China's broad goals would be difficult to achieve. Wilson promised nevertheless that he would do all that he could to help China.

When Koo met with Wilson on 26 November 1918, he did not tell him about China's most recent agreements with Japan because Koo himself did not know about them. Russell H. Fifield, after an interview with Koo more than thirty years later on 31 October 1951, quoted Koo as admitting that in late 1918—when he obtained President Wilson's promise to help China—Koo was as yet unaware of Beijing's September 1918 agreements with Tokyo.[9] By contrast, Wilson already knew that China was involved with secret diplomacy and he cautioned Koo that while "he would gladly do his best to support China at the peace conference," such treaties were "injurious to China and the world" (see Document 4).[10]

Likewise, Koo met with Secretary of State Lansing on 15 November 1918.[11] As mentioned above, the Japanese Ambassador had previously handed Lansing a memorandum outlining the most recent Sino-Japanese agreements. Therefore, Lansing carefully cautioned Koo that all parties represented at the conference, including Japan, would have to be considered.[12]

Nov. 26, 1918.
( 2:15 to 2:30 p.m.)

He first greeted me and shook hands with me and asked me to sit down with him on the sofa chair, he on right and I on left. I inquired of his health and he reciprocated, expressing sympathy to me for the loss of Mrs. Koo.

I congratulated him and through him the government and people of the United States on the victory of the American armies in Europe. I added that the government and people of China had been animated with a sincere admiration for the magnificent way in which the United States under his leadership had prosecuted the war and carried it to a victorious conclusion.

He said in reply that he had felt that China had been with the United States in the war and that only her political stress had prevented her from taking a more active part. I said that the Chinese people themselves regretted the political disturbance in China, but I expressed my hope that through it all China would emerge nearer to the goal of true democracy with which the hearts of the Chinese people are attached.

The people of China, I added, entertained the belief that the United States under the President's able leadership would play a very important role in the making of peace as it did in the prosecution of the war.

He said he hoped too, adding that it was comparatively easy to formulate principles for a peace, but their practical application was quite a task, as in the matter of defining territories for the many new-born states in Europe. He referred to Bohemia for example, and dwelt upon the difficulty of finding a boundary for her. But he said the difficulty must be faced, because the principles were important.

I said that China had great hopes for the peace Conference. She had always relied on the friendship and good will of the United States in the crises which she had to undergo in the past. Now during the present period of world reconstruction, particularly at the peace conference where stupendous problems would be dealt with, China would rely on the sympathetic support of the United States all the more, in the conviction that the ideas of the Chinese people were in full harmony with those of the United States. China would hope to present certain proposals at the peace conference concerning her territorial integrity, - the preservation of her sovereign rights, and her fiscal and economic independence---proposals which, I remarked, were designed, not to secure any material gain or any selfish advantage for herself, but merely to restore to her some of the things which, in the view of the Chinese people, had been wrongfully taken from her. So the people of China were all looking to the President and the great country which he represented for help in the realisation for their just claims and aspirations.

The President said in reply that he had always felt sympathy for China and was interested in the problems of the Far East, for in his opinion peace was more likely to be endangered there than in other parts of the world, in future. He agreed with me that the ideals of China and the United States were along the same lines and said that he would gladly do his best to support China at the peace conference. He said there was one difficulty in the case of China, i.e. there were many secret agreements between the subjects of China and other powers. He thought these agreements were injurious to China and the world, and if they had had to be published, they would never have been made at all. He said he would therefore propose at the peace conference that not only secret diplomacy but secret commercial, industrial and financial agreements between subjects of different powers should be prohibited.

**Document 4**: Excerpt from 26 November 1918 Meeting between Minister V. K. Wellington Koo and President Woodrow Wilson

## 38  CHINA'S PROPOSALS

If Koo had been informed by his government about the most recent Sino-Japanese agreements, and had therefore been in a position to tell Wilson and Lansing what the impact of these recent Sino-Japanese agreements on the Shandong question might be, then Wilson and Lansing might have expressed even more serious reservations about assisting China. Since the Beijing government never directly informed Wilson and Lansing about China's arrangements with Japan, however, any promises that they extracted from Washington to help China were actually gained under false pretenses. This makes China's later accusations of an American "betrayal" particularly unfounded.

Chinese accusers also overlooked the fact that when the Paris Peace Conference convened the American delegation brought with it a comprehensive draft program to help China attain its goals. This program was divided into nine points recommending that: 1) all foreign "spheres of influence" be eliminated in China; 2) foreign interest in Chinese railways be neutralized; 3) any "monopolistic" mining privileges be abolished; 4) all foreign concessions be put under international control with the object of returning them to Chinese control; 5) all foreign troops be removed from China; 6) China be given control over all foreign post and telegraph offices; 7) a uniform currency be adopted throughout China; 8) tariff autonomy be granted to China once the *likin* tax was abolished; and, finally, 9) all foreign extraterritoriality rights be eliminated once China met four conditions: fifty percent of Chinese children must have received at least three years of schooling, a modern civil and criminal code must be in place, China must adopt a constitutional government that could safeguard against corruption, and China must provide adequate protection for patents and trademarks.[13]

Although President Wilson and Secretary of State Lansing were eager to help China, they were extremely careful not to raise Koo's hopes too high. In Wilson's case, he had already been informed in confidence that He Weide had admitted that Beijing signed the 1915 treaty with Tokyo voluntarily; therefore, China's claims that it signed this treaty under duress rang hollow. As for Lansing, he had information from the Japanese that Beijing had just signed a new agreement with Tokyo, and that this agreement actually reaffirmed the 1915 treaty.

Furthermore, on 17 December 1918, Lansing received a confidential State Department telegram warning that "the Japanese have concluded or are attempting to conclude with the Chinese Minister of Railways an agreement to the effect that the Shandong Railway should be jointly administered by China and Japan regardless of which of them might be given a title to the railway at peace conference, the railway to be policed by Chinese military guards under instruction of Japanese." This telegram also pointed out, quite accurately as later events would show, that Japan had been guaranteed trade privileges in Shandong in return for withdrawing its civil administration from the railway lines.[14]

Although this telegram substantially corroborated the information already provided to Washington by the Japanese Ambassador, Wilson and Lansing undoubtedly went to Paris hoping that China had not actually signed any concrete agreements with Japan. As late as 5 January 1919 it appeared that Sino-Japanese negotiations were perhaps still underway, although the American Legation in Beijing reported that the Japanese minister of foreign affairs had promised to support China's larger goals at Paris in return for a rapid and amicable solution of the Shandong question. As a result, Minister Reinsch warned Washington: "All general provisions made by the Peace Conference for the protection and salvation of China would be futile if Japanese special rights in Shandong should be acknowledged."[15]

The information that Wilson and Lansing received from Beijing's representatives appeared to contradict information that China had signed an official Shandong agreement with Japan. If the existence of the September 1918 agreements had been admitted by the Chinese, then Wilson's and Lansing's support for China might have been tempered, if not lacking altogether. In particular, there is nothing to suggest that Wilson and Lansing knew that the Beijing government had already received a twenty-million yen advance from Japan in fall 1918; the transfer of funds meant that reversing the Sino-Japanese agreements would be extremely difficult, if not altogether impossible.

Ironically, Washington appears to have learned of the basic contents of Beijing's 1918 secret agreements with Tokyo before China's own delegates to the Paris Peace Conference did. Because of these agreements, Beijing ordered the Chinese delegation not to be the first to bring up the Shandong question. But once the peace conference convened in early January 1919, Koo disobeyed orders and demanded that Tokyo immediately settle the Shandong question.

As Koo explained many years later: "Japan considered it to be her right to negotiate with Germany to the exclusion of China, while we took the stand, and I was strongly urging it on the Government, that China should raise the question at the Peace Conference as a matter of her own right, ignoring the treaty which she had signed with Japan under duress."[16] This diplomatic stance, in turn, forced Japan's delegation into revealing that Tokyo had already signed official—albeit secret—agreements with Beijing in September 1918.

**The Chinese Delegation's Proposals to Paris**

The Chinese delegation's main goal at Paris was to present a series of proposals loosely based on President Wilson's Fourteen Points, which had stated that the peace treaty ending World War I should grant justice to all parties. In a clear reference to this document, the preamble to China's proposals stated: "It is the principle of justice to all peoples and their right to live on equal terms of liberty and safety with one another, whether they be strong or weak."[17] To obtain justice, equality, liberty, and security for China, the Chinese delegates proposed that not only their wartime enemies but also their allies be prepared to alter or abolish almost a century of treaties and other international agreements that were detrimental to China's sovereignty and national interests.

China's proposals were divided into two main groups, the first dealing with Germany and Austria and the second treating China's allies. With regard to the

Shandong concession, the Chinese delegation's two proposals requested that Germany return Jiaozhou bay directly to China's "lawful ownership" and that all former German and Austrian railway and mining rights be abolished.[18] The second group, entitled "Re-adjustments with Friendly States" was much longer; it encompassed no fewer than eight categories subdivided into twenty-four points. In general China's proposals can be divided into three main groups: 1) territorial integrity, 2) political matters, and 3) economic questions.

To guarantee their nation's territorial integrity, the Chinese delegation proposed the internationalization of the Manchurian railways and rivers as well as the gradual internationalization of the foreign settlements in preparation for their return to China. All foreign-leased territories fortified during World War I, however, were to be handed over to China immediately. The rationale underlying this proposal was clear: "Removal of Germany from the Far East makes the retention of these territories unnecessary."[19]

China's political proposals included the elimination of all legation guards, removal of all foreign troops stationed in China, and the abolition of extraterritorial rights. Chinese considered extraterritoriality especially onerous.[20] It gave foreigners residing in China the right to be tried in special international courts. China's rationale for eliminating extraterritoriality was that foreign courts were no longer necessary since: "Law reform in China [is] progressing satisfactorily."[21]

Fiscal independence included the full restoration to China of its right to regulate and administer tariffs, then under foreign management to insure that China promptly met its debt payments. In addition, all railways throughout China would be consolidated under the central government, which would then take out an international railway loan to be repaid from railway revenues, so the Chinese government could redeem all foreign-built railways. The nationalization of the Shandong railway was a particularly important element of this proposal.[22]

If enacted, the Chinese delegation's proposals would have revolutionized China's position in the world. In many ways these proposals were an attempt to follow in Japan's footsteps. Japan, following the Meiji restoration, had fought hard to gain an international standing equal to the Western nations; beginning in 1894, after completing the same kind of legal and tariff reforms mentioned in China's proposal, Japan was able to start eliminating extraterritoriality.

According to the American legation in Beijing, the Japanese government was perhaps responsible for urging China to make such wide-ranging proposals. Reinsch warned that Japan might be feeding China's false hopes, since "the Chinese are being encouraged by the Japanese to make demands which it is a foregone conclusion will not be granted categorically by the Powers such as abolition of extraterritoriality and of customs tariff restrictions."[23] Another interpretation, however, is that Japan intended to help China obtain its goals in return for Beijing's cooperation on the Shandong question. This issue will be discussed in greater detail below.

## Wellington Koo and the Shandong Question

In order to understand the issues that were really at the heart of the Shandong controversy it is necessary to refer to peace conference minutes of 27 and 28 January 1919. Records of these sessions—marked "secret"—prove that the Chinese delegates, and Wellington Koo in particular, did not know about Beijing's September 1918 agreements with Tokyo determining the fate of the Shandong concession. This fact was never accurately reported by the international press because it was barred from attending and reporting on the sessions. Once the Japanese delegation revealed these agreements China's entire list of proposals—not just those few concerned with Shandong—were in jeopardy; this situation threatened to become a diplomatic disaster for China.

The decision to bar the press from the official sessions, and prevent its contact with members from the various delegations, helped to obscure the real issues surrounding the Shandong question. This policy prompted sharp condemnation from American correspondents at Paris. On 14 January 1919, eleven of them petitioned Wilson: "We direct your attention to the fact that this method, if followed, will limit our information to things accomplished. It will further prevent the publication of those matters not yet closed which the public demand the right to follow through to their consummation. Unless this right be granted the public will be denied the opportunity to be informed of the positions assumed by the various elements within the Conference, and public opinion thus will have no chance to function in the way that you have always advocated and that you defined in the Fourteen Points." These correspondents concluded by offering their "vigorous protest on behalf of the American press representatives," and along with their British colleagues, who sent a similar protest to the Prime Minister, they appealed to Wilson "for relief from this intolerable condition."[24]

As explained in a 1918 memo from Wilson to Lansing, keeping negotiations at Paris secret did not contradict his support in the Fourteen Points for "open" diplomacy, since he foresaw that all agreements would be published upon completion. Wilson was concerned that talks would quickly bog down if the public was made cognizant of the details of the negotiations too soon, making it difficult for the delegates to discuss the issues and reach suitable compromises.

Although Wilson's intentions were perhaps admirable, the secrecy surrounding the meetings greatly contributed to public misunderstanding of the Shandong question. In particular, the secret minutes provide proof that Koo did not know of his government's 1918 secret agreements until the 28 January 1919 meeting. If this episode had been made public, the Chinese delegates would have had a much more difficult time later on convincing the press corps that China had been wronged.

As the minutes show, it was on 27 January 1919 that Baron Makino first recommended that Wilson, Lloyd George, Clemenceau, Orlando, and Koo grant Japan "unconditional cession" from Germany of the "leased territory of Jiaozhou together with the railways, and other rights possessed by Germany in respect of

Shandong province." According to the official transcripts (see Appendix A), after Makino finished presenting Japan's case, Koo stated that since "the question was of such vital interest to China" he "hoped the Great Powers would reserve decision until the views of China had been heard."[25] It was decided that the Chinese delegation would present its case on the following day.

On 28 January 1919, Koo presented China's proposal for "the restoration to China of the leased territory of Jiaozhou, the railway in Shandong, and all other rights Germany possessed in that Province before the war" (see Appendix B). Koo began by revealing China's sincere appreciation of Japan: "China was fully cognizant of the service rendered to her by the heroic Army and Navy of Japan in rooting out German power from Shandong. China was also deeply indebted to Great Britain for helping in this task at a time of great peril to herself in Europe. . . . China appreciated these services all the more because her people in Shandong had also suffered and sacrificed in connection with the military operations for the capture of Jiaozhou, especially in regard to requisitions for labor and supplies of all kinds."[26]

But, according to Koo, Germany's lease in Shandong had been "wrung out of China by force," and if it was not returned directly to China, but was instead transferred to "any other Power," then the Chinese delegation would conclude that Paris was "adding one wrong to another."[27]

Koo then explained that Shandong province was the "cradle of Chinese civilization." The Chinese philosophers Confucius and Mencius had been born there, and it was considered "a Holy Land for the Chinese." Koo also explained that control of this leased territory would not only give Japan virtual control over all of Shandong province but would also provide Japan a strategic "gateway" to all of North China.[28]

Koo concluded: "But, grateful as they were, the Chinese Delegation felt that they would be false to their duty to China and to the world if they did not object to paying their debts of gratitude by selling the birthright of their countrymen, and thereby sowing seeds of discord for the future. The Chinese Delegation therefore trusted that the Conference, in considering the disposal of the leased territory and other rights held by Germany in Shandong, would give full weight to the fundamental and transcendent rights of China, the rights of political sovereignty and territorial integrity, as well as to her earnest desire to serve the cause of universal peace."[29]

Responding to Koo's impassioned speech, Baron Makino informed the delegates that Japan and China had already reached agreement on the Jiaozhou concession and the Shandong railways. To President Wilson's query whether Japan would be willing to present all such agreements before the council, Makino stated that he would ask his government for permission to do so. But Makino then emphasized that because Japan was in possession of territory in Shandong that it had taken by conquest from Germany, before "disposing of it to a third party it was necessary that Japan obtain the right of free disposal from Germany." Accordingly "the cession of Jiaozhou would have to be agreed upon by Germany before it was carried out. . . . What should take place thereafter had already been the subject of an intercourse of views with China."[30]

Koo clearly did not understand that Makino was referring to the new Sino-Japanese agreements signed in September 1918. When reacting to Makino's assertion that a Sino-Japanese agreement on Shandong had already been reached, Koo revealed his ignorance of Beijing's recent secret diplomacy by declaring (see Document 5) that he "presumed that reference was to the treaties and notes made in consequence of the negotiations on the Twenty-one Demands in 1915."[31]

According to Koo, the 1915 treaty was null and void because it had been made only "after an ultimatum from Japan, . . . even if the treaties and notes had been entirely valid, the fact of China's declaration of war on Germany had altered the situation in such a way that on the principle of *rebus stantibus* they could not be enforced today."[32]

By referring only to the 1915 Twenty-one Demands, and not to the more recent agreements of September 1918, Koo all too clearly revealed that he was not aware that the Beijing government had already secretly agreed with Japan on how to handle the Shandong question. Formerly, there was a difference of opinion about when the Chinese delegation first learned of the 1918 secret agreements. According to Wunsz King, the Chinese delegation learned of these "two days before the meeting of January 27th," or in other words, on 25 January 1919.[33]

But in July 1919, Liang Qichao quoted Koo as stating in a private conversation of 4 May 1919: "[When] I brought up the Shandong Question . . . I only came to know the details of the secret pact on the evening of that day when I received a cable from the government."[34] This would suggest the evening of 28 January 1919. Koo later confirmed this interpretation: "the Shandong question was one that was kept more or less a secret. Because so many secret agreements signed with Japan were all kept secret, the legation did not know—they did not know any of it—they never notified the mission abroad."[35] In his private papers, Koo later tried to save face by claiming that a trunk full of "confidential documents relating to Manchuria, Shandong, and Mongolia and Tibet," was stolen during the voyage to France. Koo attributed this theft to Japanese agents, arguing that "nobody else would want it."[36] But no proof is available to back up his claim.

Liang's and Koo's versions agree exactly with the transcripts of the meeting, while Wunsz King's does not. This suggests that Koo did not learn about his own government's secret agreements with Japan until late in the day on 28 January 1919. Therefore, Koo's opening argument advocating the return of the Shandong concessions to China was based on the false assumption that Beijing had signed agreements with Japan only in 1915. According to Koo, when China declared war on Germany in 1917 the earlier agreements became null and void. But these arguments were undermined by the fact that the terms of the 1918 agreements were based directly on the 1915 treaty and were signed more than a year after China joined the Allies. This mistake virtually guaranteed that China's claim to Shandong would not be upheld.

## The Chinese Delegation's March and April Declarations

Faced with what was clearly a losing hand, the Chinese delegation initially tried to finesse the Shandong controversy by ignoring China's secret agreements with Japan. The Chinese delegation tried to pretend that the transfer of twenty million yen from Japan to China in fall 1918 had never happened by avoiding all discussion of this payment in its March 1919 memorandum and 11 April 1919 communiqué. Instead, these documents continued to claim that China's declaration of war against Germany had made all such treaties "null and void." When it became clear that the Chinese delegation could not avoid the diplomatic consequences of the 1918 Sino-Japanese agreements, however, they argued that the 1918 agreements violated the principles of the League of Nations and had been forced upon China by Japan.

With its diplomatic position rapidly crumbling, the Chinese delegates again stressed that Japan had used force to gain China's acquiescence to the 1915 treaty. In March 1919 the Chinese delegation released a memorandum entitled "Provisions for Insertion in the Preliminaries of Peace with Germany and Austria-Hungary." The first provision claimed that the state of war between China and Germany had "terminated all treaties, conventions, protocols, agreements, contracts and other arrangements," and that as a result all German rights "including notably the leasehold rights of Jiaozhou Bay, the Railway and Mining concessions and other rights and options in relations to the Province of Shandong, have reverted to China or ceased to exist." Provision number four added that Germany should cede to China all the "public property belonging to the German Government which are found in . . . that portion of Jiaozhou formerly leased to Germany."[37]

Once the existence of China's and Japan's 1918 secret agreements was confirmed and once copies were circulated, the Beijing government issued an official communiqué on 11 April 1919 requesting that the delegates to the Paris Peace Conference abrogate all previous Sino-Japanese agreements as being in conflict with the principles of the League of Nations: "Since the Japanese Delegate to the Peace Conference has pointedly referred to the Twenty-one Demands, it is incumbent on the Chinese Government to draw attention to the fact that China's acquiescence to terms subversive of her good government was secured by means of an ultimatum to which she was forced to surrender because of the preoccupation of the world in the European war. . . . In subsequent agreement made by Japan under a former Cabinet, the principles followed have been equally dangerous not only to China's liberty of action, but to her true independence; and if she now claims the abrogation or modification of all and sundry agreements, it is because their terms are incompatible with principles on which the League of Nations is founded."[38]

In April 1919, therefore, the Chinese delegation insisted that the 24 September 1918 Sino-Japanese agreements had been "pressed" on China by Japan.[39] Since transcripts of the sessions were not available to the press, the Chinese delegation's argument that China had signed all such agreements with Japan under duress

Mr. Koo said that China did not hold quite the same view as Baron Makino regarding the restoration of Kiaochow. He was far from desiring, in his statement of China's case, even to intimate that Japan, after obtaining the leased territory and other rights in Shantung from Germany, would not return them to China. In fact, he added, China had every confidence in Japan's assurances to her and the world that she, Japan, would not retain them herself; and he was particularly glad to hear Baron Makino confirm theses assurances before the Conference. But there was a choice between direct and indirect restitution. Of the two China would prefer the first. It was always easier to take one step than two if it had led to the same place.

As to the arrangements referred to by the Plenipotentiary from Japan, Mr. Koo presumed that reference was to the treaties and notes made in consequence of the negotiations on the twenty-one demands in 1915. It was not necessary to describe in detail the circumstances which were, to say the least, disconcerting to the Chinese Government, as the latter was constrained to agree to them only after an ultimatum from Japan. Quite apart from the circumstances of their making, however, they were at best, in the view of the Chinese Government, only provisional and temporary arrangements subject to the final review of this Conference, because they were questions arisen from the war.

Furthermore, even if the treaties and notes had been entirely valid, the fact of China's declaration of war on Germany had altered the situation in such a way that on the principle of rebus stantibus they could not be enforced to-day. China had been made to g agree that she would give full assent to whatever arrangements Japan might agree with Germany on the disposition of Germany's rights, privileges and Concessions in Shantung. But the provision did not preclude China's joining the war nor did it prevent China from participating in this Conference as a belligerent; nor could it therefore preclude her from demanding from Germany direct restitution of her rights.

**Document 5**: Excerpt from the 28 January 1919 Paris Discussion of Shandong began to have an international impact. For example, on 2 April 1919, *The Manchester Guardian* inaccurately summed up the Shandong dispute in these terms: "It is of course perfectly true that China is seeking to escape the consequences of a treaty to which she has given her adherence; but in forming any judgment of her action in so doing let us not forget that she signed the treaty under duress."[40]

By the end of April 1919 the Chinese delegation's negotiating strategy had actually changed very little from the one that Koo had first employed in January. Instead of trying to take into account China's own treaties with Japan in September 1918, the Chinese delegation tried to ignore them and direct full attention onto China's 1915 treaty with Japan. As will be shown in greater detail below, this strategy was doomed to fail once the Japanese delegation successfully argued that the 1918 agreements were based on the terms of the 1915 treaty and so could have been concluded only if the Beijing government first accepted the 1915 treaty. The transfer of funds from Japan to China made the validity of these 1918 agreements difficult to dispute.

**Direct or Indirect Restitution of Shandong**

As transcripts of the Paris discussions show, the main Sino-Japanese dispute at the conference was not about whether Japan would keep the Shandong concession indefinitely, but whether Germany would return this concession to China directly or indirectly through Japan. The distinction between "direct" and "indirect" restitution was very important to China for several reasons. First, if the Chinese delegation succeeded in gaining direct restitution of Shandong, this would be tantamount to revoking unilaterally China's international agreements with Japan dating from 1915 to 1918. Second, to regain Shandong directly from Germany would increase China's standing in the world, since Germany was considered to be one of Europe's "great powers." Third, the Chinese would regard receiving Shandong from Japan as a great dishonor—a "loss of face"—since Japan had traditionally been considered a tributary state of China.

It is important to recall that before Koo became aware that Beijing had signed a secret agreement with Japan in September 1918 he never once disputed that the Japanese government intended to return the Shandong concession to China. Koo made this claim only later. In fact, in January 1919 Koo merely argued that once China joined the war in 1917 nothing precluded it from "demanding from Germany direct restitution of her rights." On this crucial point: "Mr. Koo said that China did not hold quite the same view as Baron Makino regarding the restoration of Jiaozhou. He was far from desiring, in his statement of China's case, even to intimate that Japan, after obtaining the leased territory and other rights in Shandong from Germany, would not return them to China. In fact, he added, China had every confidence in Japan's assurances to her and the world that she, Japan, would not retain them herself; and he was particularly glad to hear Baron Makino confirm these assurances before the Conference. But there was a choice between direct and indirect restitution. Of the two China would prefer the first. It was always easier to take one step than two if it led to the same place."⁴¹

Koo's admission that he trusted Japan to turn the Shandong concession over to China shows that the main point of contention at Paris was never whether Shandong would be returned to China. This contradicts the widespread misunderstanding that the Paris Peace Conference permanently ceded Shandong to Japan. The issue was rather whether restitution would be "direct" or "indirect." The Chinese delegation at Paris tried to obscure this important point by emphasizing instead the emotional importance of Shandong to the Chinese people.

In March 1919, for example, one Chinese declaration called for the "liberation or release of China from the burdens and conditions imposed on her in the interests of an aggressive imperialism." The Chinese delegation's analysis of the origins of the Sino-Japanese dispute was similarly one-sided: "Stripped of it's minor features, the Chinese Question may be said to center on the maintenance of the independence and integrity of China, which has been guaranteed in a series of conventions and agreements concluded severally by Great Britain, France, Russia and the United States with Japan."⁴²

This and other Chinese declarations completely ignored Japan's promises that it would return the Shandong concession to China. Instead, the Chinese delegates accused Japan of wanting "the unconditional cession of the leased territory of Jiaozhou together with the railways and other rights possessed by Germany in respect to Shandong Province." They also warned that if the conferees agreed to this proposal it would give Japan permanent control over territory "greater in population and area than England [and] as the home of Confucius, it is not only packed with rare historical memories but is also sacred as the cradle of Chinese culture."⁴³

It is significant that China's seven-page public declaration of March 1919 never acknowledged that the real issue under debate was not "whether" the Shandong concession was to be returned to China but "how" it was to be returned. In sharp contrast to China's public documents, the American Commission's confidential *précis* of the "Memorandum and Appendices laid before the Peace Conference by the Chinese Delegation" makes the dispute between "direct" and "indirect" restitution quite clear.   This document summarizes the Chinese delegation's argument for direct restitution:⁴⁴

> 1. It is due the self-respect of China, as an associate in the war.

> 2. China appreciates the sacrifices of Japan, but can not admit that war between other powers can affect her territorial rights.

> 3. Japan's military occupation can not give title, and the disposition of the lease in any case is subject to determination at the Peace Conference.

4. The agreement of May 25, 1915, was extorted from China, and China signed in the belief that the question could only be settled at the Peace Conference.

5. China subsequently entered the war and abrogated all treaties and agreements with Germany, whose leasehold reverted automatically to China.

All five of these points take for granted that Japan had already agreed to return the Shandong concession to China, but they ignore completely China's own September 1918 agreements with Japan. In reality, the only outstanding decision regarding the Shandong question was over the means of transfer—whether it would be direct or indirect restitution. Therefore, what was really being disputed was form, not content.

As the first point in the "Memorandum and Appendices laid before the Peace Conference by the Chinese Delegation" makes clear, the heart of the dispute was how to return Shandong in such a way as to preserve China's "self-respect." "Self-respect" in the case of China and Japan really referred to the Asian concept known as "face." Therefore, the Chinese delegation did not question that Shandong would be returned to China, but merely how China could gain "face" by receiving it directly from Germany—a major European power—and not lose "face" by receiving it from Japan—a former Chinese tributary state.

In a meeting between Secretary of State Lansing and Viscount Chinda on 26 April 1919 Lansing admitted that "face" was the true issue under dispute when he observed that the United States government's "only desire was to find some way of reconciling the claims of Japan and China: That we wanted to save the face of Japan, but also the face of China."[45]

But of course Japan was also concerned with "face." In its response to the Chinese delegation, it reminded them that "in 1895, China, after having ceded the Liaodong Peninsula to Japan, asked Germany to intervene with the Tokyo Government in order to force them to renounce that territory." In league with France and Russia in the so-called Triple Intervention, Germany forced Japan to renounce Liaodong.[46]

Germany's price, according to the Japanese, was Shandong, and the Japanese people are "led to believe, whatever may have been said to the contrary, that the lease of Jiaozhou was the price of Germany's intervention and they regard it as an instance of the most flagrant acts of injustice committed unblushingly in international relations. The Japanese people saw in the capture of that territory from Germany not an act of revenge but of just reparation for the great wrong done to their patrician twenty-five years before. It is impossible for the Japanese Government in this connection to disregard the sentiments of the nation."[47] Clearly, for Germany to cede Shandong directly to Japan would give the Japanese enormous "face," not an insignificant issue to the Japanese populace. This important point will be discussed at greater length in Chapter Five.

## Conclusions

The Sino-Japanese dispute over Shandong in reality revolved around the Asian concept known as "face." Face was of great importance in traditional Chinese diplomacy and often "led to a rigidity in Chinese foreign policy, particularly in the mid-nineteenth century, which wore off to a degree as the Chinese learned how to use to their advantage international law and European-style balance-of-power politics." Chinese diplomats were particularly concerned about allowing China to lose face, however, since it was considered to be a crime of the "highest order." As a result, this fear had often led to "Chinese inflexibility" during diplomatic negotiations.[48] This scenario was to be replayed almost exactly during the 1919 Sino-Japanese talks in Paris.

Not surprisingly, the importance of face eluded many Western commentators at Paris. But official transcripts of the sessions reveal that China's own delegates, and Wellington Koo in particular, precipitated the dispute over face by publicly raising Shandong in front of the Japanese. Before the Chinese delegation left for Paris the Beijing government had specifically ordered its delegates not to raise the Shandong question. Koo disregarded his government's instructions. Minutes of the formerly confidential negotiations show that when Koo initially brought up the Shandong question he did so without knowing that Beijing had already secretly negotiated terms with Tokyo in its agreements of September 1918.

Koo's blunder made it impossible for China to back down. This not only soured China's relations with Japan on the Shandong question, but also ended all hope that Japan would back China's more important efforts to regain control over the other foreign concessions, protect its territorial integrity, and eliminate extraterritoriality; previously Tokyo had assured the Beijing government that it planned to support China's ambitious goals. As a result even a sympathetic Chinese observer like Liang Qichao was forced to conclude about Shandong "that the [Beijing] government was mainly responsible for this diplomatic defeat."[49]

In fact, only after Koo disobeyed Beijing and raised the Shandong question on 28 January 1919, did the true extent of China's secret diplomacy with Japan become known. Although release of these secret agreements was perhaps unavoidable, it should not be overlooked that if Koo had followed orders and not raised the Shandong question then the resulting Sino-Japanese dispute might have been avoided altogether. In particular, China would not have publicly lost face since the details of its negotiations would have remained secret. If this had happened, then China's actual gains at Paris might have been much greater; with Japan's backing, the Chinese delegation might have had more success promoting its comprehensive reform package to the assembled Western nations meeting at Paris.

Once detailed information about China's secret treaties with Japan became known, however, all hope of not losing face was gone. As a result, all further Sino-Japanese negotiations quickly became acrimonious. The spirit of conciliation that President Wilson had hoped to foster between China and Japan was thus undermined and eventually destroyed. This negative outcome would prove to have enormous and wide-ranging effects on future Sino-Japanese relations.

**Notes**

1. "Notes of a Meeting which took place at President Wilson's House, Place Des Etats-Unis, Paris," 22 April 1919, at 4:30 p.m., stamped "secret" and then "Declassified," SKH Papers, Box 382.
2. "Telegram from Li Sheng-to, President of the Senate, Wang Yi-tang, Speaker of House of Representatives, and the 100 Members of Parliament to President Woodrow Wilson, 4 March 1919," WWP Microfilm Reel #394, 11655.
3. "Chinese Contribution, in personnel, to the War," from Stanley K. Hornbeck to Colonel S. D. Embick, Tasker Bliss Papers, Manuscript Division, Library of Congress, Box # 356; Hornbeck estimated that as many as 36,925 Chinese worked in France, 97,000 in England, and 50,000 more were recruited but never sent to Europe, for a total of 183,925.
4. "Chinese Peace Commissioners," SKH Papers, Box 328; this document bears the following remark in Stanley Hornbeck's handwriting: <u>For Confidential Use</u>.
5. *Ibid.*
6. *Ibid.*
7. *Ibid.*
8. *Ibid.*
9. Russell H. Fifield, *Woodrow Wilson and the Far East* (New York: Thomas Y. Crowell Company, 1952), 187; according to Fifield, the acting foreign minister in Beijing also expressed his personal desire that the 1918 secret agreement never become known.
10. "Memorandum of a conversation at an audience with the President of the United States, Woodrow Wilson, at the White House," 26 November 1918, V. K. Wellington Koo collection, Rare Book and Manuscript Library, Columbia University.
11. "Letter from Wellington Koo to Secretary of State Lansing including an Informal Memorandum Outlining China's Upcoming Proposals at Paris," 25 November 1918, Robert Lansing collection, Box 3.
12. Chu Pao-chin, *V. K. Wellington Koo: A Case Study of China's Diplomat and Diplomacy of Nationalism* (Hong Kong: The Chinese University Press, 1981), 16-17.
13. "Essentials re China for Consideration Peace Conference," SKH Papers Box 328. Interestingly, while China eventually used a Soviet-style revolution to reclaim by force control over its territory and tariffs, the issues discussed in the last point remain at the heart of Sino-American relations to this day. In particular, the slow pace of Chinese legal reforms in the PRC has hampered legal protection of foreign patents. By contrast, American efforts to urge the Nationalists to carry out such reforms have met with great success in Taiwan. Viewed from this perspective, the United States' China policy has been remarkably consistent during the past century.
14. "Confidential telegram from Acting Secretary of State Polk to Secretary Lansing in Paris," 17 December 1918, SKH Papers Box 382; this telegram is stamped "declassified."

15. "Telegram from Minister Reinsch in Peking to Washington," 5 January 1919, SKH Papers Box 382.
16. "Reminiscences," V. K. Wellington Koo Papers, 153.
17. "China Before the Peace Conference, Preamble," SKH Papers Box 328; marked "confidential."
18. *Ibid.*
19. *Ibid.*
20. For an early, generally positive, examination of extraterritoriality, see Benj. H. Williams, "The Protection of American Citizens in China: Extraterritoriality," *The American Journal of International Law*, Vol 16 (1922), 43-58.
21. "China Before the Peace Conference, Preamble," SKH Papers Box 328; marked "confidential."
22. *Ibid.* Also Chu, 15. The 1921-22 Washington Conference later discussed some of these issues.
23. "Minister to China Paul Reinsch to the State Department," SKH Papers Box 382.
24. "Protest from Eleven American Correspondents to President Wilson About Holding Versailles Meetings in Secret," 14-21 January 1919, WWP Microfilm Reel 390, 6697.
25. "Conversation held in M. Pichon's room at the Quai D'Orsay, Paris," 27 January 1919, SKH Papers, Box 382; marked "Secret."
26. "Conversation held in M. Pichon's room at the Quai D'Orsay, Paris," 28 January 1919, SKH Papers, Box 382; marked "Secret."
27. *Ibid.*
28. *Ibid.*
29. *Ibid.*
30. *Ibid.*
31. *Ibid.*
32. *Ibid.*
33. Wunsz King, *China at the Paris Peace Conference in 1919* (New York: St. John's University Press, 1961), 9.
34. Liang Qichao, "Causes of China's Defeat at the Peace Conference," *Millard's Review*, 19 July 1919, 262-265.
35. "Reminiscences," V. K. Wellington Koo Papers, 194.
36. *Ibid,* 195.
37. "Chinese Delegation Preliminary Peace Conference, Memorandum: Provisions for Insertion in the Preliminaries of Peace with Germany and Austria-Hungary," March 1919, WWP Microfilm Reel 402, 18674.
38. "Peking Government's Official Communiqué: China's Reply to Japan," 11 April 1919, SKH Papers Box 328; from *The North-China Herald*, 19 April 1919, 144.
39. "Chinese Delegation: The Peace Conference, The Claim of China," April 1919, WWP Microfilm Reel 402, 19461.
40. "Japan's Demands on China," *The Manchester Guardian,* 2 April 1919; Hornbeck wrote on his personal copy of this article: "A very good, accurate and convincing statement of the case [on] Shantung," SKH Papers Box 328.
41. "Conversation held in M. Pichon's room at the Quai D'Orsay, Paris," 28 January 1919, SKH Papers, Box 382; marked "Secret."

42. "Address Read to Press Representatives at a Reception held by the Chinese Peace Delegation," March 1919, SKH Papers, Box 328.

43. *Ibid.*

44. "Precis of Memorandum and Appendices laid before the Peace Conference by the Chinese Delegates," 28 January 1919, SKH Papers, Box 328.

45. "Conversation between Secretary Lansing and Viscount Chinda," 26 April 1919, WWP Microfilm Reel 402, 19702-8.

46. "Some Remarks on the Chinese Memorandum Claiming Direct Restitution to Herself of the Leased Territory of Kiaochow, the Tsingtao-Chinan Railway and of Other German Rights in Respect of Shantung Province," Gaimushō, File 2.3.1-1.2(2), pp. 1289-1327.

47. *Ibid.*

48. S.C.M. Paine, *Imperial Rivals: China, Russia, and Their Disputed Frontier* (Armonk, NY: M.E. Sharpe, 1996), 13, 54-57.

49. Liang Qichao, "Causes of China's Defeat at the Peace Conference," *Millard's Review*, 19 July 1919, 262-265.

# 3
# The Japanese Delegation's Proposals to the Paris Peace Conference

> [Japan] destroyed at one stroke the German power in the Far East by the reduction of the fortress of Qingdao; hunted out the enemy warships roving the adjoining seas; patrolled the South Sea, the Indian and Pacific Oceans during the whole period of the war; convoyed the troops of Australia and New Zealand to the battlefields of Europe and Asia, co-operating on the Mediterranean with the allied fleets in their operations against the enemy submarines; prevented the [in]filtration of German influence and the spread of Bolshevism into East Siberia; subscribed to the allied loans to the full extent of her financial capacity; provided the Entente [Allied] powers with munitions and other war materials, and stood ever ready to respond to the call of her allies in case of necessity.[1]
>
> Toyokichi Iyenaga, diplomat and historian (1 August 1919)

It is important to summarize the Japanese delegation's proposals to the Paris Peace Conference. Tokyo was most concerned that its hard-won gains against Germany might be lost at Paris, just as happened before during the 1895 Triple Intervention. In particular Tokyo feared that if the United States and Great Britain backed China, then Japan's newly achieved status as the strongest economic power in Asia would be endangered. To many Japanese, a defeat at Paris would be interpreted as a defeat of Japan's entire foreign policy, a policy that attempted to promote Japan's economic and political influence throughout the Far East.

In early January 1919, immediately prior to the Paris Peace Conference, Prince Konoye openly accused the United States and Great Britain of adopting a policy of "economic imperialism" against Japan.[2] According to Konoye, the "economic imperialism with which these powers threaten the world is no less a menace to the free development of nations than military imperialism." He argued that Japan should view with suspicion vocal American and British support for "democracy and humanitarianism."[3]

As encapsulated by the American embassy in Tokyo, Konoye then warned the Japanese people: "While not opposing a League of Nations based on justice and humanity in the strict sense . . . if one such as favored by America and Great Britain is formed, the two powers will have the lion's share of the advantages while others, deprived of the arms to resist their economic aggression, will be obliged to submit to the lead of these two powers." Konoye concluded that if Japan was not allowed to expand its economic influence because of the "discriminatory treatment accorded to yellow race," Japan might soon be "obliged to assume the same attitude as Germany before the war and destroy the *status quo.*"[4]

In hindsight Prince Konoye's prediction of a future conflict between Japan and the Anglo-American *entente* proved little short of prophetic. Even in early 1919 Konoye's warnings should not be viewed as an aberration, since the Tokyo embassy ended its telegram to Washington by warning: "It is worthy of note that Prince Konoye's views are shared by a number of publicists."[5] Faced with the unsavory prospect that Japan might refuse to join the League of Nations and that this refusal might lead to war, President Wilson could not simply ignore the Japanese proposals on the Shandong question.

Beyond not wanting to upset the Japanese government, Wilson also had to be concerned about alienating the Japanese people should his actions at Paris appear to be racially motivated. Finally, the Japanese delegation came to Paris with an extremely strong diplomatic case based on a multitude of treaties and agreements signed with China, Great Britain, Russia, France, Italy, and even with the United States. Since one of the stated goals of the Allies in World War I was to uphold the sanctity of treaties, Wilson could not casually dismiss these official documents. All of these factors were to play a role in the final resolution of the Shandong question.

**The Japanese Delegation and its Proposals**

Japan sent five delegates to Paris. The oldest and highest ranking, and so the titular head of the delegation, was the Marquis Kimmochi Saionji, a former prime minister. The second highest member, and arguably the real leader, was Baron Nobuaki Makino. Makino was a member of Japan's ruling council and had held many official positions in the Japanese government, including minister of education, of agriculture, of commerce, and foreign affairs.[6] As with China's delegation, the Japanese delegation included their ambassadors to Great Britain, Vicomte Sutemi Chinda; to France, Keishiro Matsui; and to Italy, Hikokichi Ijuin. The inclusion of these three ambassadors was no doubt intended to remind Great Britain, France, and Italy of their treaty obligations backing Japan's claims to the Shandong concession.

Unlike the Chinese delegation, the Japanese delegates were thoroughly informed concerning all of Japan's treaties and agreements relating to the Shandong question; Tokyo had long been laying the groundwork for the peace conference. As early as 1917 Japan had concluded agreements with most of the major participants at Paris, including Great Britain, France, Italy, and the United States. These preparations perhaps reflected fears on the part of the Japanese government and people of again being denied the rewards of military victory. This was not an entirely unwarranted concern, as one historian of the Paris conference noted when he discussed how many participants "would fain have dispossessed Japan of the fruits of the [Shandong] campaign, and allotted to her the role of working without reward."[7]

On the afternoon of 27 January 1919, in the private room of French Minister of Foreign Affairs Stephen-Jean-Marie Pichon at the Quai d'Orsay, Baron Makino presented Japan's proposals to thirty delegates, including Woodrow Wilson, David Lloyd George, Georges Clemenceau, Vittorio Orlando, and Wellington Koo. Japan had two major claims against Germany: "The Japanese Government feel justified in claiming from the German Government the unconditional cession of: (a) The leased territory of Jiaozhou together with the railways, and other rights possessed by Germany in respect of Shandong province. (b) All of the Islands in German possession in the Pacific Ocean North of the Equator together with the rights and properties in connection therewith."[8]

When explaining the background of Japan's claim to Germany's leased territory in Jiaozhou, however, Makino made it quite clear that Japan's August 1914 ultimatum "gave notice to the German Government to surrender the leased territory of Jiaozhou with a view to its restoration to China." Japan's claims against the Jiaozhou concession and Germany's other possessions in Shandong province were mainly intended to prohibit the revival of "German activities in the Far East to the undoing of all that has been achieved at no small sacrifice [by Japan]."[9]

Makino concluded by stating that "in view of the extent of their efforts and achievements in destroying [the] German base in the Extreme Orient and the South Seas, and in safeguarding the important routes on the Pacific and Indian Oceans and the Mediterranean waters, to say nothing of their contribution in other respects, the Japanese Government feel confident that the claims above advanced would be regarded as only just and fair."[10]

The next day, after the Chinese delegation presented its case before the assembly, Makino clarified that the issue under discussion was to decide for or against the "direct restitution of Jiaozhou to China." In fact, since Japan had "actual possession" of this territory and, as Makino now revealed, Beijing and Tokyo had already concluded a "friendly interchange of views," resolution had already been achieved: "Japan had agreed to restore Jiaozhou as soon as Japan had free disposal of the place. Agreements had also been reached with regard to the leased railways." Makino appeared willing, even eager, to make the exact content of these Sino-Japanese agreements known: "As notes had been exchanged, he thought that a statement of these engagements might be worth the consideration of the members of the Council."[11]

## 56  JAPAN'S PROPOSALS

By making this public offer to discuss China's and Japan's specific arrangements on Shandong, Makino opened the door to a thorough-going review of Japan's secret diplomacy. Many of the delegates at this meeting, including the Chinese, were as yet unaware of the content of these Sino-Japanese agreements (see Document 6). Makino's offer prompted Wilson to ask whether Japan would "lay these notes before the Council?" Makino replied "that he did not think the Japanese Government would raise any objection, but as the request was an unexpected one, he would be compelled to ask its permission." But Makino soon reiterated his promise to produce copies of the agreements: "Baron Makino said that he would do so, provided his Government would make no objection. He did not think it would. If it were within his own power, he would produce these documents as soon as possible."[12]

According to these official transcripts from the 28 January 1919 session, Makino was the first delegate to volunteer detailed information concerning the contents of Japan's and China's secret agreements concerning Shandong. This is an important point, because critics were later to claim that it was the Japanese government that hoped to keep the 1918 Sino-Japanese agreements secret. In fact, it is more likely that the Chinese wanted them to remain secret.

Following these two days of meetings on the Shandong question, the issue was tabled for almost three months while additional information was collected. Among the many documents released during this period were Japan's secret treaties with Great Britain, Russia, France, and Italy as well as detailed information on its agreements with China in 1915 and 1918. Since the whole character of the Sino-Japanese debate on the Shandong question revolved around the content of these documents, it is important to clarify that these revelations deeply affected the other participants at the Paris Peace Conference. With regard to the United States, the release of this new documentary evidence undermined completely the American delegation's initial position on Shandong, eventually forcing President Wilson to create a completely new negotiating position.

**The American Delegation's Opening Position on Shandong**

Before turning to a discussion of the impact of Japan's secret diplomacy on the Paris Peace Conference, it is important to review the official U.S. record on the Shandong question prior to the conference. This position was articulated in two different documents, the first generated by the U.S. Naval Advisory Staff in December 1918 and the second by two of the State Department's leading Far Eastern experts in January 1919. Both documents agreed that Japan had taken Shandong by force and that the former German concession should be given back to China. According to the State Department's experts, the only hypothetical exception would be if the Beijing government voluntarily and without compulsion concluded a bilateral agreement with Tokyo on the future disposition of the Shandong concession, an agreement that Beijing had already secretly signed.

## JAPAN'S PROPOSALS 57

President Wilson asked Baron Makino whether he proposed to lay these notes before the Council.

Baron Makino said that he did not think the Japanese Government would raise any objection, but as the request was an unexpected one, he would be compelled to ask its permission.

President Wilson asked on behalf of China if Mr. Koo would do likewise.

Mr. Koo said that the Chinese Government had no objection to raise.

M. Clemenceau asked both the Japanese and Chinese Delegates to state whether they would make known to the Council the conditions of the restoration agreed between them.

Baron Makino said that he would do so, provided his Government would make no objection. He did not think it would. If it were within his own power, he would produce these documents as soon as possible. There was however, one point he wished to make clear. Japan was in actual possession of the territory under consideration. It had taken it by conquest from Germany. Before disposing of it to a third party it was necessary that Japan should obtain the right of free disposal from Germany.

President Wilson pointed out that the Council was dealing with territories and cessions previously German without consulting Germany at all.

Baron Makino said that the work now in hand was one of preparation for the presentment of the case to Germany. It followed therefore that the cession of Kiaochow would have to be agreed upon by Germany before it was carried out. What should take place thereafter had already been the subject of an intercourse of views with China.

**Document 6**: Excerpt from the 28 January 1919 Paris Discussion of Shandong

On 19 December 1918, Chief of Naval Operations Vice-Admiral William Shepherd Benson sent a confidential memo on the Shandong question, compiled by the U.S. Naval Advisory Staff, to four of President Wilson's closest advisers. They were Secretary of State Robert Lansing, Colonel Edward House, General Tasker Bliss, and former U.S. Ambassador to Italy and France Henry White. In this memo, Admiral Benson recommended that: "Jiaozhou should be returned to China without compensation. Japan should be permitted to remove Japanese property and should be allowed compensation for improvements and repairs made during occupation or for any Japanese property left behind." Benson's primary reason for advocating this position was that Germany's 1898 lease of Jiaozhou clearly stated that "Germany shall not cede the territory leased to any other power than China." Because of this, Japan was merely "an agent holding this territory in trust, awaiting its final disposition by the Peace treaty."[13]

Benson also presented six other reasons for returning Jiaozhou to China: 1) it impaired Chinese sovereignty; 2) for this reason, it was inconsistent with the spirit of Wilson's peace program; 3) to transfer the Jiaozhou lease from one foreign country to another could not entail a "change of jurisdiction over a nation's own sovereignty unless by the consent of the nation itself"; 4) after peace was made with Germany, German rights over Jiaozhou would be automatically revived and by the terms of its lease these rights could not be transferred to any other power; 5) allowing Japan to retain two strongholds in China—both in Manchuria and in Shandong—would not be in China's interests; and 6) since China was "associated with the Allies in a victorious war against Germany, she has earned every right to demand the return of the territory extorted from her by the enemy."[14] It should be noted, however, that since Admiral Benson's memo was prepared before the Sino-Japanese agreements were revealed, only point five—opposition to granting Japan two strongholds in China—remained completely unaffected by this revelation.

The State Department memorandum was written by Edward T. Williams and Stanley K. Hornbeck. Williams was the former Chief of the Department of State's Division of Far Eastern Affairs, while Hornbeck, listed as "Specialist on the Far East and the Pacific" was destined to become one of the longest-serving Chiefs of the Division of Far Eastern Affairs. Like Benson, they also did not know about the 1918 Sino-Japanese agreements when they wrote a twelve-page memorandum in early January 1919 entitled "Disposal of Shandong Province."[15]

Based on their historical analysis of the Shandong question, Williams and Hornbeck characterized both Germany's and Japan's activities as "militaristic." They agreed that China had been forced to sign treaties on Shandong "under duress" and recommended to President Wilson that "the whole series of Sino-Japanese agreements of 1915 be declared not binding until and unless they shall have been approved by international action." Since international support for Japan's 1915 treaty with China was unlikely, this proposal clearly recommended voiding Japan's claims to Shandong.[16]

Once the 1915 Sino-Japanese treaty had been abolished, Williams and Hornbeck proposed that the port of Qingdao be internationalized, in order that Japan not remain in sole possession of it. This memorandum also offered four reasons why all other German leases in Shandong should be returned to China: "first, the lease was taken by force; [second] there is no sufficient justification for the maintenance of a foreign jurisdiction at this point; third, it cannot be restored to Germany; fourth, China, the rightful sovereign and the lessor, wishes repossession." Most importantly, the memorandum advised that complete control over the Shandong railways be returned to China.[17]

Williams and Hornbeck had both heard many rumors claiming that Japan and China were in the process of negotiating a bilateral agreement to resolve the Shandong question. They took for granted, however, that if Japan achieved any such agreement on Shandong it would be the result of either force or bribery and so recommended to President Wilson that he not recognize it:[18]

> It has been reported that Japan is attempting to induce the Chinese government to make separate agreements with regard to disposal of rights in Shandong. Chinese officials have stated positively that there is no intention on the part of their government to make such agreements. Should it happen that any such agreements are concluded, it may be assumed, without question, that threats or bribery or both have been the instruments by means of which certain susceptible Chinese officials have been induced to sign such agreements.
>
> Your informants have recommended elsewhere that the Conference adopt a regulation to the effect that no such agreements shall be recognized in respect to any subject or any region.
>
> Refusal to recognize separate agreements would be in keeping with the principle adopted among the allied countries early in the war, although the pledges which were given to that effect may not have contemplated agreements between cobelligerents. In considering agreements which have been made and which may be made between Japan and China with reference to Shandong, it should not be overlooked that <u>British forces</u> operated jointly with Japanese in the reduction of Qingdao, and that Japan would owe to Great Britain an accounting for any separate agreement, and in turn Japan <u>and</u> Great Britain would be accountable to the other allied countries and to the United States for the fact that such agreement had been concluded.

Williams' and Hornbeck's main advice to Wilson, therefore, was that he apply pressure through Great Britain on Japan to abolish any separate agreements that Tokyo might have made with Beijing. But unknown to Williams and Hornbeck, Tokyo had previously insured that this tactic would be ineffectual by concluding in 1917 a separate secret agreement with Great Britain supporting its position in Shandong.

In their conclusions Williams and Hornbeck again addressed the question of whether the 1915 Sino-Japanese treaty, the so-called Twenty-one Demands, was valid. Their arguments, very similar in many ways to those Admiral Benson presented earlier, were that it was not valid by reason of Germany's promise in 1898 that it would never sublet its territory in China to a third party. This precluded any rights over Shandong from being passed from Germany to Japan. Williams and Hornbeck could perceive only one possible exception to this conclusion (see Document 7): "Japan will have no legal rights in the province until such shall have been admitted by the Chinese government (free from compulsion)."[19]

When Admiral Benson issued his memorandum in December 1918 and Williams and Hornbeck issued theirs in early January 1919, the U.S. government had received only unsubstantiated rumors of a secret Sino-Japanese agreement. There was still no proof that any agreement had been signed. After Makino revealed the existence of such an agreement on 28 January 1919 it became apparent that the Beijing government had voluntarily signed this agreement with Tokyo in return for a twenty million yen advance. Although this monetary transfer could be characterized as bribery, it could not be called compulsion. That Beijing willingly signed the September 1918 agreements was best shown, as mentioned above, in a signed statement from the Chinese Minister to Tokyo Zhang Zongxiang, who informed his Japanese counterpart "that the Chinese gladly agree."[20] Unfortunately for China's delegation to Paris, these new documents appeared to fulfill almost exactly the sole exception that Williams and Hornbeck had hypothesized would undermine and invalidate America's policy to support the direct return of the Shandong concession to China.

**Who Wanted the Secret Agreements Kept Secret?**

Although it was Makino who formally offered to present all secret agreements once he gained his government's permission, rumors soon began to circulate that Tokyo wanted to keep all such agreements confidential. These rumors appear to be somewhat contradictory, since it seemed to be clearly in Japan's best interests to release details of the Sino-Japanese agreements as they completely backed its claims to Shandong. The commonly held belief that Japan did not want to release these documents would appear on the whole unconvincing. By contrast, the Chinese delegation had much more to lose once these documents were released and became available to the public.

Japanese Contentions Inadmissible.

With regard to the contentions which Japan may put forward as to her right to retain either the lease or properties in Shantung:- it may be pointed out that Germany engaged at no time to sublet the territory leased to another power. The German rights, cannot by any process of legal reasoning, be assumed to have passed to Japan. Japan will have no legal rights in the province until such shall have been admitted by the Chinese government (free from compulsion).

The present American Minister to China declares in a very important cable (No. 168) of January 10, 1919, "German rights there (in Shantung) lapsed together with all Chino-German treaties, upon the declaration of war. (He obviously refers to China's declaration of war and against Germany, which occurred in 1917.) A succession of treaty rights from Germany to Japan is therefore not possible, and the recognition of a special position of Japan in Shantung could only proceed from a new act to which, conceivably, some weak Chinese officials might be induced, but which would be contrary to the recently declared aim of international policy in China, and which would amount to the definitive establishment of exclusive spheres of influence in China leading in turn to the more vigorous development of such exclusive spheres by other nations."

**Document 7**: Excerpt from the 20 January 1919 "Disposal of Shandong Province"

Accounts accusing Japan of undue secrecy need to be treated with some skepticism, therefore, since they were largely based on secondary accounts from Chinese sources. In a 3 February 1919 telegram from the American legation in Beijing, Minister Reinsch quoted China's acting minister of foreign affair's description of his conversation with Japan's minister the previous day: "[The Japanese minister] remonstrated, declaring that his Government was greatly displeased with the statement of Minister Koo to the effect that the Chinese Government had no objection to making known the secret agreements. This ought not to be done without in each case first obtaining consent of the Japanese Government. He then queried as to whom China is to rely upon, stating that England had her hands full with internal difficulties, while Japan has five hundred thousand tons [of] naval vessels, and an army of one million men waiting. He also brought up the matter of the unpaid portion of the Japanese loans, [and] suggested that, as the name of the War Participation Bureau has been changed to National Defense Bureau, it would be necessary for the Chinese Government specifically to ask for the continuance of name under this loan."[21]

While it is not possible to confirm this account of the Japanese minister's comments in Beijing, Reinsch acknowledged that the difficulties with communication—because all messages from Beijing to Paris had to go through Washington—made it impossible to keep abreast of the Japanese delegation's statements at Paris. Furthermore, although Reinsch urged China's acting minister of foreign affairs to send copies of all available Sino-Japanese agreements to Paris, he was forced to admit: "I doubt that they have everything as some arrangements seem to have been made without knowledge of Foreign Office."[22]

In Tokyo, meanwhile, it was reported in the local foreign-operated press that the Japanese military party had paid a visit to the Chinese legation to urge "the Chinese Minister to persuade the Chinese Government to repudiate the policy of Koo and Wang at the Peace Conference" because their actions at Paris were "greatly embarrassing to the Japanese Government." According to this account, the Japanese threatened that if China did not stop attempts to release the secret agreements, then Jiaozhou and Shandong might be permanently occupied. It might furthermore precipitate a "Japanese military demonstration against China."[23]

Other sources also suggested that Japan was primarily responsible for delaying the release of the as yet unseen September 1918 secret agreements. On 9 February 1919 the British legation in Beijing sent the following telegram: "As indicated in my message February 3rd cabinet favors yielding to the Japanese demands [not to release the secret agreements] but the President stands firm so far in spite of strong pressure of cabinet, diplomatic commission and military party. At his direction Premier February 6th telegraphed to Chinese peace delegation Paris approving their action and instructing them to lay before the Peace Conference all secret agreements to which China is a party. It is believed that certain secret agreements with the Japanese were negotiated by the military party without the knowledge of foreign office and are not now known to President or to Peace Delegation. Situation here is still rather tense. There is little doubt that Chinese Minister to Japan is a tool of the Japanese." This communiqué then suggested that: "If the American peace delegation will urge Chinese delegates to produce all the secret agreements entered into since the commencement of the war the best interests of America and the Chinese patriots will be served thereby."[24]

In February 1919 American reports indicated that Japan considered China's attempts to release the secret agreements as "a breach of confidence." This was allegedly reflected in Japanese bitterness against China; reportedly the Japanese even accused Chinese of organizing a propaganda campaign in the United States and other places so as "to prejudice the opinion of the world in their favor."[25] Although it was widely reported that Beijing's cabinet succumbed to Tokyo's threats not to release the secret agreements, in fact other reports show that President Xu advocated the publication of all relevant documents, supposedly sending a telegram to China's delegation at Paris on 6 February 1919 authorizing them "to lay before the Conference the Twenty-one Demands and any secret agreements that they saw fit."[26]

Tokyo's version of these on-going events was quite different. Ambassador Chinda denounced Beijing's account that it was Tokyo that did not want to release these documents. In sharp contrast to Beijing, Chinda claimed that the 1918 secret agreements were being kept "confidential at the request of China." As for the 2 February 1919 Sino-Japanese meeting in Beijing, according to Chinda's version: "The Japanese Minister informed the Chinese acting Minister for Foreign Affairs that Japan desired to place these documents before the Powers at the Peace Conference. Two days ago in Paris, Mr. Lu, the Chinese Minister for Foreign Affairs, willingly and definitely agreed to our request in this matter. It would be absurd for the Japanese Minister in Beijing to use a threat of withdrawal of financial support on February 2, when the Minister for Foreign Affairs in Tokyo, on January 21st, had announced the suspension of financial support by Japan to either the Northern or Southern Governments." Viscount Chinda also reminded the Chinese delegation that it had always been Japan's declared goal to return the Jiaozhou concession and the port at Qingdao to China some "eighty years before the time China could otherwise have secured it."[27]

Given the enormous disparities in these reports, the Japanese version of events seems to be the most reliable. For example, according to one 3 February 1919 foreign-run paper in China, the Beijing "Foreign Office and other officials have stated today that previous reports as to Japanese pressure and possible action by Japan are considerably ahead of what has actually happened . . ."[28]

A second foreign newspaper was later forced to make a rather embarrassing retraction: "Mr. Obata did not state that the secret agreements between China and Japan should not be disclosed without first obtaining the approval of the Japanese Delegates at the Peace Conference. What he said was that there should be a mutual understanding before such disclosures were made."[29]

Finally, in his personal papers Koo discussed how the Chinese delegation requested from Beijing copies of all agreements with Japan, "especially loan agreements, because this was necessary because even the Foreign Minister's files brought along by him did not contain these agreements." However, Beijing initially refused to send copies of these treaties and "C.T. Wang and Alfred Sze stated that they were under the impression that Beijing was not anxious to let the delegation have the texts of all of its agreements for political reasons."[30]

These contradictory rumors and reports make it almost impossible to determine conclusively which country—China or Japan—really wanted to keep the 1918 agreements secret. However, the minutes of the 28 January 1919 session support the Japanese account, since Makino was not only the first delegate to mention the 1918 agreements, but was also the first to offer to present copies of the various agreements. An American "confidential bulletin" dated 5 March 1919 also helps to substantiate this interpretation by pointing out that "every one who was present when China laid her claim before the Council knows that the Chinese delegates did not volunteer to lay secret agreements before the Council, but were asked by the President of the Council if China had any objection."[31]

In any event, it cannot be disputed that the Japanese delegation gave copies of the secret agreements to Wilson on 16 February 1919.[32] The Japanese delegation also presented copies of Japan's 1915 and 1918 agreements with China, as well as Japan's four other secret agreements concerning Shandong with Great Britain, Russia, France, and Italy, to the other delegations at Paris. Finally, these agreements were made public by the Japanese government in early April 1919; for example, the text of the 24 September 1918 Sino-Japanese agreement was published in the Tokyo newspaper *Chugai Shogyo* on 10 April 1919.[33] Since these six sets of agreements all solidly supported the Japanese delegation's diplomatic position vis-à-vis the Shandong concession, it is a logical conclusion that it was the Chinese delegation that opposed the public release of the agreements, not the Japanese.

### The Impact of the Secret Agreements on America's Proposals

Makino's revelation that there existed one or more Sino-Japanese agreements pertaining to Shandong was an enormous shock to the American delegation, which was trying its best to help China regain Shandong. When, on the evening of 28 January 1919, Koo received from Beijing a telegram confirming the existence of these agreements, he immediately informed E. T. Williams. According to Koo, when he "told Mr. Williams . . . about it, he told me in reply with great agitation that everything was gone."[34] As further information about Japan's extensive secret diplomacy with Great Britain, Russia, France, and Italy came to light during the spring of 1919, the American delegation's Shandong policy began to look more and more hopeless.

Through early April 1919, the American Far Eastern experts did not adjust their proposals on Shandong because texts of the secret Sino-Japanese treaties were still not available. As a result, immediately prior to the opening of intensive negotiations on the Shandong question, Williams and Hornbeck jointly tendered a five-page memorandum to President Wilson that recommended: 1) cancelling

Germany's 1898 treaty with China and Japan's 1915 treaty with China; 2) making Qingdao an international port under an international government in which China would be represented; and 3) "That the Leased Territory at Jiaozhou be restored to China, and the railway lines built under terms of the convention of 1898 be turned over to China, China agreeing to compensate Germany for the value of the properties involved, exclusive of lands."[35]

In explanation Williams and Hornbeck pointed out that the question of "treaty rights" did not apply to Shandong since both the German occupation of Shandong and Japan's later victory over Germany were the result of force and that: "The rights of Germany have been forfeited and those of Japan have not yet been established." Once the former treaties on Shandong were eliminated, it would be "possible to deal with the question of Shandong entirely on the basis of the merits of the case."[36]

By late April 1919 copies of Japan's secret agreements were available and the American delegation's position on Shandong had changed substantially (see Document 8). On 24 April Hornbeck directed an important internal memo to Williams in which he bluntly concluded that "the Japanese are first and most of all intent upon preserving appearances, or, put in the Eastern phraseology, on saving their 'face.' "[37]

In order to save Japan's "face" Hornbeck suggested that Germany transfer title over Shandong to Japan in return for Japan's assurances that "all such holdings and properties shall reverse or be transferred to China . . . within a period of one year from the signing of this treaty." Hornbeck explained that by reverting to this strategy "Japan would gain the appearance of that for which she has contended, namely of a settlement between Germany and herself, the German relinquishment being in favor of Japan, while at the same time there would be no recognition of the agreements of 1915 or 1917, and it would be made certain that the properties and privileges in question would pass to China—as they should."[38]

After receiving Hornbeck's memo, Williams sent a final memorandum to President Wilson, also dated 24 April 1919. In this memo Williams closely followed Hornbeck's advice, and by so doing conceded the overwhelming diplomatic weight of Japan's recently released secret agreements. It is important that in this memorandum Williams backed the Japanese delegation's claim that Japan be given responsibility for handing the Shandong leased concessions back to China. In other words, the formal American policy was now to support "indirect" over "direct" restitution.

To insure that the Japanese government carried through on all of its promises to return the Shandong concession, appropriate guarantees should be given to China. Williams advised:

> But with respect to former German holdings and property in Shandong province, since they were taken in military operations by Great Britain and Japan before China declared war, and since they are now in possession of Japan, it is agreed that

> Japan shall transfer them to China within one year after the signature of the Treaty of Peace upon the following conditions:
>
> 1. That an <u>international settlement</u> shall be established at Qingdao in which Chinese citizens shall enjoy the same political rights as those of foreign nations.
>
> 2. China agrees to reimburse Japan for her expenses in connection with the taking of Jiaozhou.
>
> If this should not be satisfactory to the Japanese, it might be intimated to them that the mines (which are their chief concern) could be made over to a Sino-Japanese company.
>
> It is most important that Japan shall not be left in possession of the railway.

Unlike former American documents that called for the complete abolition of Japan's 1915 treaties with China, Williams now suggested that Wilson should simply be careful not to "recognize" these treaties, a very different recommendation from that presented to Wilson in early April. Williams succinctly summarized the Sino-Japanese dispute: "Such a settlement would seem to save Japan's face while preventing the making by her of any excessive demands upon China."[39]

With the gradual release and publication of Japan's secret treaties it began to dawn on the American delegation during April 1919 that Japan had anticipated every legal pitfall and had negotiated appropriate secret treaties and agreements well in advance to avoid every one of them. As a result, in late April 1919 Williams advised Wilson that if he could persuade the Japanese delegates to 1) modify slightly Japan's four conditions on Shandong, 2) agree to publish these conditions in the final peace treaty, and 3) avoid mentioning the 1915 Sino-Japanese treaty in the text of the final peace treaty, then it might be possible to induce the Chinese delegation to accept this compromise arrangement and convince them to sign the Versailles treaty. Only in this way, Williams argued, could the problem of "direct" versus "indirect" transfer of Shandong be amicably resolved. But, Williams warned, if a solution was not found that China could stomach, then "Japan's insistence upon her pound of flesh will certainly perpetuate strife and discord in the Far East."[40]

**The Japanese Delegation's April 1919 Proposals**

On 21 April 1919 the Japanese delegation reissued its Shandong proposals. Unlike the Chinese delegation's proposals, which continued to ignore the impact of the 1918 Sino-Japanese agreements, the Japanese delegation—as with the

Suggestions as to Possible Courses of Procedure.

Mr. Williams:

I am confident that the President will, if it be within human possibility, insist upon the ideally just settlement of this question. I realize, however that that may be impossible. If a solution short of the ideal must be made, I am convinced that no such surrender need be made as would be involved in accepting either of the alternatives which I understand to have been proposed by the British Prime Minister.

If and when it may be found that there must be some concession, I submit that there are at least two possible plans of compromise which should be given fullest consideration. As the situation has developed, the Japanese are first and most of all intent upon preserving appearances, or, to put in the Eastern phraseology, on saving their "face". This being the case I am very much of the opinion that they would give favorable consideration to a proposal such as is involved in the draft of a treaty clause which we discussed recently. (1.) German rights and privileges in China having terminated, it is agreed that all holdings and property of the German State in China, with the exception of diplomatic or consular premises revert or shall pass, without compensation, to China. (2.) With regard to former German holdings and property in Shantung province, these holdings and properties, both public and private, having been taken by Great Britain and ~~China in the course~~ of military operations and being now in possession of Japan, it is agreed that all such holdings and properties shall revert or be transferred to China, the execution of this provision to be carried out by Japan and to be completed within a period of one year from the signing of this treaty. (3.) All holdings and property of the German state in China not otherwise provided for in the above articles revert or shall pass at once and without compensation to China. (4.) Germany agrees to compensate Japan for the latter's war costs in the taking of Kiaochow.

**Document 8**: Excerpt from the 24 April 1919 Memorandum from Stanley K. Hornbeck to E. T. Williams

American delegation—took these newly released documents into account. As expected, these agreements dramatically strengthened, rather than weakened, Japan's diplomatic position. In particular, the Japanese emphasized that the transfer of funds proved that the Sino-Japanese agreements were in effect. In addition, they argued that the terms agreed to in the 1918 agreements presupposed the validity of, and so therefore recognized, the 1915 Sino-Japanese treaty.

On 22 April 1919, Secretary of State Lansing forwarded a copy of Japan's most recent proposals to President Wilson. Viscount Chinda had authored these proposals, and in them he argued that the Shandong question be resolved according to the "reasonable" terms of the Sino-Japanese treaty of 1915, which specified that Jiaozhou would be opened as a commercial port, that Japanese and international settlements would be established there, and that questions concerning the disposal of German public property would be settled. According to Chinda, all of these points "can only be regarded as quite natural and matters of course and necessity."[41]

Foreseeing China's objections to Japan's diplomatic position, Ambassador Chinda once again provided the American delegation with translated copies of the Sino-Japanese agreements of 24 September 1918. Basing his remarks directly on the text of this treaty, he stated: "You seemed to entertain some apprehension as to the future status of the Province of Shandong, but what Japan and China had actually agreed upon concerns only the running of the Shandong Railway upon the basis of a Sino-Japanese Cooperation, and the loans for two railway lines to be built by China in connection with the Shandong Railway, a portion of which has already been handed over to China by Japanese capitalists. These cannot certainly be looked upon as affecting in any way the status of Shandong. These arrangements were made by an exchange of notes on September 24, 1918, copies of which are also enclosed herein for your perusal." As for returning Jiaozhou to China, Chinda promised that Japan would arrange these details with China as soon as the peace treaty with Germany had been concluded: "I need hardly assure you that my Government will be disposed to reach an agreement as to such actual arrangements with utmost speed."[42]

During a personal meeting with Secretary of State Lansing on 26 April 1919, Chinda reiterated that the Sino-Japanese treaties specified that the Shandong railway would be operated as a "joint undertaking" between China and Japan. In response to Lansing's criticism that handing over the Shandong concession to Japan would simply continue the wrong originally perpetrated by Germany, Chinda heatedly responded: "Oh, but the situation is quite different. We have express conventions with China dealing with this question and we mean to insist upon their exact fulfillment."[43]

Chinda furthermore obliquely referred to the real reason why Shandong was so important to Japan—the Japanese desire to obtain their just revenge for Germany's participation in the 1895 Triple Intervention—when he made light of China's claims that it had signed the Shandong treaties under duress. According to Chinda, Japan in 1895 "was too weak to resist these three powers [Rus., Fr., & Ger.] and acquiesced, but Japan did not go about complaining of it. It was ridiculous for a nation of 400,000,000 of people to go around complaining that they had made a treaty under duress."[44]

Because it was completely based on the treaties and agreements it had signed with China in 1915 and 1918, Japan's negotiating position immediately prior to the final round of talks on the Shandong question was much stronger than China's. In particular the Japanese had shown that since China had already accepted money from Japan, Beijing could not easily deny the validity of the 1918 Sino-Japanese agreements. By signing the 1918 agreements, Beijing, had furthermore tacitly recognized the validity of the 1915 Sino-Japanese treaty as well. Against their will, and after examining Japan's secret treaties in detail, the American delegation's Far Eastern experts had little choice but to arrive at almost the exact same determination.

## Conclusions

President Wilson hoped to balance Japan's legitimate economic rights in Shandong on the one hand and China's sovereignty and territorial integrity on the other, but given the six official agreements that all backed Japan's claims to the Shandong concession he had little room to maneuver. Initially he tried to persuade the Japanese delegation to allow Shandong to be made a trusteeship of the Five Powers meeting at Paris, but this solution was not acceptable to Tokyo. Wilson also approached the Chinese delegation and asked whether it was better for China to cede Japan the rights Germany had formerly held in Shandong, or whether China's recent treaties with Japan were less onerous; the Chinese delegation refused to choose, insisting that both options were unacceptable.[45]

Wilson turned next to his personal advisers, the majority of whom expressed their support for China. On 22 April 1919 Secretary of State Lansing warned that if Wilson fully agreed to Japan's latest proposal it "would leave the kernel to Japan and restore the shell to China."[46] Williams backed Lansing almost word for word in a 24 April 1919 memorandum pointing out to Wilson that Japan's proposal for opening a permanent settlement in Jiaozhou would be worse for China than if it were to allow Germany to complete the remaining seventy-eight years of its lease. Williams reiterated that if Japan retained control over the railway and mines in Shandong province, Japan's "offer to return Jiaozhou, therefore, is merely an offer of the shell. She would keep the kernel."[47]

Stymied on all sides by Japan's unwillingness to make Shandong a trust territory of the Five Powers, by China's intransigence in refusing to choose which of its own official treaties on Shandong it wished to uphold, and by his own advisers' warnings not to appease Japan's demands, Wilson had great difficulty crafting a compromise solution that would protect Chinese sovereignty over the Shandong concession while ceding Japan economic benefits that it had wrested from Germany in World War I and had consolidated by signing official treaties with China. During almost two weeks of intensive talks with the Chinese and Japanese delegations at the end of April 1919, the Big Three leaders at Paris turned their attention to an in-depth consideration of the Shandong question. It was during this period that President Wilson succeeded in formulating what appeared to be a suitable compromise.

**Notes**

1. Toyokichi Iyenaga, "Iyenaga Decries Shantung Charge," *New York Times*, 1 August 1919.
2. Telegram from the American embassy in Tokyo, Japan, summarizing Prince Konoye's article in *Japan and the Japanese*, 7 January 1919, SKH Papers Box 329.
3. *Ibid.*
4. *Ibid.*
5. *Ibid.*
6. It could be argued that Makino was greatly influenced by Wilson's opposition at the Paris Peace Conference to territorial imperialism, and so later became one of the most important officials to oppose Japan's imperialist policies in China. According to one Japanese Encyclopedia entry describing Makino and his political career: "With the rise of military influence in the early 1930s, Makino came under heavy criticism from the military and right wing for his support of a cooperative, nonexpansionist foreign policy and was forced to leave office in 1935. He narrowly escaped assassination in the February 26th Incident of 1936." *Kodansha Encyclopedia of Japan* (Tokyo: Kodansha Ltd., 1983), Volume 5, 86. Although it is generally ignored or overlooked by many historians of the pre–World War II period, the path to war between the United States and Japan was in no way assured. If Wilson had been successful in getting the United States to join the League of Nations, and if Washington had paid more attention to the rapidly deteriorating situation in China, then perhaps this conflict could have been avoided. This issue will be discussed in greater detail by the author in a forthcoming volume focusing on the history of Soviet-Japanese diplomatic relations during the interwar years.
7. Emile Joseph Dillon, *The Inside Story of the Peace Conference* (New York: Harper & Brothers Publisher, 1920), 323.
8. "Minutes of Conversation held in Pichon's Room at the Quai d'Orsay, Paris," 27 January 1919, SKH Papers, Box 382, marked "Secret."
9. *Ibid.*
10. *Ibid.*
11. "Minutes of Conversation held in Pichon's Room at the Quai d'Orsay, Paris," 28 January 1919, SKH Papers, Box 382, marked "Secret."
12. *Ibid.*
13. "US Naval Advisory Staff, Question II and Recommendations (Disposition of Kiao Chou)," 19 December 1918, WWP Microfilm, Series 5B: Peace Conference Correspondence, 14-21 December 1918, Reel 386.
14. *Ibid.*
15. "Memorandum on Policy from Stanley K. Hornbeck to Dr. I. Bowman," 20 January 1919, SKH Papers, Box 382.

16. *Ibid.*
17. *Ibid.*
18. *Ibid.*
19. *Ibid.*
20. Chow, 187.
21. Telegram from the American legation in Beijing, marked "Strictly Confidential," 3 February 1919, SKH Papers, Box 329.
22. *Ibid.*
23. "Telegram from the American Embassy in Tokyo," February 1919, SKH Papers, Box 329.
24. "Telegram from the British Legation," 9 February 1919, SKH Papers, Box 382.
25. "Dispatch from the American Embassy in Tokyo, sent via Washington," 19 February 1919, SKH Papers, Box 329.
26. As reported in "Telegram from the American legation in Peking," 11 February 1919, SKH Papers, Box 329.
27. "Viscount Chinda's statement: Complete Understanding Between the Governments of Japan and China," March 1919, SKH Papers, Box 382.
28. "Chinese Government Should Sit Tight," *North China Star*, 3 February 1919.
29. "A Correction: Concerning the Interview with Vice-Minister Chen Lu," *Peking Leader*, 9 February 1919.
30. "Reminiscences," V. K. Wellington Koo Papers, 200-201.
31. "E. T. Williams' Supplement to Confidential Bulletin No. 57," 5 March 1919, SKH Papers, Box 329.
32. For Wilson's copies of these agreements, dated 16 February 1919, see Ray Stannard Baker Papers, Box 8.
33. MacMurray, Volume II, 1445.
34. Liang Qichao, "Causes of China's Defeat at the Peace Conference," *Millard's Review*, 19 July 1919, 262-265.
35. "E. T. Williams' and Hornbeck's Proposal to President Woodrow Wilson," April 1919, SKH Papers, Box 330.
36. *Ibid.*
37. "Memorandum to E. T. Williams from Stanley Hornbeck," 24 April 1919, SKH Papers, Box 387.
38. *Ibid.*
39. "Memorandum from E. T. Williams to President Woodrow Wilson," 24 April 1919, SKH Papers, Box 330.
40. "Memorandum from E. T. Williams to Henry White," 27 April 1919, SKH Papers, Box 387.
41. "Viscount Chinda's 'Strictly Confidential' letter to Robert Lansing, Paris," 21 April 1919 (misdated as 31 April 1919), WWP Microfilm Reel 402, 18861-62.
42. *Ibid.*
43. "Conversation between Secretary Lansing and Viscount Chinda," Paris, 26 April 1919, WWP Microfilm Reel #402, 19702-8; underlining same as in the original document.
44. "Conversation between Secretary Lansing and Viscount Chinda," Paris, 26 April 1919, Ray Stannard Baker Papers, Box 9.

45. Roy Watson Curry, *Woodrow Wilson and Far Eastern Policy, 1913-1921* (New York: Bookman Associates, 1957), 268-270.

46. "Robert Lansing's private letter to President Wilson," Paris, 22 April 1919, WWP Microfilm Reel 402, 18860.

47. "E. T. Williams' private letter to President Wilson," Paris, 24 April 1919, WWP Microfilm Reel 402, 19363-65.

# 4
# *President Wilson's Compromise Proposal*

President Wilson said that [China's concerns] were serious considerations, but he would not like Mr. Koo even personally to entertain the idea that there was injustice in an arrangement that was based on Treaties which Japan had entered into. The sacredness of treaties had been one of the motives of the war. It had been necessary to show that treaties were not mere scraps of paper. If treaties were inconsistent with the principles on which the peace was formed, nevertheless we could not undo past obligations. If that principle were accepted, we should have to go back and France would have the treaty of 1815 and there would be no end to it. He would not like to feel that because we were embarrassed by a treaty we were disregardful of justice. Moreover, the unjust treatment of China in the past had not by any means been confined to Japan. He hoped that the quandary in which the Powers were [in] would be stated to the Chinese people. He hoped that it would be shown to them that the undoing of the trouble depended on China uniting in reality with other nations, including the Western nations. He felt absolute confidence that the opinion of the world had the greatest sympathy for the realm of China. The heart of the world went out to her 400 million people. Any statesmen who ignore their fortunes were playing a dangerous game. But it would not do to identify justice with unfortunate engagements that had been entered into.[1]

President Woodrow Wilson (Paris, 22 April 1919)

On 4 July 1914, Woodrow Wilson for the first time stated his conditions for any future peace with Germany: "The settlement of every question, whether of territory, of sovereignty, of economic arrangement or political relationship" is to be "upon the basis of the *free acceptance of that settlement* by the people immediately concerned, and not upon the basis of the national interest or advantage of *any other nation or people* which *may desire* a different settlement *for the sake of its own exterior influence or mastery.*"[2] This statement later became the basis of

Wilson's Fourteen Points and was the foundation for America's initial proposal on the Shandong question.

To bring about a lasting peace Wilson brought to Paris his plan for a League of Nations. For the League to become an effective force, however, it was imperative that Japan be a member; yet Japanese leaders and the Japanese press were already discussing the possibility of a new war between Japan and an Anglo-American *entente*. As the Japanese delegation also made quite clear to Wilson early in the Paris talks, Tokyo could not consider participating in the League until the Shandong question was resolved. As a result, a just resolution of the Shandong question that would satisfy not only the Japanese government but also the Japanese people became the linchpin determining whether or not President Wilson could realize his Fourteen Points.

Meanwhile, the Chinese government and people were counting on President Wilson to resolve the Shandong question to their satisfaction. On 1 March 1919, the Chinese Students' Alliance, which claimed to represent 1,400 Chinese students in the United States, presented him with their "plea of a quarter of humanity." According to this petition, President Wilson was the "only great champion China has," and so was the only one who could save China from "enslavement under a foreign militarism."[3] On 25 April 1919, a petition from the opposition Guangzhou government, signed by Sun Yat-sen and other South China leaders, was forwarded to Wilson: "The 21 demands of Japan and other secret conventions imposed upon China by threatening war . . . are contrary to the letter and spirit of the Fourteen Points ably laid down by President Wilson. There will not be permanent peace [in the] Far East unless they are abrogated."[4]

At Paris Wilson sought a new era of cooperation between nations. Failure risked much more than war with Japan or loss of China's friendship, however, since Wilson and his advisers viewed the major threat to the Fourteen Points to be the spread of Bolshevism. On 31 December 1918, Joseph P. Tumulty, Wilson's private secretary, noted in a private message to Wilson the differences between Russia's and America's "two ideals, one, [that] the balance of power means continuance of war; other, [that] concert of nations means universal peace." This was the primary dispute that had to be resolved at Paris, and Tumulty warned: "If the statesmanship at Versailles cannot settle these things in the spirit of justice, Bolshevism will settle them in a spirit of injustice."[5] As if to emphasize this threat further, on 8 January 1919 the American embassy in Stockholm reported to Wilson that the Bolsheviks were expanding their efforts to spread communism to China: the "Chinese Labor Association" in Russia has just adopted a "resolution to send agitators [to] China to promote social revolution and require assistance [of] Soviet Government [to] that end."[6]

On 10 January 1919, America Minister to China Paul Reinsch appealed to Wilson to conclude a "permanent settlement of the Chinese question" because Wilson had already become to "the people of China the embodiment of their best hopes and aspirations." But after explaining that "the Chinese nation asks for no better fate than to be allowed freedom to follow in the footsteps of America," Reinsch warned that if "China should be disappointed in her confidence at the present time the consequences of such disillusionment on her moral and political development would be disastrous."[7] Wilson's almost impossible task was to formulate a compromise on Shandong that would grant Japan sufficient "face" so that it would join the League of Nations, while at the same time limiting China's loss of "face" so that it would not abandon the West for Bolshevism.

**The American Delegation and its Proposals**

Of the 144 full and associate members of the American delegation to the Paris Peace Conference—a number that dwarfed the six-member Chinese and the five-member Japanese delegations—only E. T. Williams and Stanley K. Hornbeck were assigned to Far Eastern questions. President Wilson and Secretary of State Lansing also took a deeply personal interest in China's plight at the conference, as did several of Wilson's personal advisers such as Henry White and Tasker Bliss. Two sets of American proposals on Shandong were made at the end of April 1919, the first by Lansing and the second by Williams and Hornbeck.

During April 1919 the American proposals on Shandong changed radically as the American delegates had to take into account the terms of Japan's treaties and agreements dealing with Shandong. On 21 April 1919 Lansing admitted to Wilson that the Chinese demand to regain Shandong concession directly might be difficult to obtain and he recommended that Germany renounce its rights over it directly to the Five Allied and Associated Powers. There was ample precedent for this move, Lansing claimed, since similar arrangements were being made with regard to Germany's "rights, titles and privileges in territory outside her frontiers," most notably in such places as "Morocco, Egypt, Siam, Liberia."[8]

Prior to the beginning of detailed negotiations on Shandong, Wilson urged Lloyd George to approach the leader of the Japanese delegation, Viscount Chinda, and request that Japan delay talks on the Shandong question. This postponement would be the first step in turning over the Shandong question to the League of Nations. Chinda refused, explaining that the Japanese government had a "duty to perform to China" and that if the Shandong problem were not decided, then the "Japanese Delegates were under an expressed instruction from their government that unless they were placed in a position to carry out Japanese obligations to China, they were not allowed to sign the Treaty." As a result of this order Chinda warned Lloyd George that the Japanese delegation "had no power to agree [to] a postponement of this question."[9]

Once it became clear that the Japanese delegates would not postpone talks on Shandong and would boycott the peace negotiations if there were a delay, Wilson had little choice but to address the issue. On 22 April Wilson met with the Japanese delegates (see Appendix C). After it became clear that they would not agree to Lansing's proposals, Wilson was in basic agreement with Williams' and Hornbeck's view, as set forth most clearly in their 24 April 1919 notes and memorandum, that Japan should be given responsibility for handing the Shandong concessions back to China. In other words Wilson now accepted Japan's demand for "indirect" versus "direct" restitution of Shandong to China. However, Japan should also be willing to compromise: "It need not be expected that Japan will withdraw from the Conference, particularly if offered some compromise in reference to the Shandong question such as has been suggested."[10]

Wilson brought up Japan's agreements with China during private negotiations with the Japanese delegates. He urged Japan to forego these agreements:[11]

> President Wilson pointed out that in the circumstances he was the only independent party present. He would like to repeat a point of view which he had urged on the Japanese Delegation a few days before.
>
> He was so firmly convinced that the Peace of the Far East centered upon China and Japan, that he was more interested from this point of view than any other. He did not wish to see complex engagements that fettered free determination. He was anxious that Japan should show to the world, as well as to China, that she wanted to give the same independence to China as other nations possessed, that she did not want China to be held in manacles. What would prejudice the Peace in the Far East was any relationship that was not trustful.
>
> It was evident that there was not that relationship of mutual trust that was necessary if peace was to be ensured in the Far East. What he feared was that Japan, by standing merely on her treaty rights, would create the impression that she was thinking more of her rights than of her duties to China.

The only possible way out, as Wilson informed the Japanese delegation, was to find an equitable solution to the Shandong problem that would not be based on the Twenty-one Demands or on the 1918 agreements; in other words, Japan and China should negotiate a new agreement concerning Shandong.

By late April 1919, therefore, Wilson was well aware that a generally acceptable solution to the Shandong problem might prove to be impossible. This was especially true because the American government firmly upheld the sanctity of treaties, and the terms of the Sino-Japanese agreements clearly and explicitly supported Tokyo's claims. Wilson's solution was to have Japan agree to new terms. He reassured the Japanese delegation that while he "did not wish to interfere with treaties," the "validity of treaties could not be called in question if they were modified by agreements between both sides."[12] In short, Wilson hoped to persuade the Japanese to modify slightly their four conditions on Shandong in order to guarantee China's sovereignty, to agree to publish these conditions in the final peace treaty, and to avoid mentioning, and thereby recognizing, the 1915 Sino-Japanese treaty, the so-called Twenty-one Demands. All of these conditions had been set forth in great detail in Williams' 24 April memorandum.

## The Big Three's Negotiations with the Chinese Delegation

All decisions on the Shandong question at the Paris Peace Conference were made by the leaders of the United States, Great Britain, and France, three of the four great Allies in World War I; Italy, during the last week in April, withdrew temporarily from the conference because of a dispute over control of Fiume. The remaining delegates were referred to as the "Big Three," but it eventually fell mainly on Wilson's shoulders to try to negotiate compromise proposals on Shandong that would offer acceptable terms to both Japan and China. To a large degree Wilson achieved this goal in a series of separate meetings with the Chinese and Japanese delegations between 22 and 30 April.

During the initial Sino-Japanese discussions of the Shandong question in January 1919, the main participants met with the Chinese and Japanese delegations together, but during all later discussions it was decided that the Big Three leaders should meet with the two delegations separately. This change was perhaps at the request of Baron Makino, who was quoted as saying that finding a just solution to Shandong was "difficult to discuss with people who had preconceived ideas," an obvious reference to the Chinese delegation's unwillingness to change its proposals even after the terms of the 1918 Sino-Japanese agreements had been published.[13] This left Wilson almost solely responsible for defending China's views to the Japanese delegation, however, since no Chinese delegates were present at these meetings.

To make matters worse for Wilson, both Lloyd George and Clemenceau stated at the very beginning of the Shandong talks that they felt obliged to support the Japanese delegation since Great Britain and France had concluded separate agreements with Japan supporting its claims. This fact was largely kept from the press in an attempt to retain the appearance of unanimity. However, as early as 19 December 1918, Wilson's secretary in Washington, Joseph Tumulty, sent him a cablegram warning "that Clemenceau and Lloyd George are in strict agreement and . . . the cards are stacked against you."[14]

During April 1919, both of these leaders considered their agreements with Japan still in effect. As Lloyd George was quick to point out, these obligations could not simply be ignored because "the war had been partly undertaken in order to establish the sanctity of treaties." This meant that so far as Great Britain was concerned "they had a definite engagement with Japan, as recorded in the note of the British Ambassador at Tokyo, dated 18th February 1917."[15] In all subsequent meetings of the Big Three concerning Shandong, therefore, Wilson faced the combined opposition of Japan, Great Britain, and France.

The United States had always before refused to recognize officially the validity of Japan's Twenty-one Demands and had protested against the conclusion of this treaty in May 1915. Similarly, the American government also did not recognize the 1918 Sino-Japanese agreements once their contents became known. This was not the case with Great Britain and France, which generally recognized the terms of these treaties. Nevertheless, after presenting his case to the Japanese delegation during the morning of 22 April, Wilson invited Lloyd George and Clemenceau to meet later that day with members of the Chinese delegation.

After opening the session Wilson first explained to Lu Zhengxiang and Wellington Koo what had transpired that morning between the Big Three and the Japanese delegation. He then pulled out a copy of the Sino-Japanese agreement of 24 September 1918 and read out loud the seven points that were included in the agreement. According to minutes of this meeting, Wilson then turned to Koo: "The Chinese Delegation could see, President Wilson continued, the embarrassing position which had been reached. Mr. Lloyd George and M. Clemenceau were bound to support the claims of Japan. Alongside of them the Chinese had their exchange of notes with Japan. He reminded Mr. Koo that when urging his case before the Council of Ten at the Quai d'Orsay, he had maintained that the war canceled the agreement with the German Government. It did not, however, cancel the [1915] agreement between China and the Japanese Government, which had been made before [China entered] the war." Wilson then told Koo that earlier that day he had proposed to the Japanese delegation that it might be possible to "bring about an agreement by modifying the [1915] Treaty," and that the Japanese delegates had responded that "they wanted a community of interest with the Chinese in the railway, and the only reserve they made was for a residential district in Jiaozhou."[16]

Instead of accepting Wilson's proposal to modify China's own official agreements with Japan, Koo argued that both the agreements signed during 1915 and 1918 were in fact part of the same transaction. As such the 1918 agreements were a direct outcome of Japan's Twenty-one Demands. According to Koo, the only position the Chinese delegation could take was to reiterate that the Twenty-one Demands "had been made against China's free will, and the same applied to the notes exchanged in the previous year" in September 1918.[17]

After listening to Koo's lengthy explanation of the Chinese delegation's position, which differed very little from these delegates' stated position at the opening sessions in January 1919, Lloyd George bluntly asked Koo which he would prefer (see Document 9): "The Treaty with Japan, or the transference to Japan of the German rights?" When Koo tried to evade answering this question, Lloyd George repeated: "Supposing the Great Powers had to decide (and this really was his position since he was bound by a Treaty) between Japan inheriting Germany's rights in Shandong or exercising the rights under [China's 1915] treaty with Japan, which would China prefer?"[18]

After consulting with Lu, Koo responded to Lloyd George that: "He could make no choice, because both alternatives were unacceptable." Koo's answer did not resolve the Big Three's dilemma, which revolved around the fact that China's official government had signed these agreements, apparently willingly. As a result, Lloyd George even suggested to Koo that China might have avoided the difficulty it now found herself in if "in the exchange of notes of September 1918, China might have stood out" and refused to sign.[19]

Since Koo declined to answer Lloyd George's query, Wilson had to restate the question: "Hence, the question which the Chinese Plenipotentiaries had to consider

Mr. Lloyd George said that it looked that by the Treaty with China, the Japanese Government would get more than the Germans had had. He asked Mr. Koo which he would prefer:- the Treaty with Japan, or the transference to Japan of the German rights?

Mr. Koo said that the situation was so difficult that he felt he must speak very frankly. The Japanese position was so close to China; especially in Manchuria, where they occupied a railway which was connected with Pekin; that merely to transfer German rights would create a very serious situation. With the Japanese on the Manchurian railway, and the Shantung railway, Pekin would be - as it were - in a pincers.

President Wilson pointed out that the Japanese claimed that the administration of the Shantung railway would be a joint one, and they proposed to withdraw the Japanese administration.

Mr. Lloyd George said that Mr. Koo had not quite answered his point. Supposing the Great Powers had to decide (and this really was his position since he was bound by a Treaty) between Japan inheriting Germany's rights in Shantung or exercising the rights under the treaty with Japan, which would China prefer? He pointed out that Great Britain was only bound by the rights which Japan inherited from Germany.

**Document 9**: Excerpt from the 22 April 1919 Big Three Discussions on Shandong was, would they prefer to retain the rights which Japan had secured in their treaty with her or would they prefer that Japan should inherit the German rights in Shandong." But again Koo refused to answer, insisting instead that these treaties be abolished: "He thought that it would be better to undo unfortunate engagements now, if they endangered the permanence of the future peace."[20]

Spurred by what appeared to be Koo's disregard for signed treaties, Lloyd George then launched into his longest speech of the session, first reminding Koo that the "war had been fought as much for the East as for the West." If Germany had won, then it could have demanded anything it wanted from China, even including "Shandong or Beijing." Japan's contributions to the war effort were essential, especially in Shandong, where "he could say that Jiaozhou could not have been captured without Japanese support."[21]

Lloyd George then warned the Chinese delegates: "It was a solemn treaty and Great Britain could not turn round to Japan now and say 'All right, thank you very much. When we wanted your help, you gave it, but now we think that the treaty was a bad one and should not be carried out.' Within the treaties he would go to the utmost limits to protect the position of China. On the League of Nations he would always be prepared to stand up for China against oppression, if there was oppression. China was a nation with a very great past and, he believed, with a still greater future. It would, however, be of no service to her to regard treaties as [German Chancellor in 1914 Theobald] Bethmann von Hollweg had regarded them, as mere scraps of paper to be turned down when they were not wanted." After Lloyd George completed his speech, Clemenceau added "that Mr. Koo could take every word that Mr. Lloyd George has said as his also."[22]

In conclusion to what had become an entirely unsatisfactory and unproductive session, President Wilson reminded Lu and Koo that Germany's goals had included domination of the Far East: "The Kaiser had been the great exponent of what was called the 'Yellow Peril.' He wanted to get France and Great Britain out of the way and afterwards to get everything else he could. One result of the war undoubtedly had been to save the Far East in particular, since that was as [yet an] unexploited part of the world."[23]

At this point, Wilson was completely alone in trying to find a satisfactory solution to the Shandong question. Even the Chinese delegates refused to back his well-intentioned efforts to negotiate new terms with Japan that would protect China's sovereignty and territorial integrity. He persevered, however, in trying to formulate a compromise settlement that would be acceptable to all parties.

**The Big Three's Negotiations with the Japanese Delegation**

On 23 April 1919, the Japanese delegation defended its agreements with China before the Big Three. In sharp contrast to the Chinese argument that Japan was conducting an imperialist policy in Shandong, the Japanese reassured Wilson, Lloyd George, and Clemenceau that Japan intended to restore Jiaozhou to China under "conditions, none of which can be regarded in any sense as unjust or unfair, considering the part Japan took in dislodging Germany from Shandong

Province."[24] Instead of losing by these agreements, China would regain control over the Shandong concession almost eighty years earlier than its own agreement with Germany had specified.

The Japanese delegates then clarified the relationship between the 1915 and 1918 agreements. In their view China's 1917 declaration of war had no effect on the 1915 agreement, especially as "the articles of September 1918, which were made more than one year after China's declaration of war, could not have been entered into without presupposing existence and validity of the Treaty of May 1915." In addition, "China has actually received [an] advance of twenty million yen according to terms of above arrangement." For these reasons the Japanese delegation concluded that "full justice" should be accorded to Japan based "upon her sacrifices and achievements and upon the fact of actual occupation, involving [a] sense of national honor."[25]

According to the Japanese delegation, the starting point for any new arrangement would have to take into account Japan's four primary conditions to China for returning Shandong, published in the *Japanese Chronicle* on 8 November 1917: for "the whole of Jiaozhou Bay to be opened as a commercial port," "a concession under the exclusive jurisdiction of Japan to be established at a place to be designated by the Japanese Government," "if the foreign powers desire it, an international concession may be established," and "as regards the disposal to be made of the buildings and properties of Germany and the conditions and procedures relating thereto, the Japanese Government and the Chinese Government shall arrange the matter by mutual agreement before the restoration."[26]

The Japanese delegation also proposed that Germany transfer to Japan its rights over the "territory of Jiaozhou, Railways, Mines, and Submarine cables," which Germany had received as a result of its 6 March 1898 treaty with China. All railway "stations, shops, fixed materials, and rolling stock" should be transferred to Japan, along with all of Germany's movable and immovable property. Japan further specified that it wanted to acquire Germany's underwater telegraph and telephone cables running from Qingdao to Shanghai as well as from Qingdao to Qifu. Finally, Japan proposed that Japanese citizens be granted the same extraterritorial rights Germans had enjoyed before them as well as the right to have their own Japanese-controlled police force.[27]

In their subsequent meeting on 29 April 1919, Wilson expressed his concern that these claims made it appear that Japan wanted to assume Germany's former political rights in Shandong. He went so far as to ask Baron Makino detailed questions, first about the underwater cables, then about the railways and mines, to make sure that Japan was not demanding more rights than Germany had previously enjoyed. Wilson was especially concerned about Japan's demand that its citizens should enjoy extraterritorial rights along the railway lines in Shandong, strongly warning the Japanese delegates that: "He must say frankly that he could not do this. He asked the Japanese representatives to cooperate with him in finding a way out. He wanted to support the dignity of Japan, but he thought that Japan gained nothing by insisting on these leased rights being vested in the government."[28] As for Japan's insistence on using Japanese police along the railways, Wilson admitted that "he did not mind Japan asking for these rights, but what he objected to was their imposing them."[29]

Based on the recommendations set forth by Williams and Hornbeck on 24 April 1919, Wilson tried to persuade Japan to forego the Twenty-one Demands. Wilson's proposal for circumventing the Twenty-one Demands called on Japan to make a statement respecting China's sovereignty. He recommended the following wording: "Surrender to China of all rights of sovereignty and retention with regard to the railway and the mines only of the economic rights of a concessionaire; to retain however privilege of establishing a non-exclusive settlement at Qingdao."[30]

According to Japanese Foreign Ministry transcripts, Wilson urged the Japanese delegation to develop new relations with China based on respect for China's sovereignty: "President Wilson said that one of the worst features in [the] whole of these transactions had been the unfortunate 21 demands and these had included a demand for police instructors, although, of course, on a much wider basis. This had caused the greatest irritation, as it was an invasion of Chinese political and administrative independence. It was impossible to divorce transactions of this kind from the public impression they made. The present arrangement was, in public intimation, tied up with the impression made by the 21 demands. He admitted that the police point in itself was a minor one, but in its implications, both in China and the United States . . . it was very unfortunate."[31] Wilson even sent a note to Balfour, urging him to convince the Japanese delegates to accept a compromise solution (see Document 10).[32]

After deliberation the Japanese delegates agreed to Wilson's suggested wording.[33] On 30 April 1919, the Japanese delegation formally announced its intentions regarding Shandong:[34]

> In reply to questions by President Wilson, Japanese delegate declared as follows: the policy of Japan is to hand back the Shandong peninsula in full sovereignty of China, retaining only the economic privileges granted to Germany and the right to establish a settlement under the usual conditions at Qingdao.
>
> The owners of the railway will use special police only to insure security for traffic. They will be used for no other purpose.
>
> The police force will be composed of Chinese and such Japanese instructor[s] as the directors of the railway may select and will be appointed by the Chinese Government.

Wilson had convinced Japan's delegation to retain certain economic rights in Shandong but no military or political rights; even the Japanese police instructors would have to be approved by the Chinese government. Most importantly, this solution completely avoided referring back to, and thereby recognizing, the 1915

[Paris] 30 April, 1919.

My dear Mr. Balfour,

I am sending enclosed (with the Japanese proposal, which I return) a form which I hope you will be kind enough to urge upon the Japanese. I hoped that I had made it clear to them that I could not accept a settlement based on the agreements with China, which all go back for the foundation to an ultimatum connected with the wrongful Twenty-one Demands. The whole settlement must, in my view, be based upon the German rights and our _present_ understandings. What I have written is exactly equivalent in substance to their form.

Pardon typewriting: this is done by myself on my own "pen".

Faithfully Yours,

Woodrow Wilson

Hon. A. J. Balfour

**Document 10**: Woodrow Wilson's 30 April 1919 Note to Balfour and 1918 Sino-Japanese agreements' infringement on China's sovereignty. In effect Wilson had induced Japan to wipe the slate clean and build its relations with China on the basis of new agreements.

The Japanese delegation fully admitted that this new arrangement was not based on Japan's former agreements with China. But it warned that if China failed to accept and implement this new arrangement, if it refused "to cooperate in the formation of the police force or to admit the employment of Japanese instructors," then this would leave Japan with no recourse but to "fall back, in the last resort, on the Sino-Japanese agreements of 1915 and 1918." Wilson urged the Japanese delegation that "in the event of such failure on the part of China, Japan, instead of appealing to agreements, should voluntarily apply for mediation by the Council of the League of Nations."[35]

**Wilson's Rationale Behind this Compromise Solution**

In accordance with Wilson's compromise, Japan acknowledged that its much stricter treaties with China would be in effect only as a last resort and that it would attempt to base its relations with China on the public declaration drafted with Wilson's help. Although this solution was far from satisfactory from China's point of view, Wilson supported it as the only plan that would eliminate Japanese encroachments on Chinese sovereignty. Wilson later explained that the Shandong controversy had been settled "in a way which seems to me as satisfactory as could be got out of the tangle of treaties in which China herself was involved."[36]

Wilson had other weighty matters to consider. In the week prior to his discussions with Japan, Italy left Paris in a huff over its failure to secure control over the city of Fiume, which had earlier been promised to the Yugoslavs.[37] According to one memoir, since Wilson was concerned about alienating Japan, he compromised on the Shandong problem not because he was giving up his high ideals but because the danger of pushing Japan away from international cooperation would have been a much greater threat to these ideals: "[Wilson] knew his decision would be unpopular in America, that the Chinese would be bitterly disappointed, that the Japanese would feel triumphant, that he would be accused of violating his own principles, but nevertheless, he must work for world order and organization against anarchy and a return to the old militarism."[38] Another observer reported that Wilson regretted that he could not do more for China, but that he was compelled to work with Japan in order to "save the League of Nations," which required Japan's support if it was to be accepted by the Paris Peace Conference.[39]

Members of the American delegation to Paris, however, blamed mainly Great Britain and France. Vance McCormick described in his diary how the secrecy surrounding the negotiations on Shandong resulted in President Wilson's role being misunderstood: "I am thoroughly disgusted with Allies' selfishness and constant effort to use the United States for their own selfish purposes and throw the blame for delay on us when we have been ready for some time and they are temporizing and playing politics; afraid to tell their people they cannot get them what they promised them at election time. I feel more discouraged today than at any time since I came over." He continued: "I really pitied him [Wilson] as they [the other Allies] are trying to make him the goat and he is powerless to fight publicly in the open because it would only help Germany by showing serious discord among the Allies."[40]

Tumulty later recounted that: "Not love of China, but hatred of Woodrow Wilson led partisan Republicans, without careful investigation of the actual situation, to seize on the Shandong affair as an opportunity to embarrass the President." When it came down to the facts underlying this resolution, Tumulty was equally clear: "Even I felt bitterly critical of what seemed to me to be the President's surrender to Japan in the matter of Shandong. But when he returned and told me the whole story and explained the complicated and delicate world situation which confronted him, I agreed with him that he had obtained out of a bad mess the best possible settlement."[41]

All of these accounts are consistent in showing that Wilson tried to find the best solution possible in difficult circumstances. Wilson was later accused of betraying China, in part because the compromise he reached with the Japanese delegation was not widely read or understood. Even Secretary of State Lansing grumbled that he was not kept informed.[42] Although the negotiating minutes prove that Japan promised to respect China's sovereignty in Shandong and to turn over control of the concession to China once Germany completed all paperwork transferring it to Japan, this pledge was made separately from the final peace treaty. Williams and Hornbeck had earlier recommended that the Japanese delegation be persuaded to allow a copy of its promises to be included with the terms of the peace treaty, but Wilson either forgot or decided against asking the Japanese delegates to agree to this condition.

Instead, Wilson telegraphed a copy of the Japanese promises to his private secretary in Washington for public distribution. On 1 May 1919, Tumulty cabled back: "I have not made use of the Japanese statement, but am keeping my ear to the ground and waiting. My feeling is that an attempt to explain the compromise, when no demand is made, would weaken our position instead of strengthening it. I will therefore do nothing about the Japanese matter unless you insist" (see Document 11).[43]

Wilson responded on the following day by agreeing that he was "perfectly willing to have you use your discretion about the use you make of what I sent you about the Chinese-Japanese settlement."[44] To this Tumulty said: "Sympathetic editorial in *New York World* with reference to Japanese settlement. I have not given out statement as yet. It does not appear now as if any would be necessary."[45] Since Tumulty all along had a letter from Wilson explaining the Shandong resolution and Japan's promises, it is unclear why the White House did not do more to explain its actions. In hindsight, this proved to be a major mistake, because it made it look as if Wilson had something to hide. As one commentator later wrote: "At the Peace Conference, the Japanese delegates verbally promised to restore to China certain sovereign rights in Shandong but this promise was never confirmed either in writing or by formal public declaration."[46]

When the Shandong decision was announced, it came as a shock.[47] The shock was greatest in the Far East, and to China in particular. Rumors began to spread that Paris had granted the Shandong concession to Japan in perpetuity. When Reinsch heard the news in Beijing, he cabled his incredulity to Washington: "I consider the telegram an imposture because it is impossible to conceive such a disregard of right and justice and such submission to Japanese military ambitions since the question between China and Japan is not local but is a test of world-wide application and effect as to whether the principles for which we fought are actually to prevail or not." Reinsch warned Washington that if this decision was true, it would "terribly arouse the whole Chinese people if it should be published."[48]

General misunderstanding over what Wilson's compromise terms were and what they meant contributed to the myth that Wilson betrayed China. Since no one could possibly have foreseen the storm of protest that arose over the Shandong decision, it would have been difficult, if not impossible, adequately to prepare the ground for this decision. As Tumulty reasoned, since there was no immediate demand for an explanation, why produce one? As will be shown in greater detail below, the consequences of this decision were to cause endless problems for the American delegation.

**The Impact of Wilson's Compromise**

Although Japan did not receive any political rights in Shandong, it did acquire the economic advantages that Beijing had already agreed to and had been partially reimbursed for by Tokyo. Sovereignty over the Shandong concession was not actually ceded to Japan, therefore, and certainly not in perpetuity. And since the peace treaty avoided officially recognizing Japan's 1915 and 1918 treaties with China, the special rights and economic privileges that Japan received at Paris were actually more limited than those specified by China's own treaties; in this regard it was Japan that lost at Paris, not China.

In addition, Woodrow Wilson's compromise proposal envisioned including both China and Japan in the newly created League of Nations. This would provide China with international guarantees against renewed Japanese aggression. Although many Americans—including Secretary of State Lansing[49] and E. T. Williams[50]—thought Japan was bluffing and insisted that Japan would certainly sign the treaty and join the League of Nations no matter what happened to Shandong, according to a 1951 analysis by Russell Fifield of Japanese foreign ministry documents: "Japan would not have signed the peace treaty with Germany or have joined the League of Nations if her Shandong demands had not been substantially accepted."[51]

Furthermore, as discussed by Frederick Dickinson, to Japanese officials Wilson's denunciation of Japanese territorial imperialism in China and his "appeal for a new order packed a force equivalent to Perry's 'black ships' in 1853." In particular: "By denouncing German militarism and imperialism, Wilson condemned modern Japan's preferred path to national development and reinvigorated the debate over national identity that had complicated the politics of modern Japan since its

# The White House,
## Washington.

CODE                                                                1 May, 1919.


The President of the United States,
        Paris.

I have not made use of the Japanese statement, but am keeping my ear to the ground and waiting. My feeling is that an attempt to explain the compromise, when no demand is made, would weaken our position instead of strengthening it. I will therefore do nothing about the Japanese matter unless you insist. It would help if I could unofficially say: First. The date of your probable return to the country; Second. Whether tour country to discuss the League of Nations is possible. The adoption of the labor program as part of the peace program, is most important, but not enough emphasis is being placed upon it. Could you not make a statement of some kind that we could use here, showing the importance of this program as helping toward the stabilization of labor conditions throughout the world.

20633                                            TUMULTY.

**Document 11**: Tumulty's 1 May 1919 Cable to Woodrow Wilson founding. In the place of arms, the American president counseled arms reduction. Instead of 'autocratic' government, he proposed 'democracy.' And in the place of empire, he advised economic, rather than territorial, expansion and a peaceful international association of states instead of a balance of power."[52]

To put Wilson's plan into effect, Secretary of State Lansing proposed that the United States, Britain, France, and Japan organize a banking consortium to regulate foreign loans to China. A draft agreement was prepared on 12 May 1919 and was submitted to each government for its approval. On 18 June 1919, the Japanese delegation proposed that all of Manchuria and Mongolia be excluded from the "operation of the consortium," but after Washington and London protested, Tokyo limited its exclusion request to include only Japanese-run railways in these areas. On this basis the final consortium agreement was signed in New York City on 15 October 1920. According to Secretary of State Charles Hughes, the consortium "will be effective in assisting the Chinese people in their efforts towards a greater unity and stability, and in affording to individual enterprises of all nationalities equality of commercial and industrial opportunity and a wider field of activity in the economic development of China."[53]

The American State Department fully agreed with Wilson's compromise. On 21 July 1919, it produced a memorandum outlining the many secret agreements that Japan had signed with China and with the Great Powers:[54]

> Under such circumstances it was manifestly out of the question for the Council to sit in equity upon the case. The practical question presented by the Chinese claim was therefore not one of law or of equity, but of policy—a question on which the attitude of all of the Principal Powers, other than the United States, was irrevocably fixed. It would therefore have been impossible, as a matter of practical affairs, to hope for a decision favorable to China's claim . . . [and so] the only feasible alternative was to accept the claim made by Japan . . .

The State Department furthermore concluded that not only had China not lost by the Shandong agreement, but that it had gained significant new advantages:[55]

> From this analysis it appears that the peace treaty transfers to Japan the several categories of German rights and interests in Shandong, in accordance with the Japanese claims as approved by the other Principal Allied Governments in February and March, 1917; it created no new rights in enlargement of the original grants of rights and privileges to Germany by virtue of the Jiaozhou Convention of 1898 and subsequent agreements, but rather affords to China the possibility of improving its situation in regard to the leasehold of Jiaozhou by accepting the restoration offered by Japan, and it gives ground for confidence that the new beneficiary of the Jiaozhou treaty of

1898 will not seek to avail itself of any such interpretation of the grant of commercial and industrial preference as would be repugnant to the principle of the Open Door.

The Chinese people did not, however, see eye to eye with the State Department. With China divided between competing governments in the North and South, and faced with even further disintegration at the hands of military warlords, many Chinese nationalists hoped that a foreign policy victory at Paris might help unite the country. Instead, China's failure at Versailles was perceived to be yet another domestic defeat. Demonstrations against the Beijing government quickly erupted. As noted by Shinkichi Eto: "The impact of foreign affairs on domestic politics was never more clearly demonstrated."[56]

## Conclusions

In the end, the Paris Peace Conference did decide that Germany must cede China "all the buildings, wharves and pontoons, barracks, forts, arms and munitions of war, vessels of all kinds, wireless telegraphy installations and other public property" in the Shandong concession. It also ordered Germany to return the ancient astronomical instruments that German troops had taken from Beijing in 1901.[57] But the key matter was the legal right to the Shandong concession itself, which the Paris delegates decided Germany should cede to Japan.

In the final analysis, the issue under dispute at Paris was whether China should regain Shandong directly from Germany or indirectly from Japan. Wilson supported indirect restitution, but in return he persuaded Japan to eliminate all encroachment on China's sovereignty or territorial integrity. Wilson considered his compromise to be a clear victory for China, especially when compared with Beijing's own secretly signed agreements with Tokyo.

But, according to the intellectual and author Liang Qichao, the real issue at stake was that the Paris delegates had backed Japan's equivalent of a "Monroe doctrine" for Asia: "Here in a treaty to be signed by practically all the Powers of the world Japan is allowed to act as an arbitrator between China and Germany. Jiaozhou, a piece of Chinese territory, is to be restored to China, not directly by Germany, with whom China is also at war, but through the hands of Japan. Thus a diplomatic precedent is created the importance of which is hard to exaggerate." As such, the Paris decision meant a victory for Japan: "What Japan has been striving for during the last few years is that she should be recognized by the Powers as the only spokesman of Eastern Asia." Liang further warned that if China "must submit to a foreign yoke she will not do so without a struggle," and that if China were driven "to desperation, [and] she attempts something hopeless, those who have helped to decide her fate cannot escape a part of the responsibility."[58]

It was as a result of this struggle, a struggle that even Liang granted was "hopeless," that Bolshevik calls for China to rebel against the West and join with

Soviet Russia in building socialism took on new importance. Ironically, Wilson appears to have unwittingly pushed China toward Bolshevism, a result that was exactly the opposite of what he had sought to accomplish at the Paris Peace Conference.

Chinese policies also backfired. Had China cooperated with Wilson to obtain his goals, it would have ultimately been the winner. Not only would China have received the Shandong concession from Japan more quickly, but America's entry into the League of Nations would have made this organization a more effective tool to regulate future encroachments on Chinese sovereignty, especially from Japan. However, instead of helping Wilson obtain his lofty objectives, the Chinese delegation to Paris actively hindered him, in the process creating the myth that it was Wilson who had betrayed China.

**Notes**

1. "Notes of a Meeting which took place at President Wilson's House, Place Des Etats-Unis, Paris," 22 April 1919, at 4:30 p.m., SKH Papers, Box 382; stamped "secret" and then "Declassified."
2. "Memorandum from E. T. Williams to Henry White," 27 April 1919, SKH Papers, Box 387.
3. "Petition from the Chinese Students' Alliance to President Wilson," 1 March 1919, SKH Papers, Box 328.
4. "A Petition to President Woodrow Wilson, signed by Wu Tingfang, Tang Shaoyi, Sun Yat-sen, Then Chuan, Tang Chiyas, Lu Yungting, and Lin Paoyi," 25 April 1919, Henry White Papers, Manuscript Division, Library of Congress, Box 47; this petition was transmitted unofficially to Washington by the American Consul General at Canton.
5. "Cablegram from Tumulty to Wilson," 31 December 1918, WWP Microfilm Reel 388.
6. "Report from American Embassy in Stockholm to Paris," 8 January 1919, WWP Microfilm Reel 388, 5626-7.
7. "Telegram from American Minister to China Paul Reinsch to Woodrow Wilson," 10 January 1919, WWP Microfilm Reel 389, 5955-64.
8. "Letter from Robert Lansing to Woodrow Wilson," 21 April 1919, WWP Microfilm Reel #402, 18673.
9. Gaimushō, File 2.3.1-3.4.
10. "Memorandum from E. T. Williams and Stanley Hornbeck to President Wilson," 24 April 1919, Ray Stannard Baker Collection, Box 9.
11. Gaimushō, File 2.3.1-3.4.
12. Gaimushō, File 2.3.1-3.6.
13. Gaimushō, File 2.3.1-3.4.
14. "Cablegram from Tumulty in Washington to Wilson in Paris, quoting Cobb in New York," 19 December 1918, WWP Microfilm Reel 386, 3512.
15. Gaimushō, File 2.3.1-3.4.

16. "Notes of a Meeting which took place at President Wilson's House, Place Des Etats-Unis, Paris," 22 April 1919, at 4:30 p.m., SKH Papers, Box 382. These minutes show that only Wellington Koo and Lu Zhengxiang were at this meeting with Wilson, Lloyd George, and Clemenceau; no member of the Japanese delegation was present.
17. *Ibid.*
18. *Ibid.*
19. *Ibid.*
20. *Ibid.*
21. *Ibid.*
22. *Ibid.*
23. *Ibid.*
24. Gaimushō, File 2.3.1-3.1.
25. *Ibid.*
26. *Ibid.*
27. *Ibid.*
28. Gaimushō, File 2.3.1-3.4.
29. *Ibid.*
30. *Ibid.*
31. Gaimushō, File 2.3.1-3.4.
32. Note from President Wilson to Balfour, 30 April 1919, Balfour Papers, Add. MSS 49751, British Library.
33. According to one account, Balfour was instrumental in urging the Japanese delegation to accept Wilson's draft compromise. Morinosuke Kajima, *The Diplomacy of Japan 1884-1922* (Tokyo: Kajima Institute of International Peace, 1980), 379-380.
34. Gaimushō, File: 2.3.1-3.1.
35. Gaimushō, File: 2.3.1-3.2.
36. Roy Watson Curry, *Woodrow Wilson and Far Eastern Policy 1913-1921* (New York: Bookman Associates, 1957), 279.
37. Baker, Volume One, 30; Versailles' apparently opposite decisions on Fiume and Shandong have often been portrayed as signs of Wilson's indecisiveness. In fact, the Croatians had received assurances at the beginning of World War I that Fiume would be turned over to them. On 23 April 1919 Wilson reiterated this point: "Fiume was not included in the Pact of London but there definitively assigned to the Croatians." Wilson's "Statement in Re Adriatic," SKH Papers, Box 328. In addition, a 19 December 1918 report to Wilson by Wickham Stead, a member of the American delegation to Paris, warned: "Were the present city and territory of Fiume to be assigned to Italy, the Southern Slavs would inevitably create a better port at Buccari, a few miles away, connect it with the Agram railway and divert all their trade to it. The prosperity of Fiume would thus be jeopardized." WWP Microfilm Reel 386, 3500-3502. Although the Chinese delegation tried to compare Fiume to Shandong, it should be emphasized that—unlike with the Croatians—the 1918 secret agreement on the Shandong concession was willingly signed by Beijing. For this reason, Fiume and Shandong are not analogous situations.
38. Baker, Volume Two, 266.
39. Curry, 280.
40. "Unpublished diary of Vance C. McCormick," 3 April 1919, entry 63, Vance C. McCormick Papers, Hoover Institution Archives.

41. Joseph P. Tumulty, *Woodrow Wilson as I Know Him* (New York: Doubleday, Page & Company, 1921), 380-391.

42. In a letter to William Phillips, Assistant Secretary of State, Lansing said: "The Council of Four has been meeting now nearly two weeks and practically nothing comes out of the cloud of mystery which envelopes them. . . . It is a rather difficult position the Commissioners are in and one not to be envied. We want to help but have no opportunity. Were it not that it would cause an unfortunate situation I would be disposed to ask to be allowed to go home, as I apparently render little or no service as an adviser." 5 April 1919, Robert Lansing collection, Box 3. Later, he wrote: "What discussion [on Shandong] took place in the latter council I do not know on account of the secrecy which was observed as to their deliberations. But I presume that the President stood firmly for the Chinese rights, as the matter remained undecided until the latter part of April." *The Peace Negotiations: A Personal Narrative* (New York: Houghton Mifflin Company, 1921), 254.

43. "Telegram from Tumulty to Wilson," 1 May 1919, WWP Microfilm Reel 404, 20633.

44. "Telegram from Wilson to Tumulty," 2 May 1919, WWP Microfilm Reel 404, 20858.

45. "Telegram from Tumulty to Wilson," 2 May 1919, WWP Microfilm Reel 404, 20848.

46. Wilson Leon Godshall, *The International Aspects of the Shantung Question* (Ph.D. Diss., University of Pennsylvania, 1923), 165-166.

47. Ray Stannard Baker, "How Japan Forced Shantung Clause," *New York Times,* 17 August 1919.

48. "Telegram from the American Legation at Peking to Washington," 5 May 1919, SKH Papers, Box 383.

49. Lansing thought the Japanese were bluffing, and advised telling them: "If you do not give back to China what Germany stole from her, we don't want you in the League of Nations," Robert Lansing collection, Box 7, 81 .

50. After it was too late, Williams denounced Wilson's compromise, calling it a "flagrant violation of the Fourteen Points." See E. T. Williams, "The Conflict Between Autocracy and Democracy," *The American Journal of International Law*, Vol. 32 (1938), 663-679.

51. Russell Fifield, "Documents: Japanese Policy Toward the Shantung Question at the Paris Peace Conference," *The Journal of Modern History*, Vol. XXIII, No. 3 (Sept. 1951), 265-272.

52. Frederick R. Dickinson, *War and National Reinvention: Japan in the Great War, 1914-1919* (Cambridge, MA: Harvard University Press, 1999), 207, 236.

53. George A. Finch, "American Diplomacy and the Financing of China," *The American Journal of International Law*, Vol. 16 (1922), 25-42.

54. "Memorandum on the Shantung Question," 21 July 1919, John V. A. MacMurray Papers, Box 22.

55. *Ibid.*

56. Shinkichi Eto, "China's International Relations, 1911-1931," John K. Fairbank and Albert Feuerwerker, eds., *The Cambridge History of China*, Vol. 13, Part 2 (New York: Cambridge University Press, 1986), 103.

57. Department of State, *The Treaty of Versailles and After* (Washington, 1947), 287-288.

58. Liang Qichao, "China and the Shantung Settlement," *Manchester Guardian,* 16 June 1919.

# 5
# *The Myth of Woodrow Wilson's Betrayal*

> Germany cedes to Japan all rights, titles and privileges, notably as to Jiaozhou, and the railroads, mines, and cables acquired by her treaty with China of March 6, 1898, and by other agreements as to Shandong. All German rights to the railroad from Qingdao to Jinan, including all facilities and mining rights and rights of exploitation, pass equally to Japan, and the cables from Qingdao to Shanghai and Qifu, the cables free of all charges. All German state property, movable and immovable, in Jiaozhou, is acquired by Japan free of all charges.[1]
>
> "Summary of the Conditions of Peace" (10 May 1919)

In the end the Chinese delegation failed to obtain its primary objective at the Paris Peace Conference: regaining the Shandong concession directly from Germany. Unfortunately for China, its own internationally-recognized Republican government in Beijing had signed treaties and accepted money in exchange for transferring economic rights in Shandong to Japan. The resulting Sino-Japanese agreements, which the Chinese delegation failed to prove were signed under duress, solidly supported Japan's diplomatic position. Delegates at the Paris Peace Conference—led by the Big Three—believed that they had little choice but to adhere to these bilateral agreements and to recommend that the Shandong concession be turned over to Japan. To do otherwise would have left the Western delegations open to the just accusation that Japan was being treated differently only because of racial prejudice. This would have most likely led Japan to boycott the League of Nations.

Since Japan formally promised to transfer control of the Shandong concession to China, which Tokyo subsequently did in 1922, the end result between direct and indirect restitution was actually the same. The intense emotions that were stirred in China cannot be understood without referring to the concept of "face." To the Chinese, having Japan as the intermediary in this transaction was a grave insult. This was because for centuries Japan had been considered a tributary state of China and therefore not equal, much less superior, to China. When Tokyo assumed responsibility for returning Shandong to China, it put Japan in the position of superior and placed China in the position of inferior. This enormous "loss of face" was overwhelmingly rejected by the Chinese delegation at Paris, by the Beijing government, and by the Chinese people.

The Chinese delegation's major dilemma was how to explain its failure at the Paris Peace Conference in order to "save face" for itself and for China. The delegates could not very well blame Beijing for negotiating the 1915 and 1918 treaties. They also could not reasonably be expected to criticize themselves for their losing diplomatic hand or acknowledge their lack of advance knowledge of the 1918 agreements. They could certainly blame Japan for China's plight, but this tactic had already been tried and had failed to achieve results; accusing Great Britain and France would have been equally futile, since both nations had signed agreements with Japan well in advance of Paris.

This left the United States. It should not come as a total surprise, therefore, that the Chinese delegation should suddenly turn on their strongest supporter and blame Wilson for China's predicament. Beginning in early May 1919 the Chinese delegates began to criticize Wilson in public for failing to uphold his Fourteen Points. They also publicly misrepresented or completely ignored Wilson's compromise with the Japanese delegation. The Chinese delegates' efforts to make Wilson the scapegoat for China's diplomatic failure were particularly successful in China, where public demonstrations against the Shandong resolution became more and more anti-American. These public demonstrations, known as the May Fourth Movement, helped create and popularize the myth that it was Woodrow Wilson who had betrayed China.

**The Importance of "Face" in China**

It is all too often overlooked that the Paris Peace Conference gave China many financial and territorial benefits (see Document 12). First, it terminated all of Germany's and Austria's former treaties with China. Second, it returned to China all of Germany's concession property in Tianjin and Hankou. Third, it reaffirmed the abolition of the German and Austrian shares of the Boxer indemnity. But all of these positive points were overshadowed by the decision to turn Germany's former concessions in Shandong over to Japan before their return to China, a decision that the Chinese delegation at Paris portrayed as an affront to Chinese sovereignty and to China's self-esteem. To understand the Sino-Japanese conflict over Shandong one must refer to the Chinese term "face."[2]

By terminating Germany's and Austria's former "unequal" treaties with China, Paris eliminated at one stroke almost a half century of German diplomacy with China. The most important example of this was the Shandong concession itself, which was eventually returned to China more than seventy-five years before the 1898 Sino-German treaty came due. Because this move served as a legal precedent, it became an important first step on the road to eliminating almost a century of international treaties that Beijing claimed were to China's disadvantage.

The return of the German concessions in Tianjin and Hankou to China also set a precedent. Not only were these concessions quite valuable in their own right, but their elimination stripped Germany of the final territorial levers through which it had exerted diplomatic pressure on China. Later, the Beijing government

China.

Germany renounces in favor of China all privileges and indemnities resulting from the Boxer Protocol of 1901 and all buildings, wharves, barracks, forts, munitions of war, ships, wireless plants and other public property, except diplomatic or consular establishments, in the German concessions of Tientsin and Hankow and in other Chinese territory except Kiao-Chow, and agrees to return to China at her own expense all the astronomical instruments seized in 1900 and 1901. China will, however, take no measures for disposal of German property in the Legation Quarter at Pekin without the consent of the Powers signatory to the Boxer Protocol.

Germany accepts the abrogation of the concessions at Hankow and Tientsin, China agreeing to open them to international use. Germany renounces all claims against China or any Allied and Associated Government for the internment or repatriation of her citizens in China and for the seizure or liquidation of German interests there since August 14, 1917. She renounces in favor of Great Britain her State property in the British concession at Canton, and of France and China jointly of the property of the German school in the French concession at Shanghai.

Shantung.

Germany cedes to Japan all rights, titles and privileges, notably as to Kiao-Chow, and the railroads, mines, and cables acquired by her treaty with China of March 6, 1898, and by other agreements as to Shantung. All German rights to the railroad from Tsingtao to Tsinanfu, including all facilities and mining rights and rights of exploitation, pass equally to Japan, and the cables from Tsingtao to Shanghai and Chefoo, the cables free of all charges. All German state property, movable and immovable, in Kiao-Chow, is acquired by Japan free of all charges.

**Document 12**: 7 May 1919 "Summary of the Conditions of Peace" was able to argue with some success that, since German militarism had been the greatest threat to the Far East, once this threat had been eliminated the other powers should also return their concessions to China. Beijing officials were thus able to use the Paris decision returning these two German concessions to apply diplomatic pressure on the other major powers to follow suit.

Finally, the abolition of Germany's and Austria's combined twenty percent share of the Boxer indemnity redirected enormous funds into China's coffers. According to one estimate, the savings amounted to $88,000,000 over the twenty-three year period from 1917 to 1940.[3] By contrast, Japan's financial gains were estimated to be as high as $100,000,000, but military expenses in driving Germany from China were estimated at $50,000,000.[4] It could be argued, therefore, that Japan's financial gains at Paris were considerably less than China's.

As a result of the Versailles Peace Treaty, China received an enormous share of the German spoils in the Far East from minimal involvement in the war. Although this would suggest that the Chinese public should have been satisfied with the treaty, it was not. In fact, while many Chinese had applauded Japan's victory over Germany in 1914, they did not acknowledge Japan's rights to the Shandong concession, even if these were only partial economic rights.

As correctly summarized by the 30 June 1919 edition of *La Petite République*, the real underlying problem was face: "It is known that the Chinese delegates so as to avoid complications inclined for a long time towards the adoption of a provisional solution which would have 'saved the face' of all parties."[5] Saving face has continued to be a powerful motive force in China, especially in diplomatic settings. For example, Mao Zedong's personal physician, Li Zhisui, refers to it repeatedly to explain Mao's political decisions vis-à-vis the Soviet Union.[6] The April 2001 Sino-U.S. standoff over the EP-3 "spy plane" is another good example.

China's extreme displeasure with Wilson's solution was due in part to the centuries-old historical relationship between China and Japan. In Sino-Japanese relations China had traditionally played the dominant role, even referring in its history books to the Japanese as "wokou," or "midget pirates."[7] Sun Yat-sen, the leader of the opposition government in Guangzhou, later alluded to this relationship between the two states in a 1924 speech when he referred to Japan as China's "younger brother" and said: "It is our hope that Japan, as the younger brother, will assist the elder brother in his efforts to abolish these Unequal Treaties, and to secure emancipation from his serfdom."[8]

From China's point of view, therefore, it was bad enough that the Europeans had forced concessions out of China, but now Asian powers were being allowed to do the same. This increased Chinese frustration at what they perceived to be a century of foreign mistreatment. As a result, the Chinese public concluded that China had "lost face" at Paris. This attitude was often difficult for foreigners to understand, since China gained a tremendous amount from the Versailles Peace Treaty—arguably even more than Japan did—in terms of abolished treaty rights, returned concession territory, and cancelled indemnity payments, while having to contribute virtually nothing to the war effort.

## The Chinese Diplomatic Reaction to the Shandong Resolutions

The American delegation was worried that the Shandong resolutions might be either misunderstood or rejected by the Chinese delegation because of "face." As early as 2 May 1919, Hornbeck and Williams began explaining to the Chinese delegation exactly what the Japanese delegates had promised during their confidential talks with President Wilson. They also reassured the Chinese that the United States would continue to support China's efforts to regain the Shandong concession indirectly through Japan. Regardless, the Chinese delegation chose to blame Wilson for their own failure to regain Shandong directly from Germany.

On 2 May 1919, Hornbeck sent Williams a note warning that since the final Shandong resolution appeared to grant "all that Japan asked and nothing that China asked," it was of the utmost importance to clarify the "various restrictions and pledges" that the Japanese delegates had agreed to in their private talks with Wilson. Hornbeck suggested that "one of the American Commissioners confer with one or several of the Chinese delegates with a view to explaining to them the reasons for the decision and giving them some assurance as to the continued adherence of the American Government to its policy of good will toward China."[9]

Hornbeck was particularly concerned that the Chinese delegates' disappointment with the Shandong resolutions might turn them against the United States. Even though they knew that President Wilson had stood up for China's rights to Shandong in opposition to the combined forces of Japan, Great Britain, and France, Hornbeck warned that the Chinese delegation "must inevitably hold the American Government particularly responsible."[10] Hornbeck's prediction proved accurate. On 3 May 1919, the Chinese delegation made a public announcement that it had received news of the final Shandong resolutions with "disappointment and dissatisfaction."[11]

Overall, the Chinese delegation's public protest was quite similar to previous documents outlining China's proposals. But the Chinese delegation's 3 May declaration had a key impact on public opinion in one regard: it falsely implied that Japan would gain control of all of Shandong province in perpetuity. It passionately argued that "Shandong is China's holy land, packed with memories of Confucius and Mencius, and hallowed as [the] cradle of her civilization."[12]

Japan's direct control of Shandong province did not in fact extend beyond the railway line and the 200-square-mile Jiaozhou concession that had formerly been under German, not Chinese, jurisdiction. Furthermore, Japan's economic influence was limited to those commercial concessions that the Sino-Japanese agreements of 1915 and 1918 had specified. This Chinese declaration and others like it, however, helped to promote the myth that all of Shandong province and its entire population was being ceded to Japan in perpetuity.

On 4 May 1919, Lu Zhengxiang presented China's real concerns in a confidential three-page protest to President Wilson (see Document 13). Lu acknowledged that all political rights in Shandong would be returned to China and that Japan would retain only economic rights. He admitted that Japan had formally promised that it would "strictly observe the principle of the Open Door in letter and spirit." He even agreed that Japan had promised to return the Shandong concession to China once Germany formally ceded it to Japan. What Lu actually opposed was the indirect method for restoring Shandong to China: "If the Shandong peninsula is to be restored in full sovereignty, according to the proposed settlement to China, the reason does not appear clear why recourse should be had to two steps instead of one, why the initial transfer should be made to Japan and then leave it to her to 'voluntarily engage' to restore it to China."[13]

In this secret protest Lu brushed aside the controversy over the September 1918 Sino-Japanese agreements, which were the single strongest evidence that the Japanese delegates had presented at Paris to back their case. Lu dismissed them by claiming that officials in the "Chinese Government were obliged to exchange the 1918 notes" with Japan. Describing the final Shandong resolution as a "grievous disappointment" to China, Lu concluded by blaming Wilson for China's defeat: the Chinese delegation had come to Paris naively relying on Wilson's Fourteen Points, on the "spirit of honorable relationship between states," and on the "justice and equity of her case."[14]

China's public statements differed greatly from those expressed in private. This was to disguise the fact that the real dispute was not over the return of the Shandong concession but over direct and indirect restitution. That this maneuver was effective is well illustrated by referring to just a few of the many Chinese-American telegrams and letters the U.S. delegation in Paris received.

For example, one protest from a group called the "Chinese American Citizens Alliance" begged Wilson to stop Japan from "dismembering China by taking Shandong." Another, from the "Chinese Association of Oregon" pleaded: "We pray for fair treatment to China and nullification of all secret Sino-Japanese treaties." Finally, the "Chinese Press Association of America" pointedly reminded the President: "Council of three decision of Shandong Jiaozhou settlement is in direct violation of principles you [sic] propounded. We appeal for reconsideration."[15]

As a result of the White House's earlier hesitation to publish Japan's promises, and because of the Chinese delegation's determination to avoid responsibility for failing to regain the Shandong concession directly from Germany, large sections of the American and Chinese public generally assumed that Paris had ceded to Japan all of Shandong province in perpetuity. This assumption could not have been further from the truth. The stage was now set, however, to create and perpetuate the myth that it was Wilson alone who had betrayed China and Chinese national interests at Paris.

**The Japanese Diplomatic Reaction to the Shandong Resolutions**

The Japanese were proud of their success at the Paris Peace Conference. They had gone to Paris with certain objectives and had met most of them. Concerned, as it turned out justifiably, that Japan's hard won victories on the battlefield

AMERICAN COMMISSION TO NEGOTIATE PEACE.

S-H Bulletin No. 238.

Paris, May 4, 1919.

Sir:

    The Rt. Hon. Arthur J. Balfour, on behalf of the Council of Three, verbally informed the Chinese Delegates on May 1, 1919, of the settlement arrived at by the Council in regard to the Kiaochow-Shantung question. They were given to understand that the clause to be inserted in the Peace Treaty would be very general, to the effect that Germany should renounce all her rights in Kiaochow-Shantung to Japan, that the conclusions reached by the Council of Three regarding Kiaochow-Shantung was that all political rights formerly enjoyed by Germany were to be restored to China, and to Japan were given only the economic rights such as a settlement at Tsingtao, the railway already built (Tsingtao-Chinan railway), the mines connected therewith, and two other railways to be built.

    If the Shantung peninsula is to be restored in full sovereignty, according to the proposed settlement to China, the reason does not appear clear why recourse should be had to two steps instead of one, why the initial transfer should be made to Japan and then leave it to her to "voluntarily engage" to restore it to China.

    The Chinese Delegation feel it to be their duty to register a formal protest with the Council of Three Against the proposed settlement of the Kiaochow-Shantung question.

        I have the honour to be
           Sir,
           Your most obedient.
              Humble Servant,
       Signed    Lou Tsengtsiang.

To the President
  The Council of Three
    Peace Conference, Paris.

**Document 13**: Excerpts from Lu Zhengxiang's 4 May 1919 Letter to President Wilson might be taken away at the negotiating table, Japan was able to present an array of agreements on the Shandong question. China's portrayal of Japan's claim to Shandong as blatant imperialism angered the Japanese. In response, Tokyo proclaimed on numerous occasions its intention to return the Shandong concession in full sovereignty to China. Clearly, "saving face" was also important to Japan.

Immediately after the Paris Peace Conference, the reaction of the U.S. delegation and American journalists was generally favorable toward Japan. According to one account: "The Japanese never said anything; they took the palm for silence at the Conference.... The Japanese had their minds made up when they came as to what they wanted: they let it be known; and then they waited and said nothing—but never let go. They were the one-price traders of the Conference; they possess the genius—perhaps the oriental genius—of knowing how to wait. Though the disposition of . . . Shandong was almost the first question to be discussed in January, it was almost the last to be settled in May."[16]

But face was clearly an issue, and one author concludes that "Japanese honor was at stake."[17] Described by American delegates as "immobile as the Sphinx" or as "enigmatic as the Mona Lisa," the Japanese delegation spoke very little but "were perhaps listened to with all the more interest and attention on that account."[18] Wilson's goal was to help China while making sure that the Japanese did not lose face: "Wilson had hoped to 'find some outlet to permit the Japanese to save their face and let the League of Nations decide the matter later.' "[19]

That Wilson succeeded was shown when news of Japan's victory reached Tokyo. The American embassy reported that the Japanese were anything but tranquil and trumpeted their delegation's complete diplomatic victory at Paris: "The Japanese public is clearly elated over the results of the Peace Conference especially as it had anticipated more opposition as to Japan's claims in Shandong. The public announcement of the settlement of this question together with the lunch tended to the Embassy staff and newspaper men by the Minister of War have caused a very rapid decline in the anti-American campaign." Japan's former gloomy forecasts of a future war with the Anglo-American *entente* had already changed to official reaffirmation that "Japanese-American friendship together with the Anglo-Japanese Alliance forms the fundamental basis of Japan's policy."[20]

However, international press services were slow in reporting Japan's guarantees to respect China's sovereignty (see Document 14). By the middle of May, misrepresentations of the Shandong question in American and European newspapers became commonplace; the Hearst papers ran sensational headlines like: "SOLD—40,000,000 People."[21] The resulting misunderstanding was exacerbated when the Chinese delegation's declaration opposing the settlement came out immediately on 3 May 1919, while only on 6 May 1919 did *The London Times* publish Baron Makino's 4 May 1919 statement of intent. This statement clarified that "Japan's policy is to hand back the Shandong Peninsula in full sovereignty to China, retaining only the economic privileges granted to Germany and the right to establish a settlement under the usual conditions at Qingdao."[22] By then, however, the damage to public opinion was irreparable.

*London Times May 6, 1919*

(May 4)

THE SHANTUNG PENINSULA. - In explanation of Japan's position in regard to the Shantung question, Baron Makino states that Japan's policy is to hand back the Shantung Peninsula in full sovereignty to China retaining only the economic privileges granted to Germany and the right to establish a settlement under the usual conditions at Tsingtau.

In regard to the railway, which will become a joint Chino-Japanese undertaking, Baron Makino further states that the special police force which is to be created will be used only to ensure security for traffic, and for no other purpose. The organization of this police force is provided for in Notes exchanged between China and Japan on September 24, 1918, in which the Chinese Government undertake to organize a police force to guard the railway from TSINFTAU to TSINAN. Provisions were made for the Japonese to be employed at the headquarters of the force, its training stations, and the principal railway stations.

**Document 14**: 6 May 1919 *The London Times* reprint of Japan's 4 May 1919 Statement

On 17 May 1919, the Japanese issued a second official declaration publicly reaffirming Baron Makino's 4 May statement at the Paris Peace Conference. The American embassy in Tokyo reported the text of the minister of foreign affairs' statement the following day: "Japan will keep every word which she has passed. Shandong peninsula will be handed back to China in full sovereignty and all agreements made to promote the mutual benefit of the two nations will be loyally observed.... China, by entering the war secured from the associated powers the suspension of the payment of the Boxer indemnity and the raising of the tariff to an effective 5% also that other terms of value to China would be included in the peace treaty.... Japan gladly supported China in her legitimate aspirations and Japan will adhere to the policy announced at the last session of the Diet which places Sino-Japanese relations on a basis of Justice."[23] Although the Japanese government had acted quickly to dissipate the confusion that surrounded the Shandong resolutions, its efforts were largely unsuccessful.

The American press in particular continued to publish mainly the Chinese contention that Japan had gained control over all of Shandong province. This not only muddied the diplomatic waters but greatly angered Japan. On 1 August 1919 Toyokichi Iyenaga, a former Japanese diplomat and lecturer at Columbia University, wrote a rebuttal in the *New York Times* in which he called "sheer nonsense" the general misconception that Paris had ceded Japan Shandong's 55,000 square miles and its 36 million population.[24]

Iyenaga did provide his readers one possible explanation for the confusion: "I am at a loss to understand all this fuss about the Shandong settlement. I cannot but take it as the result of either ignorance or of 'deliberate exaggeration' to serve some purpose. This outcry seems to have originated in a large measure by the mixing up of Jiaozhou and Shandong. The latter is a big province the size of Illinois, while Jiaozhou has a land area of 200 square miles." He concluded: "The Shandong settlement does not infringe upon the territorial integrity of China or her independence, rather does it serve to recover China's sovereignty which Germany had overrun at Jiaozhou—for Japan proposes to restore the leasehold to China."[25]

On 2 August 1919, Viscount Uchida again announced Japan's intentions "to restore to China the whole territory in question and to enter upon negotiations with the Government at Beijing as to the arrangements necessary to give effect to that pledge as soon as possible after the Treaty of Versailles shall have been ratified by Japan."[26] Although the Japanese delegation at Paris and the Japanese government in Tokyo both tried to correct public misunderstandings concerning the Shandong resolutions, they could not counteract the impact of the pro-Chinese sympathies of the press. Japan's public reassurances were largely ineffectual and by the middle of May 1919 many Chinese students and intellectuals had already turned against Japan and, perhaps more gradually, against the Western system that had allowed Japan to mistreat China.

## The Shandong Resolutions, the May Fourth Movement, and Wilson

It has long been acknowledged that there was a direct and immediate connection between the publication of the Shandong resolutions and the birth of the May Fourth Movement, the primarily student-led movement that was initially created to express the Chinese public's outrage at Versailles' decision. What has been less clear to historians is that there was also a firm link between news of the Shandong resolutions and Chinese condemnation of Woodrow Wilson as the perceived perpetrator of this decision. As will be shown below, the American legation in Beijing first warned of this link during May 1919.

News of Shandong's transfer to Japan was initially released on 30 April 1919, but Japan's statement of intent was not widely published until many days later. The negative impact of the Shandong resolutions was much greater than Wilson had expected. Tens of thousands of Chinese organized demonstrations throughout China. The leaders were mainly students, teachers, and university professors, arguably some of the best educated and most pro-Western segments of the Chinese population. Because of Shandong many of these leaders later turned away in disgust from American democracy and capitalism, choosing instead to embrace Soviet Russia's socialist experiment. In some cases—most notably, Peking University professor Chen Duxiu and the soon-to-be Peking University library assistant Mao Zedong—the leaders and participants of the May Fourth Movement later became important figures in the Chinese Communist Party.

As early as 2 May 1919 the U.S. legation in Beijing warned Washington that China's Ministry of Foreign Affairs was already fearful of "a great national uprising," based on "universal popular indignation and despair." The legation agreed with this assessment, warning that: "It would not be surprising if the indignation of outraged opinion in China would find vent in a violent anti-foreign movement, powerless as yet to produce more than danger and sufferings to individuals, but leaving behind lasting results of a total failure of confidence in the power, justice, principles, and action of the Western nations. After this complete disillusioning and after futility of popular demands for justice has been demonstrated the way would be open for organizing the forces of the Asiatic mainland in cynical hostility to Western civilization [sic]."[27]

Considering China's later turn toward Soviet Russia and its eventual adoption of communism, this warning was prophetic. Reinsch also pleaded with the American delegation in Paris: "A demand made by United States or Great Britain that Japan comply with the principles of international justice would guarantee peace."[28] When this "demand" was not made, subsequent events proved Reinsch correct: the next day he reported that protest meetings had been called in Beijing, Shandong, and Shanghai. These demonstrations opposed the Paris decision and called on the "Chinese delegates in Paris not to sign the Peace Treaty."[29]

Shandong was clearly the motivating force behind the "May Fourth" Movement. Even though it was well-known that the Paris Peace Conference had justified its decisions "partly on the basis of agreements between Japan and Duan's [Beijing] government," the annoucement of the resolution sent shockwaves through China: "This flagrant denial of the new Wilsonian principles of open diplomacy and self-determination touched off the May Fourth incident."[30]

As described by one historian: "May Fourth was a movement of intellectuals, and primarily of academics at that . . . to protest the decision . . . that transferred Germany's rights in Shandong province to Japan."[31] Public demonstrations and student protests quickly spread throughout China. Student groups marched through the foreign legation quarter on 4 May 1919 and left protest notes at the American, British, French, and Italian embassies. When the police arrested thirty-two students, one was mortally wounded, which led to further demonstrations.[32]

On 5 May 1919 an American military attaché in Beijing named Drysdale cabled his views to the American delegation in Paris. After describing how a mob composed of 3,000 students had set fire to the residence of the minister of communications, Drysdale warned that further demonstrations were set for 7 May 1919, the fourth anniversary of Japan's Twenty-one Demands. Led by Beijing's "influential residents" such as "members of Parliament [sic], university professors, merchants, students and others," a newly formed People's Self-Determination Society was leading efforts to boycott all Japanese goods. Although the movement did not appear to be strictly anti-foreign in nature, it did threaten to spread all throughout the Yangzi river valley: "Public opinion against Chinese officials under Japanese influence and against Japanese due to their unscrupulous political methods and the likelihood of Japanese control of Qingdao [sic] is developing strength greater than at the time of the Twenty-one Demands."[33]

This warning also proved accurate. A 16 May 1919 telegram from the Beijing legation reported that "particularly around Shanghai a general anti-foreign movement is feared." Moreover, the so-called "Shanghai Peace Conference" between Guangzhou and Beijing had been disrupted, with the southern delegates demanding that Beijing refuse "to recognize Paris decision regarding Shandong."[34] The center of the demonstrations then shifted from Beijing to Shanghai, where a general strike of students, workers, and businessmen reportedly attracted 100,000 people and virtually paralyzed Shanghai.[35]

By 20 May 1919 the May Fourth Movement had produced repercussions throughout China. Students from middle schools and universities went on strike and in early June government troops arrested over a thousand protestors. On 11 June 1919, Chen Duxiu, one of the most famous leaders of this movement and later the first leader of the Chinese Communist Party, was arrested and imprisoned for 83 days for distributing Bolshevik propaganda.[36] According to one of Chen's biographers, it was the "failure of Wilsonian democracy" and Versailles' proof of the "hypocrisy of the West" that first attracted him to Marxism.[37] Mao Zedong also began to study Marxism shortly afterward. Later he acknowledged that the May Fourth Movement had "marked a new stage in China's bourgeois-democratic revolution against imperialism."[38]

As a result of Chinese public anger, the U.S. legation in Beijing reported in early June that "three so-called traitors" who were responsible for signing China's secret agreements with Japan —"Zao Julin, Lu Zhongyu Chief of Currency Board, and Zhang, Minister to Japan"—had all been forced to resign. President Xu was also under attack. Xu had "formally threatened to resign unless Parliament and Nation will support him in his foreign and domestic policies."[39]

The May Fourth demonstrations also had a tremendous impact on the Chinese delegation. On 1 May 1919 the Beijing daily *China Press* reported that China's loss at Paris was because of the Beijing government's " 'gladly agree' exchange of notes with Japan in September 1918 in respect to the Shandong question." In particular, Chow reports that the Chinese delegates were "fearful of being held responsible for the failure."[40] This fear may explain, in turn, why the Chinese delegates in Paris later tried to blame Wilson for their own mistakes.

Throughout May, the Chinese people progressively became more and more critical of Wilson. According to one firsthand account, news of the Shandong resolutions meant that China "could no longer depend upon the principles of any so-called great leader like Woodrow Wilson."[41] One well-known historian of these events also concluded: "Woodrow Wilson's promises of self-determination and social justice for all peoples had bred the hope that in the general postwar settlement, China would be relieved of Japanese and Western overlordship . . . at Versailles, these illusions were cynically spiked by horse-trading politicians."[42]

During June 1919 the Beijing legation reported increased xenophobia among the Chinese public. In particular the Chinese accused the United States of helping Japan take control of the Chinese railways. In response, the American delegation in Paris instructed the Beijing legation on 20 June 1919 to "combat efforts to make the United States appear associated with or sympathetic toward any aggressive policy." But the telegram admitted that the root cause of the anti-American fever could not be resolved: "No present revision of Shandong decision can be expected."[43]

Chinese dissatisfaction with the Shandong resolutions, and the resulting disillusionment with Wilson, led many Chinese intellectuals to search elsewhere for answers. The search often led them to communism. Most recently, the anonymous Chinese author and the American editors of *The Tiananmen Papers* have pointed to the important link between the Shandong question and the birth of the Chinese Communist Party: "The May Fourth Movement in favor of 'science and democracy' was initiated by the May Fourth Incident of 1919, when students in Beijing, protesting international approval of Japan's claims to Shandong Province after World War I, marched to the house of a cabinet minister and burned it down. The movement is viewed both as the high tide of Chinese liberalism and as the starting point of the Chinese Communist revolution."[44]

**Liang Qichao's Interpretation of the Shandong Resolutions**

As discussed in the preceding sections, the unexpected strength and depth of the Chinese reaction to the Shandong resolutions can be explained, in part at least, by a misunderstanding of what Versailles had actually decided. On 19 July

1919, *Millard's Review*, a popular journal specializing in East Asian news and commentary, published a lengthy article by Liang Qichao entitled "Causes of China's Defeat at the Peace Conference." In addition to being one of China's most famous intellectuals, Liang had previously been China's minister of finance and justice and so had a thorough understanding of how the Chinese government worked. Unlike China's delegation at Paris and the leaders of the May Fourth Movement, it is notable that Liang did not blame Wilson but the Beijing government for China's failure. He pointed particularly to the secret September 1918 Sino-Japanese agreements, which had effectively negated China's ability to claim that it had been coerced into signing Japan's Twenty-one Demands in 1915.

After outlining the Shandong agreements that had preceded the Paris Peace Conference, Liang explained how the Japanese delegates had early raised the issue of racial equality, a preemptive tactic that he openly admired: "It must be admitted that such high diplomacy is skillful." Liang also related how British Foreign Secretary Arthur Balfour told the Chinese delegates that the Shandong resolution was partly based on the fact that Japan had carried out important military duties during World War I. This caused Liang to lament: "Had China therefore made serious preparations to participate in the war immediately after the declaration of war on Germany and despatched some troops to the Western front last spring, China [would] have come to the front rank when an account was taken as to the degree of services rendered."[45]

According to Liang, it was the September 1918 Sino-Japanese agreement that really destroyed China's chances for success in the negotiations at Paris. Beijing had not only denied in the fall of 1918 that it had signed such an agreement, but it did not even inform its own delegation at Paris of this document until 28 January 1919. Liang chastised the Beijing government: "We should inquire into the question with whom lies the responsibility for this failure. The secret pact concluded with Japan was effected at the time when Germany was fast collapsing. Who instigated it? Where was the moving spirit? Why was no conversation held with some of the European states on this matter before and during the conclusion of the pact? Why were our diplomatic officials and peace delegates so grossly ignorant of the government's doings, so much so that when they were called upon to meet the situation they were utterly at a loss and failed? Who is to bear the whole blame? If those who are responsible for such an impasse are not located how can the whole nation be appeased? So long as China continues to send abroad diplomats of the Mandarinate type, or the new but unprincipled type, so long China will suffer diplomatic defeat. One day the people may wake up to find that the whole country had been signed away by them."[46]

In sharp contrast both to the Chinese delegation and the leaders of the May Fourth Movement, Liang acknowledged that during the Paris Peace Conference China's "main support was America." Wilson was seriously handicapped by China's own secrecy about the 1918 agreements, since he was "not fully conversant on the Shandong problem." Liang therefore placed responsibility for China's failure on Beijing, concluding that: "But in justice it must be said that the government was mainly responsible for this diplomatic defeat."[47] Unfortunately, Liang Qichao's English-language article had little impact on Chinese public opinion, which had already decided that Wilson was to blame.

## Conclusions

When the Chinese delegation failed to obtain the direct restitution of the Shandong concession, it turned on Wilson and blamed him for China's defeat. American Far Eastern experts accurately predicted this possibility and tried to counter it, but to no avail. The Chinese delegates' attempt to divert responsibility onto Wilson was largely a face-saving measure to protect themselves from criticism. The tactic worked especially well in China: during the long period of public demonstrations against the Shandong resolution that began on 4 May 1919, the mood of the demonstrators became progressively more and more anti-American.

The May Fourth Movement helped create and spread the myth that Wilson betrayed China at Paris. According to one account, Wilson "gave in" to Japan and so was accused by "liberals" of "nothing less than a sell-out to old-style power politics."[48] This belief that Wilson had betrayed them had an important impact on the early leaders of the Chinese Communist Party. In particular, Chen Duxiu exclaimed that all of "President Wilson's fourteen-point declaration have [been] turned into hollow words not worth a cent," while Li Dazhao called Wilson a hypocrite: "The American president talked of self-determination and then betrayed that principle and China's hopes."[49]

Later Communist leaders, like Mao Zedong, were also influenced by the Shandong issue. One historian has described how Mao's "trust that the Western powers would uphold justice [was] shattered" and how the "U.S. compromise with the Japanese at the Paris conference dashed Mao's high hopes for the United States."[50] Recent authors have even gone so far as to say that "Mao's expectations for the United States and other Western countries were dashed" and that "Mao's anger also turned on Wilson."[51]

The concept of "face" played an important role in the Shandong question. Although Japan had officially promised to transfer control of the Shandong concession to China once it legally gained control from Germany, allowing Japan to be the middleman was considered a grave insult to China. This perceived "loss of face" was at the heart of the many protests by the Chinese delegation at Paris, by the Beijing government, and by the Chinese people, to overturn the Shandong resolutions. Because of face, the controversy over direct and indirect restitution of Shandong became especially bitter.

Western observers had trouble understanding why the Chinese were so upset. After all, hadn't Japan promised to return Shandong some seventy-five years earlier than Germany's treaty with China had stated? Furthermore, they questioned why the Chinese delegation did not better publicize Japan's promises. On 19 July, Balfour even accused Koo of intentionally obscuring Wilson's compromise solution. According to the minutes of this private meeting from the Koo papers:

> Mr. Balfour said that this feeling in China was uninstructed. He was surprised that the Chinese Government had taken no step to inform the Chinese people of the existence of the other part of the arrangement, namely the Japanese assurances to the Council. Besides the Government and the Delegation knew its existence, and he was at a loss to know what had been the real reasons for China not signing the treaty.

What Balfour was referring to when he mentioned "real reasons" was face. It was this unspoken factor at Versailles that made all the difference to the Chinese.[52]

One way of visualizing China's bitterness is to realize that if Germany had returned Shandong directly to China, then China would have gained great face. By transferring Shandong through Japan, China not only did not gain face but lost it twice: once when Germany gave face to Japan by ceding it Shandong and again when China was forced to accept Shandong from Japan. In other words, the difference between direct and indirect restitution to China was not one degree, or even two, but represented a total separation of three degrees.

Likewise for Japan, obtaining Shandong from Germany—still a major European power in 1919—meant gaining face, as well as wreaking long-sought revenge on Germany for its role in the Triple Intervention. Jacob Gould Schurman, President of Cornell University and later the U.S. minister to China, summed up this situation in a July 1920 speech before the members of the Council of Foreign Relations: "the troublesome question of the hour was how the [Shandong] matter might be arranged so that both Japan and China might save their faces."[53]

The largely invisible but enormous disparity between direct and indirect restitution helps to explain why the Chinese delegation—with America's support—did everything it could to persuade Japan to sign a declaration attached to the final peace treaty guaranteeing Shandong's swift return. Only a public declaration by Japan would show that it had made specific promises to China, and thus place Japan in the position of a subservient. This, in turn, would save China's face and allow the Chinese delegation to sign the treaty. Wilson's last-ditch attempts to obtain just such a declaration, and thereby resolve the Shandong question, will be discussed in the next chapter.

## Notes

1. Revised copy of "Summary of the Conditions of Peace as Presented to the German Plenipotentiaries at Versailles, May 7, 1919," 10 May 1919, SKH Papers, Box 328.

2. For a better understanding of "face," see Andrew J. Nathan, *Peking Politics, 1918-1923: Factionalism and the Failure of Constitutionalism* (Berkeley, CA: University of California Press, 1976); S. C. M. Paine, *Imperial Rivals: China, Russia, and Their Disputed Frontier* (Armonk, NY: M.E. Sharpe, 1996), 54-57; S. C. M. Paine, *The Sino-*

*Japanese War, 1894-5: Perceptions, Power, and Primacy* (New York: Cambridge University Press, 2002), especially chapter 9.

3. "China in the Peace Treaty," undated (probably May 1919), SKH Papers, Box 328.

4. *Ibid.*

5. Gustave Gouin, *Why China did not sign the Peace Treaty* (Paris: La Vérité, 1919), 35.

6. Li attributed many of Mao's actions to face, such as Mao's reaction to the 1958 famine, his aversion to official banquets, his willingness to placate his wife Jiang Qing, and his desire for younger and younger mistresses. Li Zhisui, *The Private Life of Chairman Mao* (New York: Random House, 1994), 283, 286, 335, 341, 361, 374, 381, 408.

7. History texts published in Taiwan as late as the 1950s still used this derogatory term. Wu Xiangxiang (吳相湘). 俄帝侵略中國史 (*The History of Imperial Russia's Aggression in China*), (1954; reprint, Taiwan, 1968).

8. From a speech by Sun Yat-sen on 28 November 1924, in Kobe, Japan. Reprinted in Sun Yat-sen, *The Vital Problem of China* (Taipei: China Cultural Service, 1953), 161.

9. "Memorandum from Stanley Hornbeck to E. T. Williams," 2 May 1919, SKH Papers Box 383.

10. *Ibid.*

11. Gaimushō, File 2.3.1-3.1.

12. *Ibid.*

13. "Communication from M. Lou Tseng Tsiang, protesting for the Chinese Delegation against the proposed settlement of the Kiauchow-Shantung question," 4 May 1919, SKH Papers, Box 383; stamped "Secret" and then "Declassified."

14. *Ibid.*

15. "The following additional telegrams regarding Shantung have been received from Chinese sources," 14 May 1919, SKH Papers, Box 328.

16. Ray Stannard Baker, *What Wilson Did at Paris* (New York: Doubleday, Page & Company, 1919), 73.

17. David Steigerwald, *Wilsonian Idealism in America* (Ithaca, NY: Cornell University Press, 1994), 81.

18. Edward Mandell House and Charles Seymour, eds., *What Really Happened at Paris* (New York: Charles Scribner's Sons, 1921), 94, 408.

19. Frank Ninkovich, *Wilsonian Century: U.S. Foreign Policy since 1900* (Chicago, IL: The University of Chicago Press, 1999), 73.

20. "Telegram from Acting Secretary of State Polk in Washington retransmitting the 13 May 1919 telegram from the American Embassy in Tokyo, Japan," 16 May 1919, SKH Papers, Box 382.

21. Thomas A. Bailey, *Wilson and the Peacemakers* (New York: The Macmillan Company, 1947), 283.

22. "Japan's Guarantees on Shantung," *The London Times*, 6 May 1919, SKH Papers, Box 329.

23. "Telegram from American Embassy in Tokyo, Japan," 18 May 1919, SKH Papers, Box 382.

24. Toyokichi Iyenaga, "Iyenaga Decries Shantung Charge," *New York Times*, 1 August 1919.

25. *Ibid.*

26. "Future of Shantung, Japanese Declaration of Policy," *The London Times,* 6 August 1919.

27. "Evidence leading to the conclusion that little or no support is to be expected from Mr. Balfour toward securing Japanese declaration," 21 July 1919, SKH Papers, Box 382.

28. *Ibid.*

29. "Dispatch from American Minister, Peking," 3 May 1919, SKH Papers, Box 383.

30. John K. Fairbank, ed., *The Cambridge History of China,* Vol 12, Part 1 (New York: Cambridge University Press, 1983), 311, 407.

31. Lucien Bianco, *Origins of the Chinese Revolution, 1915-1949* (Stanford: Stanford University Press, 1967), 32.

32. Chow, 113-114.

33. "Dispatch from Military Attaché Drysdale, Peking," 5 May 1919, SKH Papers, Box 382.

34. "Telegram from Peking Legation," 16 May 1919, SKH Papers, Box 382.

35. Wang Shih-han, "May 4th Movement," in *China Reconstructs* (Beijing, 1962), 64.

36. Meisner, 103.

37. Feigon, 140-142.

38. Mao Zedong, *The May 4th Movement* (Beijing: Foreign Languages Press, 1969), 1.

39. "Telegram from Peking Legation," 14 June 1919, SKH Papers, Box 328.

40. Chow, 92.

41. *Ibid.,* 93.

42. Harold R. Isaacs, *The Tragedy of the Chinese Revolution* (Stanford, CA: Stanford University Press, 1961), 54.

43. "Telegram from American delegation in Paris to Peking Legation," 20 June 1919, SKH Papers, Box 328; including handwritten note "O.K.ed by Mr. Lansing."

44. Andrew J. Nathan and Perry Link, eds., *The Tiananmen Papers: The Chinese Leadership's Decision to Use Force Against Their Own People–In Their Own Words* (New York: Public Affairs, 2001), 13.

45. Liang Qichao, "Causes of China's Defeat at the Peace Conference, " 19 July 1919, *Millard's Review,* 262-268.

46. *Ibid.*

47. *Ibid.*

48. Ninkovich, 73.

49. Michael H. Hunt, *The Genesis of Chinese Communist Foreign Policy* (New York: Columbia University Press, 1996), 66-68.

50. Michael H. Hunt and Niu Jun, eds., *Toward a History of Chinese Communist Foreign Relations, 1920-1960s* (Washington, D.C.: Woodrow Wilson Center Asia Program, 1992), 4.

51. Xu Guoqi, "The Age of Innocence: The First World War and China's Quest for National Identity," Harvard University Ph.D. Dissertation, 1999, 362.

52. "Notes of a meeting between Wellington Koo and Balfour," 19 July 1919, V. K. Wellington Koo Papers, Box 1.

53. "Notes of a Speech by Jacob Gould Schurman to the Council of Foreign Relations Luncheon," 14 July 1920, John V. A. MacMurray Papers, Box 22.

# 6
# Wilson's Failed Attempts to Secure a Japanese Statement of Intent

President Wilson went to Europe with lofty ideals and his one great conception which he hoped to realize was the League of Nations idea. When he reached Europe he found the narrow minded nationalistic idea was predominant which was diametrically opposite to his ideal. In America the opposition to the League of Nations ideal was strong. His foster child seemed to suffer seriously from external as well as internal dislike. How could he face his countrymen in the event his League of Nations proposal fell to the ground. Herein was Mr. Wilson's weakness. . . . Japan threatened to decline to be a signatory to the League of Nations clause. Great Britain and France were tied down by their secret treaties. The outcome of all this was that China was made the scapegoat. But, alas, President Wilson made an irrevocable mistake. What is Fiume or the League of Nations Clause compared with the vital Shandong Question? He, however, fought a hard battle on behalf of the Southern Slavs on Fiume, but yielded to Japan her Shandong claim. I am afraid America's day of anxiety commenced on that day and will run its bitter course.[1]

Liang Qichao (Paris, July 1919)

Public opinion in the United States, in China, and throughout much of the rest of the world condemned the Shandong resolutions even though few outsiders could claim that they either understood what the resolutions said or could explain what they actually meant for China. Wilson received the lion's share of the blame for this even though he was the only member of the Big Three to stand up for China. This public criticism greatly disturbed Wilson. On 15 May 1919 he complained to Vance McCormick that the other leaders were "mad men," and he recounted "his struggles with Clemenceau and Lloyd George to hold them down to justice and reason."[2]

What Wilson needed was a way to make known what had really transpired in his private meetings with the Japanese delegation. On 6 May 1919, Thomas F. Millard, a journalist and publisher of *Millard's Review*, suggested just such a method. According to Millard, now that the British and French governments had fulfilled their obligations, as defined by their 1917 secret agreements with Japan, they were "free to join with America in supporting China's claims for just treatment." Millard recommended, therefore, that the American, British, and French delegations jointly sponsor a declaration explaining the resolution of the Shandong situation and detailing Japan's obligations to China. Such a declaration would go far "to diminish the causes for a great war in the Far East."[3]

This suggestion proved attractive to the American delegation. Beginning in late May 1919, Hornbeck began to extol to Secretary of State Lansing and President Wilson the advantages of spelling out Japan's exact obligations to China in a formal statement of intent. The most important reason would be to induce China to sign the final peace treaty, which the Chinese delegates had been hesitant to do because of strong public opposition in China.

The American delegation worked hard to persuade Japan to sign a formal statement on Shandong. It also urged the British and French delegations to sign a joint statement with the United States. But as the deadline for signing the Versailles Treaty neared, the Japanese delegates continued to stonewall the release of such a statement. Once again "face" played an important role, since such a statement might make Japan appear subservient to China.

Fearful of a public outcry if they accepted the treaty, and forbidden from signing the treaty with reservations, at the last minute the Chinese delegates refused to sign. By not signing the Versailles Peace Treaty, the Chinese delegation not only risked losing the many advantages embodied in Wilson's compromise with Japan, but it threatened to delay Japan's transfer of Shandong to China indefinitely. Like a self-fulfilling prophecy, China's refusal to sign appeared to hand Japan the very thing that Wilson had been so unjustly accused of permitting—Japanese control over Shandong in perpetuity. Meanwhile, the American delegation's failure to secure a Japanese statement of intent appeared to confirm the myth that Wilson betrayed China at Paris.

**America Decides to Obtain a Japanese Statement of Intent**

From late April through early June 1919 the American delegates urged Japan to sign a statement of intent on Shandong. The Japanese delegates declined, correctly pointing out that the Versailles Treaty was with Germany, not China. But as the May Fourth Movement grew both in size and importance, the American delegation hoped that such a statement would satisfy the Chinese public's demand for justice. In particular, a definite time limit for the return of the Shandong concession as well as a Japanese promise not to treat Shandong province as an exclusive sphere of interest were considered essential for this statement to be successful.

Early attempts by the American delegation to secure a Japanese statement of intent met with failure. The reason was simple and was perhaps best expressed by Viscount Chinda on 26 April 1919 when he told Lansing not only that "the treaty of peace was with Germany and not with China," but also that "Japan had already proclaimed her generous intentions . . . in the Convention [with China] which had been published to the world." Chinda also tersely reminded Lansing that all the delegations at Paris were representatives of "sovereign states" and that "no one could call in question the actions of another."[4] This comment suggests once again that the real issue at stake for Japan was not to lose "face."

In late May Hornbeck renewed his efforts to induce Japan to sign a statement on Shandong. On 27 May 1919, he sent a memorandum to both Wilson and Lansing asking that they request from Japan definite guarantees to carry through on its commitments to China. Hornbeck warned that the Shandong resolutions appeared to award Japan more than just economic privileges: control of Shandong, in connection with Japan's position of strength in Korea and Manchuria,"puts her potentially in control of North China (and perhaps East Siberia)."[5]

According to Hornbeck, the history of Japanese expansion in Asia was clear: "Japan has in the course of twenty-five years defeated China in war, defeated Russia in war, occupied South Manchuria, annexed Korea, defied the United States, driven Germany from Shandong, coerced China into signing a series of iniquitous agreements, enticed Great Britain, France and Russia into immoral pledges and levied blackmail on the Peace Conference." Hornbeck warned that the Versailles decision left to the League of Nations the "whole burden of safeguarding democracy in a region which at the moment of the creation of the League has virtually been surrendered to imperialism."[6]

Hornbeck then quoted a 22 May 1919 telegram from Beijing in which the American Chamber of Commerce in China requested a document from Japan that included a time limit: "Americans in China view with gravest concern the decision of Peace Conference to give over to Japan German rights and interests in Shandong, irrespective of pledges which Japan will make to return these to China unless those pledges are accompanied with guarantees which make it patent to all that they will be made effective within reasonable time, otherwise all pledges regarding the maintenance of the open door or equal opportunities will become mere scraps of paper and China is endangered with a militarism controlled by Japan, which may involve the world in another great catastrophe."[7]

Hornbeck stated that he considered this explanation to be "a sound and sober view of the situation." He recommended that Japan be asked to sign a statement of intent on Shandong that would fix a specific time limit for returning the concession to China and also for giving up the former German right to treat Shandong as an exclusive sphere of interest. Hornbeck's draft statement included the following two articles:

> 1. Japan agrees to restore to China within two years the whole of the Leased Territory of Jiaozhou, with all rights and privileges appertaining thereto, on condition that China compensate Japan for the properties relinquished by Germany to Japan within that area and make of the port of Qingdao an international settlement.

2. Japan agrees to the cancellation of that portion of Article IV of Section II and III of the Convention between Germany and China of March 6, 1898, which reads: The Chinese Government binds itself in all cases where foreign assistance, in persons, capital or material, may be needed for any purpose whatever within the Province of Shandong, to offer the said work or supplying of materials, in the first instance to German manufacturers and merchants engaged in undertakings of the kind in question.

Hornbeck concluded by urging Wilson and Lansing to secure these guarantees from Japan, "guarantees such as do not now appear in the treaty and are not to be found in the pledges and assurances which the Japanese have made."[8]

On 29 May 1919 the Beijing legation transmitted a message from Chinese President Xu requesting that America "induce Japan to make to the Great Powers or for all conjointly to cable a definite statement as to the Shandong arrangements, particularly as to the date of the return of the territory." Xu also warned that if the "Chinese Government is to sign the Treaty, popular disapproval would be less violent if these arrangements were definitely stated."[9] Minister Reinsch supported this action: "Public confidence here [in China] can be restored only by a definite statement which Japan ought to make if her purposes are honest."[10]

On 3 June 1919 Lansing acted on Hornbeck's recommendations and President Xu's request when he sent a memorandum to President Wilson (see Document 15). It suggested "that an effort be made to secure from the Japanese Delegation a statement, in the form of an official undertaking so enunciated that it may be considered a binding part of the Peace settlement, as to what the Japanese Government intends to 'restore' in Shandong and the time within which it is intended that the restoration shall take place."[11] After Wilson granted his approval, the wheels were set in motion to begin negotiating with the Japanese delegates a suitable statement of intent on Shandong.

**The Chinese Delegation Fails to Sign on a Provisional Basis**

While the Americans were working to obtain a statement of intent on Shandong, the Chinese were trying to obtain permission to sign the Versailles Peace Treaty with reservations, most notably with regard to the Shandong resolutions. Throughout May and June 1919 this contingency was discussed by the delegates. It appeared that this method was acceptable to everyone. Immediately prior to the formal ceremony to sign the treaty, however, Clemenceau told the Chinese delegation that not only would reservations "not be allowed" but that all reservations made previously would no longer have any effect.[12] Instead Clemenceau determined that the Chinese delegation would have to sign the treaty in full, and all reservations would have to be made in a separate, non-binding document. Faced with this unsavory prospect, the Chinese delegation refused to sign.

*China (Shantung)*

THE SECRETARY OF STATE
OF THE UNITED STATES
OF AMERICA

                                Hotel de Crillon, Paris,
                                June 3rd, 1919.

My dear Mr. President:

    With reference to the telegram from the American Chamber of Commerce of China regarding the Shantung decision which, in accordance with your request has been dully acknowledged, I am transmitting herewith a memorandum prepared by the Far Eastern Division of the Commission regarding the possibility of procuring additional guarantees in connection with the execution of the Treaty provisions regarding Shantung.

                                Faithfully yours,

                                *Robert Lansing*

The President,
   11 Place des Etats-Unis,
      P A R I S .

24/584-A-465

**Document 15**: 3 June 1919 Letter from Robert Lansing to Woodrow Wilson

During May it was still an open question whether China could sign the final treaty with reservations. On 26 May 1919, members of the Chinese delegation indicated to Hornbeck that they thought that China should be able to sign the Versailles Peace Treaty with "such reservations as it sees fit to make."[13] But only two days later the Beijing legation reported that President Xu was concerned that China "may not be able to effect signature with broad reservations."[14]

To support China's hopes of signing with reservations, Hornbeck contacted Lansing on 31 May 1919 and suggested that a telegram be sent to Beijing reassuring it that the Chinese delegation "has given confidential official notice of intention to sign treaty with reservations." He further recommended that the American delegation fully support this decision with the following statement: "We consider this procedure legal and proper. Reservation or exception may be as extensive as they choose to make." But in a handwritten note on his personal copy, Hornbeck made it clear that Lansing had "not approved" this addition.[15]

Questions about whether or not China would be allowed to sign with reservations continued to fester during June. On 25 June 1919, Hornbeck reported that Koo told him in confidence that Clemenceau had told the Chinese delegates that it was his "painful duty of informing the Chinese Delegation that the making of reservations would not be allowed." Hornbeck condemned this action and suggested that the American commissioners make it clear that they would "support the Chinese in their contention for the right to enter a reservation."[16]

Two days later, however, Wilson appeared to reach a compromise whereby China could make its reservations in a separate document. On 27 June 1919, Hornbeck reported to Lansing that the Chinese delegation had apparently agreed to "sign the Treaty without reservations if it were permitted to make its reservations in a separate document."[17] On 28 June 1919 the Chinese delegation issued its reservations (see Document 16). Signed by Lu Zhengxiang representing Beijing, and C. T. Wang representing Guangzhou, the note was addressed to Clemenceau. Describing the Shandong resolutions as "unjust," the Chinese stated that they would sign the Versailles Peace Treaty on a provisional basis only, proclaiming that "in the name and on behalf of their Government, that their signing of the Treaty is not to be understood as precluding China from demanding at a suitable moment the reconsideration of the Shandong question, to the end that the injustice to China may be rectified in the interest of permanent peace in the Far East."[18]

Unfortunately for China its reservation was non-binding, since it had already been decided that reservations could not be attached to the final treaty. According to Hornbeck: "Reduced to simple terms, not only are China's rights being sacrificed, but the Chinese Delegation is being asked to approve the sacrifice, as a contribution toward success for the efforts of the American Government to insure the founding of the League of Nations."[19] If the Chinese delegation actually signed the final treaty under these conditions, Hornbeck concluded it would only "be because of loyalty to President Wilson."[20]

On 28 June 1919, the date of the official ceremony to sign the Versailles Treaty, the Chinese delegation was still debating whether or not to sign. Throughout

## THE JAPANESE STATEMENT OF INTENT

In proceeding to sign the Treaty of Peace with Germany today, the undersigned, Plenipotentiaries of the Republic of China, considering as unjust articles 156, 157 and 158 therein which purport to transfer the German rights in the Chinese Province of Shantung to Japan instead of restoring them to China, the rightful sovereign over the territory and a loyal co-partner in the war on the side of the Allied and Associated Powers, hereby declare, in the name and on behalf of their Government, that their signing of the Treaty is not to be understood as precluding China from demanding at a suitable moment the reconsideration of the Shantung question, to the end that the injustice to China may be rectified in the interest of permanent peace in the Far East.

      (Signed) Lou Tseng Tsiang

            Chengting Thomas Wang

Paris, June 28, 1919.
To His Excellency Georges Clemenceau,
 President of the Peace Conference.

**Document 16**: 28 June 1919 Chinese Reservations to the Versailles Peace Treaty

June the Beijing government ignored all demands by the May Fourth demonstrators that the Chinese delegation refuse to sign. The student union in Beijing was a major leader of this public protest. It marshalled hundreds of representatives from different student groups to stand outside President Xu's office for two days and nights to pressure him to order China's delegation not to sign. Reportedly at the last minute President Xu caved in to student demands and sent a telegram to Paris to rescind his previous order; but his message was not expected to arrive before the scheduled time for the signing.

On 28 June 1919, Chinese students supposedly surrounded the Chinese delegates' hotel, thus stopping them from signing the treaty. Interestingly, no newspaper from the period reported this event. In fact, this story was probably just a face-saving excuse, since on 27 June the delegates already announced they would not sign. Even though they had not yet received President Xu's official order to this effect, the delegates received thousands of telegrams from Chinese students and workers in France and abroad who opposed the treaty terms. Under this intense public pressure the Chinese delegation took the unusual step of unanimously refusing to sign the treaty; C. T. Wang appears to have been the most vigorous in opposing the treaty, with Wellington Koo joining only later.[21]

Koo and Wang became instant heroes for refusing to agree to the Shandong resolutions. This decision gave these American-trained diplomats enormous prestige, which they later used to gain almost a free hand in determining the Beijing government's foreign policy.[22] According to one of Koo's biographers: "This Anglo-American group was in control of China's foreign policy for almost the entire span of the Republican governments, be it a warlord government in Beijing or the Nationalist Government in Nanjing and Taiwan."[23]

But the long-term negative impact of not signing the treaty was also great, since all the above-mentioned benefits that Versailles gave to China were also postponed indefinitely. On 3 July 1919, Hornbeck suggested that Lansing meet with Koo and explain that the American delegation had already taken action to secure from Japan a declaration of intent with regard to Shandong: "I am strongly of the opinion that it would be advantageous to inform Dr. Koo of the fact that steps are being taken toward persuading the Japanese to make a declaration concerning their Shandong policy."[24]

**The Creation of a Draft Statement of Intent**

At Wilson's behest, Hornbeck formulated an eight-point draft statement of intent that Lansing presented to Baron Makino on 28 June 1919. The major features of this draft statement were that Japan would not infringe on Chinese sovereignty, would not retain Shandong for more than two years, and would not try to make Shandong an exclusive Japanese sphere of interest. When Baron Makino refused to sign this statement, Lansing tried to exert pressure on him through the British and French delegations. When the British Foreign Secretary refused to comply, however, the Japanese statement of intent on Shandong was doomed.

Throughout May, Minister Reinsch's requests for further information became more and more insistent. On 31 May 1919, he pleaded that he needed this information to save America's "face," which he described in terms of American credit and prestige: "If their [American delegation's] opinion is indicated to me in a confidential and personal manner it would make it possible for me to meet the difficult situation with a saving of American credit and prestige and to influence action here in conformity with American policy. This is impossible if no information is given."[25] By 9 June 1919, the May Fourth Movement in China had intensified to such a degree that Reinsch sent the following urgent message: "This situation cannot be solved by use of force or repressive measures. The only adequate solution would be revision of the Paris decision re Shandong or a frank statement on the part of Japanese to do justice to China."[26]

Wilson apparently agreed with this assessment and wrote Lansing on 12 June 1919 requesting that he talk with Baron Makino and formulate an official statement of Japan's intentions: "I have been impressed by Colonel Hornbeck's recommendation and am interested to know that our Minister in Beijing repeats it. Will you not be kind enough to see Baron Makino and present the matter to him very earnestly in the light of the desirability, not to say necessity, of quieting opinion in China and making the fulfillment of the Treaty provisions possible without serious friction? I think you cannot urge it upon him too strongly."[27] In response, Lansing wrote on 16 June 1919 that he still thought that a Japanese statement would be best, since anything less would "complicate rather than improve the situation, but I shall be glad to see Baron Makino if you think it desirable."[28]

Lansing's letter elicited a longer and much more detailed letter from Wilson dated 20 June 1919. This letter is worth reproducing in full because it helps to show Wilson's attitude toward the Shandong resolutions:[29]

> I am afraid that I did not make my meaning clear in my earlier letter. I meant to express the hope that you would take up with Baron Makino the question of the formulation and formal entrance into just such engagements as you suggested in your letter of June third; namely, the assurances and obligations which were orally assumed by Baron Makino and Viscount Chinda when they were in consultation with our little conference here with regard to the Shandong matter.
>
> It will seem perfectly natural for us to take the initiative in this matter, through our own Secretary of State, because Baron Makino will understand without explication that the interests of the United States are very deeply involved, and it ought to be clear to him, as it is to me, that extended unrest in China, which will certainly ensue unless the most explicit reassurance is given, might not only immediately but for a long time to

come disturb the peace of the East and might lead to very serious international complications.

I beg that you will take the whole matter up with him very earnestly, and I am sure you will know how to handle it, in view of your past discussions of kindred subjects, in a way which will be entirely with[out] irritation to the Japanese.

The very next day Hornbeck received a request from Lansing to prepare just such an outline for a "conversation with Makino."[30]

By 27 June 1919, Hornbeck had completed his draft statement of intent. He emphasized to Lansing how important it was to "do everything possible to safeguard China's interests" by securing "a set of definite pledges from Japan."[31] The next day Lansing presented am eight-point draft to Baron Makino:

1. Japan claims no right of sovereignty in Shandong Province.

2. Japan will restore the Lease of Jiaozhou and will relinquish to China all rights, titles and privileges acquired by Japan from Germany within the Leased Territory, except as regards railways, on condition that China compensate Japan for properties thus relinquished and that China agree to make of the city of Qingdao an international settlement and of the port an open port.

3. Japan will endeavor to make this restoration complete within two years from the signing of the Peace Treaty.

4. Japan relinquishes the benefit of any provision or provisions in the conventions and agreements between Germany and China which gave an exclusive preferential position in the Province of Shandong.

5. In the administration of the existing railways which have been conceded to her, Japan will not discriminate against the trade of China or of other nations.

6. The new railway lines, for the construction of which concessions have been accorded to Japan, shall be built by the Japanese for the Chinese Government.

7. Japan will use special police only along the railways and only to ensure security for traffic. These police shall be Chinese, with such Japanese instructors as the Directors of the Railway

# THE JAPANESE STATEMENT OF INTENT     121

may select, these instructors to be appointed by the Chinese Government.

8. Japan will withdraw all military forces from Shandong as soon as practicable, it being the intention, if conditions permit, that the withdrawal shall be completed within a period of not more than two years.

This exchange was confirmed by Hornbeck, who penned on his copy of the statement: "Presented to Baron Makino by Mr. Lansing, June 28, 1919."[32]

Lansing and Makino met for three-and-a-half hours on 28 June, the very day that the Versailles Treaty was to be signed. In the Lansing papers at Princeton, there is a detailed description of this meeting. In it, Lansing claims that he "labored" with Makino to convince him to sign the statement, and thus remove the last obstacle for China to sign the peace treaty:

> I asked him again to study the draft and to act for his government in a way to relieve the situation and insure China's participation. I felt, however, that, while Makino was very courteous and apparently impressed, I had not made a dent in his armor of oriental inscrutability. In a word, I knew that I had completely failed in persuading him.

As a result of this failure, the Chinese delegation refused to attend the signing ceremony. At the ceremony, Lansing pointed this problem out to Wilson:

> The President was greatly disturbed at the absence of the Chinese. When I pointed it out to him, he exclaimed: "That is most serious. It will cause grave complications." I told him of my interview with Makino and he said that he was sorry that they had not listened to me, as he believed trouble would result. He then added: "This is most unfortunate, but I don't know what we can do."

Contrary to popular belief, Lansing's description confirms that the United States completely supported China up to the treaty signing. In fact, Lansing even urged Makino to sign the draft "or else the Chinese wouldn't come."[33]

Although the Chinese delegation boycotted the signing ceremony, they could always sign the peace treaty later. To make this possible, during the next month the American delegation tried to exert indirect pressure on the Japanese delegation to sign the eight-point statement of intent. On 23 July 1919, Hornbeck reported a conversation in which Koo stated that the French government had high hopes that Japan would accept the statement; according to Koo, the matter would be decided at a committee meeting set to convene five days later.

In fact, on that very day *The Beijing Leader* reported that the Beijing government had received a telegram from the Chinese delegation to this effect. The telegram stated that they had nearly completed an agreement "clearly stating how and when Jiaozhou will be returned to China." Once this agreement was completed, it would be attached to "the peace treaty."[34]

To guarantee that Clemenceau backed this plan, Hornbeck asked Lansing to speak with him and reiterate that the U.S. Senate might use the Shandong clause to reject the Versailles Treaty altogether. This in turn would "endanger the treaty pledging the U.S. to come to the aid of France." Hornbeck concluded: "Therefore, measures which tend to weaken the opposition on the question of Shandong tend by just so much to lessen the likelihood of effective opposition to other agreements in which France is much more directly interested."[35]

In a private conversation between British Foreign Secretary Balfour and Baron Makino on 23 July 1919, however, Makino still refused to sign the statement of intent. His excuse was the fact that "in view of there being now only one telegraphic cable available to Japan, which is very much overworked, it is not possible to count upon cables reaching Tokyo under five or six days, and he feared that period, doubled, with additional time for his Government to consider the matter, would involve too long a delay for any Japanese statement to be of use insofar as public opinion in America is concerned."[36]

In fact, the Japanese Foreign Ministry does contain a telegram from Makino, dated 24 July 1919, listing these eight points. A crucial difference between this telegram and the American proposal, however, was that in place of the time limit "two years" in point eight the text was left blank.[37] Clearly, this firm deadline worried the Japanese, since China could use it to exert pressure on Japan. But Makino perhaps revealed the true reason for not wanting to sign the eight points—fear of losing "face" by making Japan appear subservient to China—when he explained to Balfour that Japan had already made a public statement and that the Japanese "pride themselves on always keeping their word."[38]

On 26 July 1919, the American delegation was forced to telegraph Lansing, who in the meantime had returned to Washington, the bad news that Balfour had been unable to obtain a signed statement and that the Japanese delegates "are unwilling to make any further public declaration in regard to their intentions and obligations to the Allies than that which was made by Baron Makino to the press some weeks ago."[39] Although Makino's excuse may have appeared feeble, especially in light of the fact that he had been in possession of the draft document for almost four weeks, there was no way for the American delegation to force him to sign the statement of intent on Shandong. In desperation the American delegation next turned to Great Britain and France for help.

**Plans to Issue a Big Three Statement of Intent**

In a final effort to clarify the actual meaning of the Shandong resolutions, the American delegation sought to issue a statement of intent signed by the American,

British, and French delegations. This statement would be based directly on the Japanese delegation's promises to Wilson in their confidential meetings during late April 1919. Unfortunately, this attempt also failed because it turned out that only the British government had accurate and complete minutes of conversations between President Wilson and Baron Makino. Since the American delegation did not have its own copy of the minutes, it proved to be impossible to publish a statement of intent based on these confidential exchanges. In the end, Wilson's decision to support secret meetings at Paris proved to be his undoing.

In early July Lansing had given Balfour a copy of the U.S. eight-point statement and asked him to intercede on America's behalf by bringing the matter to the attention of Clemenceau, which Balfour agreed to do. On 7 July 1919, Lloyd George's private secretary, Philip Kerr, told Hornbeck that while Balfour favored having the Japanese delegation sign the statement of intent, the British delegation did not see how Japan could add anything to what it had already promised in its public statements in May. This response clearly showed that London was unwilling to upset Japan to help save China. On 10 July 1919, therefore, Lansing had little choice beyond simply giving Clemenceau a copy of the proposed American statement of intent on Shandong.[40]

Kerr did propose, however, that if the Japanese delegation refused to sign a statement of intent, "the other Allies might make public the assurances which had been given to the Council."[41] Almost a week later, on 17 July 1919, after much urging, Balfour promised Henry White to prepare a draft of the Allied statement of intent. But in a conversation with Koo only two days later, Balfour reportedly gave "the impression that he had given no particular attention to the subject." On 21 July 1919, Hornbeck was forced to report that Balfour had apparently done nothing at all, leading Hornbeck to recommend strongly: "That it should be undertaken to secure from Mr. Balfour an explicit statement, in which he shall either decline to act in support of the American effort or shall agree to act, shall say what he will do and within what time he will do it."[42]

Over time the Americans' energies were directed away from obtaining a statement of intent from Japan and toward obtaining Great Britain's promise to support a combined American, British, and French statement of intent. Without Balfour's active cooperation, however, it was difficult for the American delegation to act alone, especially since it was not in possession of detailed minutes of Wilson's April meetings with the Japanese; one American memorandum explained that Sir Maurice Hankey had been in charge of keeping minutes of the meetings and that "President Wilson had no one with him."[43]

During late May and early June, Lansing had requested on numerous occasions that the British circulate copies of the minutes from Wilson's meetings with the Japanese delegation. On 5 June 1919, Hankey issued instead a summary of these minutes, which was too general to prove that the Japanese delegates had actually made certain pledges. While Hankey did eventually present a copy of the full minutes to Wilson, it was on the same day that he embarked on a ship for the United States.

## 124   THE JAPANESE STATEMENT OF INTENT

As a result, Wilson took these crucial minutes with him to Washington, so the American delegates in Paris did not have access to his copy. Years later, when Ray Stannard Baker wrote Wilson to ask for permission to use his personal papers to write a history of the conference, Wilson replied: "I have a trunk full of papers, and the next time you are down here I would like to have you go through them and see what they are and what the best use is that can be made of them. I plunked them into the trunk in Paris and have not had time or physical energy even to sort or arrange them."[44] Clearly, Wilson's copy of the missing minutes never found their way into the hands of the American delegates in Paris.

Although Balfour acknowledged that Great Britain had the right to publish the minutes of the Paris meetings that exactly detailed Japan's promises, he insisted that he would do so only after notifying the Japanese government, a matter "which requires very delicate handling." While the American delegation could also publish the records, Hornbeck warned Lansing on 21 July 1919 that if it was the "Hankey memorandum" that was to be published, then it should be the British government's responsibility. According to Hornbeck, the "memorandum has inadequacies both in form and in substance, and it would seem better not to establish the impression that we approve and accept it as satisfactory."[45]

This series of delays and bureaucratic setbacks—whether intentional or accidental on the part of Great Britain is impossible to say—led Hornbeck to request in late July that the American delegation again ask Balfour for a copy of the minutes. Hornbeck suggested that if Balfour did not "promptly" fulfill this request, that a telegram should be sent immediately to Washington asking Wilson to let the Chief of the Far Eastern Division of the State Department see his personal copy of the minutes so that a "comprehensive précis" could be sent at once to Paris.[46]

Apparently nothing was done regarding Hornbeck's last-ditch proposal. As a result, since the American delegation did not have a copy of the minutes proving that Japan had promised to return the Shandong concession to China, its hopes of releasing a separate statement of intent on Shandong were dashed. This final failure allowed the widespread public condemnation of the Shandong resolutions to continue unopposed. Japan—with Great Britain's tacit assistance—appeared more than willing to sacrifice America's "face" to save its own.

**Shandong and the League of Nations**

It is often overlooked that Wilson's Shandong solution included two separate and distinct parts. The first part guaranteed that China retained sovereignty over the Shandong concession even while granting Japan limited economic benefits. Wilson accomplished this. The second was to create an international organization—the League of Nations—that would allow the United States to join with the other major powers in order to continue to observe, criticize, and even regulate Sino-Japanese relations if necessary. Wilson utterly failed to achieve this second goal.

## THE JAPANESE STATEMENT OF INTENT    125

In his discussions with the Chinese delegation, Wilson persuasively argued that if they signed the Versailles Treaty the creation of the League of Nations could in the future help China avoid additional foreign encroachments:[47]

> In the establishment of the League of Nations, the territorial integrity and political independence of China would be safeguarded. China would have a protection. Other nations would also have a right of intervening in things unfair to China. In 1915 Japan could have better replied to us that we had no business to intervene. But with the establishment of the League of Nations, the Powers would have right to intervene in China's behalf.

After Wilson signed the Versailles Peace Treaty, he returned to Washington to promote its ratification by Congress. In Wilson's view, perhaps the most essential element of the treaty was the creation of the League of Nations, since it would be the responsibility of this organization to keep the peace that he had so laboriously made in Paris. However, it was just this part of the treaty that many Americans objected to. Their criticism of the League was that Americans might again be called into battle to fight on behalf of others.

The Shandong issue soon became linked with the ratification debate. Unaware of Japan's assurances to China, many Americans believed that Wilson really had sacrificed China. According to Lansing:

> I believe that the Shandong decision has done more than anything else to strengthen the opposition to the Treaty. It seems to have been the proverbial "last straw." You see the arguments in its favor which appealed to the President and the Colonel [House], do not go with the average American anymore than they did with White, Bliss and me. You constantly hear, "was it right to sacrifice China to save a League of Nations such as was worked out by the British?"

Lansing further described how the League was—rightly or wrongly—thought to be a British device to insure American support in a future war and that many Americans dismissed it as simply "some more of this British diplomacy."[48]

When Robert Lansing was asked to appear before the Senate Committee on Foreign Relations on 6 August 1919, he firmly denounced the Shandong resolutions. He later explained: "I told the Committee that, in my opinion, the Japanese signatures would have been affixed to the Treaty containing the Covenant even though Shandong had not been delivered over to Japan, and that the only reason that I had yielded was because it was my duty to follow the decision of the President of the United States."[49] Elsewhere in his memoir, however, Lansing fully admitted that he was not present at the Council of Four meetings and so did

## THE JAPANESE STATEMENT OF INTENT

"not know [what discussions took place] on account of the secrecy which was observed as to their deliberations."[50]

Because Japan would not sign a statement of intent, Wilson was also forced to defend his Shandong compromise before a hostile Senate. On 19 August 1919, Wilson was asked by Senator George H. Moses about Japan's promises:[51]

> **Senator Moses:** Mr. President, are these *procès verbaux* to be deposited anywhere as a matter of public record?
>
> **The President:** That has not been decided. Of course, if they were deposited as a matter of public record, there would be certain very great disadvantages.
>
> **Senator Moses:** Are they are to be deposited with the Secretariat of the League of Nations?
>
> **The President:** No, sir.
>
> **Senator Moses:** Without some such depository how otherwise would this engagement of Japan, as embodied in the *procès verbal*, be brought forward for enforcement?
>
> **The President:** There would be as many copies of the *procès verbal* as there were members of the conference in existence, much longer than the time within which we shall learn whether Japan will fulfill her obligations or not.
>
> **Senator Moses:** You mean in the private papers of the personnel of the Council of Four.
>
> **The President:** I would not call them private papers. I have a copy, Senator. I regard them as a public trust, not private papers, and I can assure you they will not be destroyed.
>
> **Senator Moses:** Suppose that each member of the Council of Four had passed out of office, out of any position of power at a time when it became evident that Japan was not keeping the engagement as it was embodied in the *procès verbal* on the day when this record was made; in what manner would you expect that engagement to be brought forward for enforcement?
>
> **The President:** I should deem it my duty—I cannot speak for the others—to leave those papers where they could be made accessible . . .

Without a doubt, Lansing's criticism of Wilson's Shandong compromise helped to undermine the Versailles Treaty's chances of being accepted by Congress. The Senate was also concerned because Wilson was unable or unwilling to produce an official document detailing Japan's promises to China.

As a result, Senator Henry Cabot Lodge firmly denounced the treaty, in the process linking Shandong and the League of Nations in a manner that was completely contrary to Wilson's goal in Paris of protecting China:[52]

> I do not think that a more dishonorable agreement can be found in all history, for this agreement aims at the division of the territory not of an enemy but of a friendly nation.
>
> If we sanction and ratify the treaty such as it is, we sanction not merely the decision already taken but the method employed. If this treaty is to be put into operation and if later on the forty million Chinese in Shandong revolt against the Japanese and if China lends assistance to her old subjects, in the United States we shall be forced by article 10 of the Treaty of the League to sacrifice American lives in battle in helping Japan to keep her sovereignty over Shandong.
>
> The Treaty must be amended, and I am of the opinion that if the American people knew the faults, the wicked faults it contained, it would condemn it unanimously.

Wilson's supporters responded by comparing the Treaty's opponents to "the Israelites who were worshipping the golden calf when Moses first extolled the Ten Commandments."[53] Ignoring all such criticism, the Senate's subsequent decision not to sign the treaty as written or join the League of Nations undermined the basis of Wilson's Shandong solution. Specifically, it precluded the United States from participating in the League's attempts to resolve future Sino-Japanese conflicts. This proved to be especially important during the early 1930s, when Japan invaded Manchuria.[54] Although the League of Nations backed China on this issue, without America's participation Japan could simply ignore this criticism; in fact, Japan decided to leave the League of Nations as a result of this dispute.

Largely as a result of division on the American home front, therefore, Wilson's vision of peace in Asia did not come to pass. Strange as it may seem in hindsight, the first part of his Shandong solution—alienating China by granting Japan limited economic rights in Shandong—succeeded in helping to knock out the second, arguably more important, part: America joining the League of Nations and securing a lasting peace through mutual security. According to Frederick Dickinson, "the American president's compromise with Japan over the Chinese province played a critical role in both the U.S. Senate rejection of the peace treaty and the rise of Chinese nationalism."[55]

In the end, the United States did not ratify the Versailles Peace Treaty and so did not join the League of Nations. The long-term consequences in Asia from this unexpected debacle were catastrophic, inadvertently leading to decades of tensions and war between China and Japan. During an interview in the 1950s, Wellington Koo tacitly admitted that signing the Versailles Treaty without reservations would have been far better for China: "One could wonder what would be the situation in China [today] either if China had succeeded in settling the Shandong question at Paris to her satisfaction or if she had signed the treaty without the reservation."[56]

## Conclusions

The American delegation tried and failed to persuade the Japanese delegation to issue a statement of intent on Shandong. It also tried and failed to obtain from Great Britain a copy of the complete minutes of Wilson's talks with the Japanese delegation so that Japan's exact promises to China could be published. While this drama was still unfolding, the Chinese delegation decided to take matters into its own hands. On 28 July 1919, the *Beijing Daily News* published a letter from the Chinese delegation addressed to the U.S. Senate. In the letter China called upon the Senate not to ratify the Versailles Peace Treaty. Its primary argument was to blame the Shandong resolutions on Wilson: "[The] President's counsel finally brought about China's entry into war. On him, as trustee of American honor, China rested hope of settlement enabling her to live untrammeled and unthreatened by Japanese imperialism."[57]

On 3 August 1919, Wilson responded publicly to this accusation by denying that his compromise solution with Japan was "in any way dependent upon the execution of the agreement of 1915" and so did not support Japanese imperialism. Wilson further insisted that he had never recognized China's 1915 treaty with Japan, the Twenty-one Demands: "Indeed, I felt it my duty to say that nothing that I agreed to must be construed as an acquiescence on the part of the government of the United States in the policy of the notes exchanged between China and Japan in 1915."[58]

It was now all too clear to the White House that the Chinese delegation was determined to make Wilson the scapegoat for its own mismanaged diplomacy with Japan. The Chinese delegation's open letter to the U.S. Senate greatly strengthened the myth that Wilson had "betrayed" and "sacrificed" China at Paris. This myth, in turn, led to America's rejection of the League of Nations.

But the validity of this myth is undermined (see Document 17) by a 5 July 1919 diary entry by Vance McCormick. He quoted Wilson as saying: "He told us frankly of the Shandong settlement because it was in his opinion the most criticized and most difficult part of Treaty to defend. . . . He said it only gave Japan an economic control, not political in any sense, and by this settlement they kept Japan in the conference and made her a party to the Allied policy toward China in all other respects and by getting her in the League of Nations will

*THE JAPANESE STATEMENT OF INTENT* 129

July 5 (Saturday)—

A perfect day but warm, drifting along at about 315 miles per day. We have settled down for the long voyage and everybody knows everybody else by this time.

The President sent for Lamont, Davis, Baruch and me with Dr. Taussig to come to his room after lunch to read us his message to Congress to get our suggestions and criticisms. Mrs. Wilson, Miss Wilson and Grayson were also present in his stateroom.

We had few changes to suggest as it was an excellent general statement of the situation at Paris and the problems that confronted him. We raised the question as to the praise given his colleagues and developed from him a real feeling of friendship for his colleagues whom he said privately were in accord with the principles we were fighting for but were hampered and restricted by their own political conditions at home, due to the temper of their people. He said he was surprised to find they had accepted the Fourteen Points not for expediency only but because they believed in them. He told us frankly of the Shantung settlement because it was in his opinion the most criticized and most difficult party of Treaty to defend. He referred to the agreement made by France and England with Japan, binding them absolutely to the Shantung agreement. This he said Lloyd George criticized himself and said it had been made by Asquith when Gray was sick, that the War Cabinet was astounded when it was presented but had to accept it. He said it only gave Japan an economic control, not political in any sense, and by this settlement they kept Japan in the conference and made her a party to the Allied policy toward China in all other respects and by getting her in the League of Nations will maintain the open door policy in China and make it possible to compel Japan to give up an exclusive sphere of influence in that country, and you could see he was far from satisfied but felt it was the best that could be done under all the circumstances. He further stated Japan had agreed with him verbally to pull out of Shantung but would not put it in writing as it reflected on their good faith.

We all discussed the advisability of reading message to Congress as a whole or to Senate alone. He said he had cabled to Tumulty to get advice from friends in Senate on this point. He also told us he was ready to make a tour of the country if necessary to speak for the League of Nations and read us topics of his speeches.

Baruch, Davis, Grayson and I dined in Captain McCauley's cabin on the bridge and had an excellent dinner. Captain McCauley is a fine young officer and is one of the reasons for the great success of the Navy. It makes you proud of our country when you get close to the men who really run our Army and Navy. They have attained their leadership because they delivered the goods.

**Document 17**: 5 July 1919 Entry from the Unpublished Diary of Vance McCormick, Quoting Woodrow Wilson maintain the open door policy in China and make it possible to compel Japan to give up an exclusive sphere of influence in that country, and you could see he was far from satisfied but felt it was the best that could be done under all the circumstances. He further stated Japan had agreed with him verbally to pull out of Shandong but would not put it in writing as it reflected on their good faith."[59]

According to all of the available documentary evidence, Wilson in fact succeeded in negotiating a compromise solution with Japan that represented a significant diplomatic victory for China. This was especially true because the terms of his compromise represented an enormous improvement over China's own 1915 and 1918 agreements with Japan. He also worked hard to guarantee China's future security through the auspices of the League of Nations.

By refusing to sign the Versailles Peace Treaty and by rejecting Wilson's Shandong compromise, however, the Chinese delegation also rejected Wilson's attempts to safeguard China. In a strange twist, China was later able to join the League of Nations even while refusing to sign the Versailles Treaty. As explained by Wilson Godshall: "By declining to be a party of the Versailles Treaty China also had been excluded from the League of Nations, the Covenant of which was embodied in that treaty. However, the Treaty of St. Germain with Austria likewise contained the Covenant, so that by signing it, September 10, 1919, the Chinese Republic had become enrolled as a member of the League without consenting to the objectionable features of the German treaty, and was entitled to whatever advantages and protection might be afforded by the new experiment."[60] Unfortunately for China, the League's "protection" proved to be inadequate without America's full participation.

Finally, it is often overlooked that so long as China refused to sign the Versailles Treaty, Japan was unable to carry out arrangements to transfer the Shandong concession back to China. It was therefore Chinese intransigence, not Japanese "imperialism," that delayed the ultimate return of the Shandong concession to China until 1922. Japan even protested the unwarranted delays. On 19 October 1921, Tokyo complained to Beijing: "[M]ore than twelve months have elapsed since when the Japanese Government invited the Chinese Government to enter into negotiations on this subject."[61]

It was during this chaotic period between 1919 and 1922 that the Beijing government as well as a small but influential group of China's intellectuals decided to turn away from the West and Japan and put their faith in the generosity of Soviet Russia. On 25 July 1919, immediately after the Paris Peace Conference ended, the Bolshevik government in Moscow issued a manifesto promising to abolish all of Tsarist Russia's imperialist treaties with China and to treat the Chinese people as equals. As the next chapter will discuss, the early Sino-Soviet contacts fostered by this manifesto proved to be a major turning point in twentieth-century Chinese history.

# Notes

1. Liang Qichao, "Causes of China's Defeat at the Peace Conference," *Millard's Review*, 19 July 1919, 262-265.
2. "Unpublished diary of Vance C. McCormick," 15 May 1919, entry 86, Vance C. McCormick Papers, Hoover Institution Archives.
3. Thomas F. Millard, "The Case of China and Its International Reactions," 6 May 1919, SKH Papers, Box 329; underlining in the original.
4. "Conversation between Secretary Lansing and Viscount Chinda," Paris, 26 April 1919, WWP Microfilm Reel 402, 19702-8.
5. "Letter from Stanley Hornbeck to the President and the Secretary of State," 27 May 1919, SKH Papers, Box 382.
6. *Ibid.*
7. *Ibid.*
8. *Ibid.*
9. "Letter to Secretary of State Lansing from the American Legation in Peking," 29 May 1919, SKH Papers, Box 382.
10. "Letter from Secretary of State Lansing to President Wilson," 16 June 1919, SKH Papers, Box 328; on 6 June 1919 Hornbeck sent a similar request to Lansing, see SKH Papers, Box 382.
11. "Secretary of State Lansing's Memorandum to President Wilson," 3 June 1919, SKH Papers, Box 328.
12. "Letter from Secretary of State Lansing to President Wilson," 16 June 1919, SKH Papers, Box 328; according to Koo, Pichon explained that reservations were not possible "On the grounds that if one reservation was accepted, other countries would likewise make their [own], as the settlements which had been made from many of the Allied nations had been found by them to be not entirely satisfactory." "Reminiscences," V.K. Wellington Koo papers, 225.
13. "Letter from Stanley Hornbeck to Secretary of State Lansing," 31 May 1919, SKH Papers, Box 382.
14. "Telegram from Peking legation to American delegation in Paris," 28 May 1919, SKH Papers, Box 382.
15. "Memorandum from Stanley Hornbeck to Secretary of State Lansing, entitled *Request of Minister to China for information*," 31 May 1919, SKH Papers, Box 382.
16. "Letter from Stanley Hornbeck to the American Commissioners," 25 June 1919, SKH Papers, Box 328.
17. "Letter from Stanley Hornbeck to Secretary of State Lansing," 27 June 1919, SKH Papers, Box 328.
18. "Protest signed by Lou Tseng-tsiang and C. T. Wang and addressed to Georges Clemenceau," 28 June 1919, SKH Papers, Box 328.
19. "Letter from Stanley Hornbeck to Secretary of State Lansing," 27 June 1919, SKH Papers, Box 328.
20. "Letter from Stanley Hornbeck to Mr. Kirk," 27 June 1919, SKH Papers, Box 328.
21. Chow, 165-166, see footnote w.
22. In the midst of the constant cabinet changes which the Beijing government went through between 1912 and 1928, there were 45 changes in the Beijing government's

cabinet but only 19 changes of foreign ministers. Nathan, 67.

23. Chu, 2.

24. "Memorandum from Stanley Hornbeck to Secretary of State Lansing, entitled *Information to Dr. Koo*," 3 July 1919, SKH Papers, Box 382.

25. "Memorandum from Stanley Hornbeck to Secretary of State Lansing, entitled *Further Request of Minister to China for Information. Draft of Reply*," 6 June 1919, SKH Papers, Box 382.

26. "Memorandum from Stanley Hornbeck to President Wilson, entitled *Request for further consideration of the Shantung Situation*," 5 June 1919, SKH Papers, Box 382.

27. "Letter from President Wilson to Secretary of State Lansing," 12 June 1919, SKH Papers, Box 328.

28. "Letter from Secretary of State Lansing to President Wilson," 16 June 1919, SKH Papers, Box 328.

29. "Letter from President Wilson to Secretary of State Lansing," 20 June 1919, SKH Papers, Box 328.

30. "Memorandum from Kirk on behalf of Secretary of State Lansing to Stanley Hornbeck," 21 June 1919, SKH Papers, Box 328; marked "confidential."

31. "Letter from Stanley Hornbeck to Secretary of State Lansing," 27 June 1919, SKH Papers, Box 328.

32. "Copy of the Eight Pledges prepared by Stanley Hornbeck for Secretary of State Lansing," 28 June 1919, SKH Papers, Box 382; marked "Draft."

33. "The Signing of the Treaty of Peace with Germany at Versailles on June 28th, 1919," 28 June 1919, Lansing Papers, Box 4, Folder 1: May-Aug. 1917.

34. "The Shantung Question, Latest Views and News," 23 July 1919, *The Peking Leader*. Although this newspaper article gives the impression that the Beijing government was pleased that an agreement was finally being reached, it also reported that the Chinese delegation's telegram from Paris was too vague to know for sure. Therefore, the report states: "Naturally the Government felt that something more than a vague 'how and when' was required, as the clear statement might not be satisfactory. As one official says, 'Neither the date nor the method might be acceptable.' The Government, therefore, has asked for further information." *Ibid.*

35. "Memorandum from Stanley Hornbeck to Secretary of State Lansing, entitled *Conversation with Dr. V. K. W. Koo, Chinese Minister and Delegate, regarding Japanese Declaration*," 23 July 1919, SKH Papers, Box 382.

36. "Telegram from Henry White to Secretary of State Lansing," 26 July 1919, SKH Papers, Box 382.

37. "Draft Eight Points from Makino in Paris," 24 July 1919, Gaimushō, File 2.3.1-3.2.

38. "Telegram from Henry White to Secretary of State Lansing," 26 July 1919, SKH Papers, Box 382. While most historians have examined the Shandong question from the point of view of China and have concluded that Wilson did too little, Noriko Kawamura has examined it from the Japanese side and suggests that Wilson did too much. She concludes that "the Japanese felt that President Wilson's interference in Sino-Japanese negotiations over Shandong was humiliating" and that the "Japanese viewed Wilsonian universal internationalism simply as hypocritical rhetoric that hindered the advancement of their country." Noriko Kawamura, *Turbulence in the Pacific: Japanese-U.S. Relations During World War I* (Westport, CT: Praeger Press, 2000), 149.

39. *Ibid.*

40. "Memorandum from Stanley Hornbeck, entitled *Evidence leading to the conclusion that little or no support is to be expected from Mr. Balfour toward securing Japanese declaration*," 21 July 1919, SKH Papers, Box 382.
41. *Ibid.*
42. *Ibid.*
43. *Ibid.*
44. "Letter from W. Wilson," 27 December 1920, Ray Stannard Baker Papers, Box 1.
45. "Telegram from Henry White to Secretary of State Lansing," 26 July 1919, SKH Papers, Box 382.
46. "Memorandum from Stanley Hornbeck, entitled *Request for minutes of meeting of the Council at which Japan's assurances with regard to Shantung were made (about April 26)*," 21 July 1919, SKH Papers, Box 382.
47. Wunsz King, *Woodrow Wilson, Wellington Koo, and the China Question at the Paris Peace Conference* (Leyden: A. W. Sythoff, 1959), 17.
48. "Letter to John W. Davis, U.S. Ambassador to London," 2 September 1919, Lansing Papers, Box 4, Folder 2.
49. Robert Lansing, *The Peace Negotiations: A Personal Narrative* (New York: Houghton Mifflin Company, 1921), 263-264.
50. *Ibid.*, 254.
51. Charles Burke Elliott, "The Shantung Question," *The American Journal of International Law*, Vol. 13 (1919), 687-737.
52. Gouin, 45.
53. Edward B. Parsons, *Wilsonian Diplomacy: Allied-American Rivalries in War and Peace* (St. Louis, MO: Forum Press, 1978), 190.
54. E. T. Williams, "Japan and Jehol," *The American Journal of International Law*, Vol. 27 (1933), 215-224.
55. Dickinson, 207.
56. "Reminiscences," Wellington Koo Papers, Columbia University, 251.
57. Gaimushō, File 2.3.1-3.3.
58. *Ibid.*
59. "Unpublished diary of Vance C. McCormick," 5 July 1919, entry 119, Vance C. McCormick Papers, Hoover Institution Archives. There are many examples in both the memoir literature and in biographies to substantiate McCormick's diary. For example, Inga Floto has also commented in his biography of Colonel House: "Wilson himself, the Experts Hornbeck and Williams, Commissioners Lansing, White and Bliss, and R.S. Baker–all, in fact, except House–sympathized with China. This became quite clear at the meeting Wilson held with his Commissioners on 26 April, at which only House seems to have been in favour of a compromise with Japan, on the grounds that 'it would be a mistake to take such action against Japan as might lead to her withdrawal from the Conference'. This was the argument that, in the end, proved decisive for Wilson's acceptance of the Japanese demands. But was this due to House's influence? There is nothing, in fact, to indicate that House had any influence at all on Wilson's decision on the matter. His standpoint should rather be taken as support for the view that House was, in spite of everything, the only adviser whose aims harmonized well with the fundamental principles behind Wilson's policy." Inga Floto, *Colonel House in Paris* (Princeton, NJ: Princeton University Press, 1973), 233.

60. Wilson Leon Godshall, *Tsingtau Under Three Flags* (Shanghai, China: The Commercial Press, Ltd., 1929), 275.
61. Gaimushō, File 2.3.1-3.6.

# 7
# *Shandong and the Origins of the Chinese Communist Party*

> The Soviet government restores to the Chinese people without exacting any kind of compensation, the Chinese Eastern Railway, as well as all concessions of minerals, forests, gold, and others which were seized from them by the government of Tsars, the government of Kerensky, and the brigands Horvath, Semenov, Kolchak, the former generals, merchants, and capitalists of Russia. . . . If the Chinese desire to become free like the Russian people, and to escape the destiny prescribed for it at Versailles in order to transform it into a second Korea or a second India, it should understand that its only allies and brothers in the struggle for liberty are the Russian worker and peasant and the Red Army of Russia.[1]
>
> Lev Karakhan, Soviet diplomat (Moscow, 25 July 1919)

The general misperception that Wilson had betrayed China caused enormous anger and disappointment among Chinese. This in turn opened the door to Bolshevik propaganda and influence. This outcome was exactly the opposite of what Wilson wanted and what he had worked so hard to prevent, with Tumulty even warning him that if the decisions at Paris did not appear just, then China might turn to the Bolsheviks.[2] Even though it was China's own 1915 and 1918 agreements that forced the Paris delegates to adopt the Shandong resolution, and even though pro-Chinese scholars have since admitted that "China could only blame itself,"[3] the Chinese delegates publicly blamed Wilson for sacrificing China. The myth of Wilson's betrayal led to a Chinese reaction against Western democracy and capitalism, a reaction that ultimately led to closer intellectual and diplomatic ties with Soviet Russia.

As a result of the Shandong resolution, intellectual ties soon formed between Chinese radicals and the Bolshevik Party, as represented internationally by the Moscow-based Communist International (Comintern). Li Dazhao and Chen Duxiu, two of the most famous leaders of the May Fourth Movement, were instrumental in bringing about this change. Beginning in 1921, Chen began to encourage his former students from Peking University to form the Chinese Communist Party (CCP). After becoming its first leader, Chen advocated that the CCP become a member of the Comintern. Thereafter, he played a crucial role in forming a United Front with Sun Yat-sen's Nationalist Party.

In addition to forming intellectual and political ties with Soviet Russia, anger over the Shandong resolution also played a pivotal role in the disillusionment of Chinese intellectuals and diplomats with the United States. To a large degree the Chinese rejected the American model because they truly believed that Wilson had betrayed China's national interests; by contrast, the Chinese believed that Soviet Russia would treat China fairly. This perception eventually led to China's decision to turn to the Soviet Union as the model for its twentieth-century modernization and development.[4]

Unfortunately for the pro-Soviet Chinese intellectuals, later events proved that their trust in Soviet Russia was ill-founded.[5] While Moscow's anti-Versailles declarations promising to treat China as an equal appeared attractive on the surface, these promises turned out to be merely propaganda. But before the full truth became clear, the Chinese intellectuals' widespread misunderstanding of America's role in the Shandong question, matched with their new-found faith in the Soviet Union's promises of better treatment, had led to the 1921 formation of the Chinese Communist Party and to the 1923 creation of the Communist–Nationalist United Front policy. These two events were instrumental in leading China down the path toward communism.

**The May Fourth Movement and Chinese Radicalization**

As shown above, the 1919 May Fourth Movement turned many Chinese intellectuals away from Western democracy and capitalism. In the wake of the Paris Peace Conference, Chinese intellectuals became more receptive to reports about the Bolsheviks' political, economic, and social reforms. The "New Culture Movement" included the teachings of many of China's most famous intellectuals such as Li Dazhao, Chen Duxiu, Li Da, and Lu Xun. These intellectuals took the lead in forming closer ties between China and Soviet Russia. Li Dazhao and Chen Duxiu, in particular, soon began to urge Chinese students to emulate Soviet Russia to order to save China from the false promises of the West.[6]

The 1917 February and October Revolutions (using the Western calendar, these events took place in March and November) in Russia caught most Asian diplomats and intellectuals by surprise. War and revolution quickly disrupted much of Siberia.[7] As a result, it took many years for even the most fundamental outlines of Leninism to come under discussion in Asian countries like China and Japan.[8] Even though as early as 1902 Lenin had begun to advocate a small, disciplined, secret organization of professional revolutionaries to carry out a proletarian revolution, the Chinese intellectuals' anarchist leanings meant that most had never really heard about, much less understood, Lenin's particular contributions to Marxism.

For this reason, the 1917 October Revolution did not have an immediate impact on China. According to Jerome Ch'en, it was only as a result of the end of World War I and Wilson's failure to resolve the Shandong question that Chinese intellectuals first decided to turn to Soviet Russia:[9]

> China's continued moral degeneration, political instability and economic deterioration provided the context for the repeated attempts at imperial restoration and foreign encroachment. In a wide context, the war in Europe revealed the inherent weaknesses of the much admired Western civilization, and the triumph of the Bolsheviks with its consequent abrogation of the Czarist privileges in China pointed a new way to China's emancipation. As if these epochal events were not enough, the Paris Peace Conference decided to hand the former German possessions in Shandong to Japan, instead of their just rendition to China. Under the combined impact of these events and decisions the intellectual and political climate of China suddenly was transformed—the hegemony of Confucianized social Darwinism was shattered. In its wake there was intellectual confusion in which Chinese scholars were open to persuasion and conversion by the views of Russell or Bergson, Nietzsche or Comte, Kropotkin or Marx.

It was not until the beginning of 1920 that the new Soviet government was widely acknowledged and studied by Chinese revolutionaries. This general lack of information about the Bolsheviks meant that prior to 1920 the Chinese intellectuals generally misunderstood the most fundamental characteristics of the Soviet government, even mistaking it for an anarchist government.[10]

In November 1918, Li Dazhao became one of the first Chinese to praise the October Revolution for its "universal significance." But he mistakenly used traditional anarchist terminology to describe the revolution as the victory of the "common people" over the issue of "bread."[11] Furthermore, Li incorrectly stated that worker's Soviets would form a "central governing congress" and a world government, but that this government "would not have a Congress or Parliament, would not have a President, a Prime Minister, a Cabinet, a Legislative branch, or politicians" and the full Congress would "decide all matters."[12] Elsewhere, Li enthusiastically explained that the Bolshevik revolution proved that on a social level "capitalism was defeated, and the proletariat was victorious."[13] Chen Duxiu also showed his dawning awareness of the importance of socialist revolutions by emphasizing in an April 1919 article that: "Our Chinese people do not fear it."[14]

Few Chinese intellectuals had studied the Bolshevik revolution prior to the May Fourth Movement. As a result, their understanding of the party-based organization of the Bolsheviks and the political history of the October Revolution was incomplete. Therefore, instead of stating that the Soviet state embodied a future model for China, these Chinese intellectuals portrayed Soviet Russia as merely one revolutionary alternative.[15]

Chinese intellectuals were radicalized by the May Fourth Movement, however, which was sparked in turn by the worldwide publication of the Shandong resolution. Since Japan's promise to return Shandong was published several days later, most Chinese assumed that Japan was given the right to keep this concession forever. According to John King Fairbank, this decision "provoked" an extreme Chinese reaction: "The incident of May 4, 1919, was provoked by the decision of the peacemakers at Versailles to leave in Japanese hands the former German concessions in Shandong."[16]

Widespread misunderstanding of what Versailles had sought to accomplish quickly led to a nationalist explosion in China. John Israel's study of Chinese student nationalism during this period shows that the most important factors included easily available newspapers, extensive telegraph and railway systems, and the emergence of modern political parties. However, "the catalyst that activated these explosive ingredients was the decision of the Versailles powers to sanctify Japan's occupation of Shandong."[17]

As discussed above, the belief that Wilson had betrayed China became widely accepted. Noel H. Pugach clearly linked Wilson to the Chinese students' disillusionment, stating that after "Wilson's abandonment of China . . . Chinese resentment and nationalism exploded in the May Fourth Movement."[18] Robert C. North further argued that Chinese students lost their faith in Western principles, even quoting one Peking University student as stating: " . . . we could no longer depend upon the principle of any so-called great leader like Woodrow Wilson."[19]

Finally, scholars have also linked the Shandong question to Chinese radicalism and revolution. For example, Lucien Bianco has stated that in its "narrowest sense," the May Fourth Movement was a demonstration staged in Beijing "to protest the decision of the Paris Peace Conference that transferred Germany's rights in Shandong province to Japan," but that in its "broadest accepted meaning" it was a "movement of cultural renewal and revolution."[20] Marilyn Levine has also described the Chinese reaction against Versailles as including "feelings of betrayal and disillusionment [that] were all prominent factors in forming a sense of spiritual loss that often translated into an inability to act. Those that did act were often attracted to the extreme of fascism or communism because they had been alienated from liberal forms of democracy."[21]

The tremendous post-Versailles wave of nationalism, plus the general disillusionment with Woodrow Wilson's failed principles, forced many Chinese students and intellectuals to search for an alternative to Western liberalism and capitalism. Soviet Russia actively sought to capitalize on this situation. Therefore, the origins of Chinese communism can also be dated to these seminal events.

**The Karakhan Manifesto and the Birth of Chinese Communism**

Soon after the May Fourth Movement, radical journals like *New Youth* publicly advocated looking at Soviet Russia for solutions to China's problems. Moscow sponsored this important shift away from the West. Interest in Soviet Russia increased even more when news of the 25 July 1919 "Karakhan Manifesto" was widely published during spring 1920. In this manifesto, Assistant Commissar of Foreign Affairs Lev Karakhan promised to abolish all of Tsarist Russia's unequal treaties with China. He also said that the Bolsheviks would return the Chinese Eastern Railway in Manchuria without compensation. This promise, in particular, was directed at Japanese attempts to retain economic control over the Shandong railway, and so was a direct challenge to Japan.

Beginning in the summer of 1919 a propaganda pamphlet written by a Soviet government official, Vladimir Vilenskii, was published and circulated in China. Entitled "China and Soviet Russia," this pamphlet predicted that "revolutionary Russia will find for itself a reliable ally in China against the imperialist predators."[22] It also reprinted the Bolsheviks' "Karakhan Manifesto," which appeared to grant what Versailles had denied China. According to Tony Saich, this manifesto played directly on China's dissatisfaction:

> One further reason for putting out the [Karakhan] Declaration was to highlight the contrast between the new Soviet Government and the old ways of the imperialist powers. It was intended to show up the shabby treatment of China at Versailles where the allies were proposing the prolongation of the Japanese occupation of Shandong. China had fully expected that following Germany's defeat . . . the province would be returned to Chinese jurisdiction. The actions at Versailles created a strong upsurge in nationalist feeling in China, best symbolized by the May Fourth demonstration (1919) in Beijing. The fervour of the reaction in China led the government to tell the delegation in Paris not to sign the treaty. What better time could exist for the Soviets to score a few good propaganda points off their Western allies?

The Karakhan Manifesto spurred Chinese intellectuals to study Marxism, since the trend of the May Fourth Movement was to "flow into more and more radical channels, leading finally to Communism."[23]

According to George Moseley, this shift was aided by Moscow: "That the Chinese revolution would ultimately require the assistance of the Soviet Union was indicated in the summer of 1919 by the hostile reaction of the powers to the May Fourth movement, which was enthusiastically applauded by the Russians. While student agitation was being suppressed in the foreign concessions, the new government in Moscow announced its determination to break with the past by renouncing all special rights acquired in China by the Czarist regime. It went on to denounce the other powers for clinging to theirs."[24]

The United States was not completely unaware of the Bolshevik efforts to influence foreign countries, including China. On 7 August 1919, Secretary of State Lansing wrote a letter warning about the Bolshevik threat to President

Wilson (see Document 18). In this letter, Lansing expressed his wish that Wilson would make use of his status as the "principal leader of progressive thought" in order to oppose the Bolshevik "world-menace" by making "a frank declaration against the Bolshevist doctrines which are certainly extending far beyond the confines of Russia."[25]

Without a doubt, the Bolshevik promises of immediate and unconditional equality, in contrast to Wilson's apparent betrayal of China at Paris, made Soviet Russia appear morally superior to the United States. These Soviet promises were especially important because they "gave face" to China, while the decisions at Versailles had made China "lose face." By offering to grant such enormous benefits to the Chinese, the Bolsheviks appeared to be kowtowing before the superior Chinese, the exact opposite of Woodrow Wilson. Allen S. Whiting has discussed this crucial difference, concluding: "Taken by themselves, the Comintern resolutions pertaining to Asia would have seemed utopian to many observers," but by taking advantage of the nationalist outpouring in China: "The Comintern had fertile ground for sowing its seeds of protest against the West."[26]

Soviet Russia's act of supplication was received positively by the Chinese people. In fact, as discussed above, if American support for the indirect restitution of Shandong was seen as representing a total loss to China of three degrees—one degree by not receiving Shandong directly, one by having Germany cede it to Japan, and one by being forced to receive Shandong from Japan—then the Soviet promises were clearly one or more degrees in the positive range. Therefore, in the minds of the Chinese people, the difference between the positions proposed by the United States and Soviet Russia was not simply one degree of separation, but was actually perceived to be as many as four or more degrees apart.

In order to convince China to join Soviet Russia against the capitalist nations, the Comintern early on sent representatives to meet with Chinese intellectuals, like Chen Duxiu and Li Dazhao, who soon became instrumental in helping form the Chinese Communist Party. It also made contact with Sun Yat-sen during the fall of 1920.[27] These Soviet actions quickly developed into an important foreign policy initiative: actively promoting colonial revolutions in Asia by training and funding native revolutionaries. As such, the Bolsheviks clearly hoped that Li Dazhao, Chen Duxiu, and Sun Yat-sen would soon develop into China's most important anti-imperialist leaders.

**The Shandong Resolution's Impact on Li Dazhao and Chen Duxiu**

Perhaps the greatest historical importance of China's decision not to sign the Versailles Peace Treaty was that it was brought about, in part at least, because of the huge outpouring of Chinese public disapproval at the terms transferring Shandong to Japan. Although the Chinese delegation's refusal to sign the Versailles Peace Treaty temporarily ended the May Fourth Movement in China, the Chinese anger at the settlement remained. Good examples of this were Li Dazhao and

August 7, 1919.

My dear Mr. President:

After a talk which I had this morning with Mr. Tumulty I feel it my duty to write you in the hope that there may be opportunity for you to make a frank declaration against the Bolshevist doctrines which are certainly extending far beyond the confines of Russia. I think it is time for this Government to take a very definite stand since there is growing up a propaganda in favor of classism in contradistinction to nationalism which seems to me to menace our present social order. Your well-recognized position as the principal leader of progressive thought makes you the most effective agent to check this dangerous movement and I sincerely hope that you may seize an occasion to make public your views upon this great world-menace and assume the leadership against it to which your position and record entitle you.

In this connection I am enclosing a memorandum which I asked Mr. D. C. Poole, our former Chargé at Archangel (who had so wide an experience throughout European Russia) to prepare. He apologises for its incompleteness in that the work was done in about three hours.

Faithfully yours,

ROBERT LANSING

**Document 18**: 7 August 1919 Letter from Secretary of State Robert Lansing to President Woodrow Wilson

Chen Duxiu, the two May Fourth leaders who eventually also became the first leaders of the Chinese Communist Party.

Li Dazhao has been described by his biographer Maurice Meisner as being "virtually alone" in his support of Marxism during the spring of 1919, and even Li admitted that "the most advanced discussions in our country are separated from Bolshevism by several thousand *li*." Therefore, Li saw Versailles' "betrayal of Chinese interests . . . as less a disillusionment than a confirmation of the deep-seated suspicions and intense distrust with which he had long looked at the Western world." Li asked rhetorically: "When we look at what has been decided at the Paris Conference, where is there the slightest shadow of humanity, justice, peace, or brightness? Where have the freedom and rights of the small and weak peoples not been sacrificed to a few big robber states?"[28]

Chen Duxiu, like many other Chinese intellectuals at this time, supported a resurgence of China into a "strong, independent, and prosperous nation." It was this goal that led Chen to adopt a "sense of nationalistic pride in Chinese traditions" and that prompted Chen initially to call on China's youth to join the positive features of Japan and the West with the traditional strength of the Chinese people. For example, in 1915, Chen's opening essay for the *New Youth* magazine called upon the youth in China to face bravely the challenge of rebuilding Chinese society. This article helped launch the beginning of the "New Culture" movement, and as Peking University's dean of the School of Arts and Letters, Chen was acclaimed as one of China's most influential intellectuals.[29]

Of all the leaders of the May Fourth Movement, Chen Duxiu perhaps felt particularly betrayed by the Shandong resolution because he had initially supported declaring war on Germany. Chen saw World War I as "a struggle against imperialism—an issue, he felt consistently, that was the most pressing matter facing China."[30] Therefore, Chen interpreted the terms of the Versailles Peace Treaty not just as a victory for Japanese imperialism, but as a personal betrayal. His disillusionment with Versailles was subsequently directed against the Western capitalist countries and Japan, as well as against the Chinese central government in Beijing, which he perceived as having failed in its diplomatic efforts to regain the Shandong concession from Germany.

In the meantime, Soviet Russia was actively engaged in pushing China to adopt communism. For example, the Bolsheviks began a propaganda campaign in Asia soon after the October Revolution, even allocating two million rubles for the needs of the international revolutionary movement. During March 1919, when Moscow hosted the founding congress of the Communist International, two Chinese delegates attended. On 6 March 1919, an article in *Izvestiia* discussed the importance of the revolutionary movement in China.[31]

Moscow also supported the publication of pro-Soviet books, such as the aforementioned 1919 Vilenskii pamphlet *China and Soviet Russia*. Two reports from the American consulate in Shanghai to the Beijing government in early 1920 identified eighty-three examples of Bolshevik-supported radical literature in circulation throughout Shanghai. While the largest single group was concerned with anarchism and the second largest with socialism, works discussing the October Revolution were also numerous and included such titles as *The Two Most Important People of the Russian Revolution*, *An Analysis of Lenin*, and *The Policies Enacted by the Russian Radicals' Faction*.[32]

By early 1920, therefore, the diplomatically-isolated Soviet government had organized and was executing its strategy of obtaining the support of sympathetic Chinese intellectuals. On 26 March 1920, a copy of the original 25 July 1919 Karakhan Manifesto was telegraphed directly to the Foreign Ministry in Beijing. Additional copies were delivered simultaneously to newspapers in Harbin and Vladivostok, where they were published immediately in Chinese translation. The Chinese consulate in Vladivostok reported the arrival of the Comintern official, Gregorii Voitinskii, on the same day.[33]

Voitinskii was the Far Eastern Secretariat's China expert. His assignment was to help organize a communist party in China. The publication of the Karakhan Manifesto in Chinese newspapers all over China was timed precisely to guarantee him a warm welcome. For most Chinese, this was the first time they were able to read actual copies of the Soviet promises to abolish all unfair treaties, extraterritoriality, the Russian concessions, and the Russian share of the Boxer indemnity, and to give back the Russian-built Chinese Eastern Railway to China without compensation. During this same period, Sino-Japanese negotiations on the fate of the Shandong concession and the Jinan-Qingdao railway remained deadlocked. This made the Bolsheviks look particularly good.

The Chinese public response to these promises of Sino-Soviet equality and friendship was instantaneous, as the Chinese press cheered the Soviet government. For example, the *Shanghai National* newspaper stated that the news of the Karakhan Manifesto caused an "incredible shock in the hearts of the Chinese people"; the *Shanghai Save the Country* newspaper commented that if the reports were true, then a "world in which harmony, equality, and justice prevail has already arrived"; and the Chinese Worker's Union published a statement which simply said that the Russian peasants, workers, and soldiers were the world's most "lovable people."[34]

After the publication of the Karakhan Manifesto, public interest in the October Revolution soared. The *New Youth* magazine issued a special appendix to its May 1920 issue on the impact of the Karakhan Manifesto. It also began publishing articles almost every month about the Soviet government, education system, labor unions, etc.

Voitinskii took advantage of the positive public response to visit Beijing during April 1920, where he met Li Dazhao.[35] Li then introduced Voitinskii to Chen Duxiu.[36] According to Thomas C. Kuo, the Karakhan Manifesto made Chen receptive to Marxism: "Chinese intellectuals responded to the Soviet declaration with enthusiastic admiration, and Chen Duxiu called it a progressive policy of the Lenin government aimed at helping China." Therefore, the "historical events that resulted from the May Fourth incident and the Versailles Peace Conference laid the organizational and ideological foundations for the founding of the CCP."[37]

Chen was in many ways the perfect choice as the leader of the new Chinese communist movement. He was a well-know leader of the May Fourth Movement and had gained notoriety after being arrested and imprisoned. Chen not only had the prestige of being one of China's most celebrated revolutionary leaders, but he was no longer employed at Peking University. Therefore, he was also unencumbered by official ties, which gave him a freedom of action few of his academic colleagues could match.

Voitinskii arrived on the scene at a crucial time in Chen's life, since Chen was torn between his former loyalty to Western ideas and his bitterness over Versailles' mistreatment of China; for example, during late 1919, Chen briefly called on China to follow the American democratic example by creating a federalist government with ordinary people founding associations and societies in order to accelerate the growth of local governments.[38] Interestingly enough, this same message was at that point being publicly espoused by Jacob Gould Schurman, the American minister to China, who said that the federalist "experience shows that no other system of Representative government is capable of operation over a vast territory like that of the U.S. or of China."[39]

Chen was swayed away from federalism, however, and toward communism during his discussions with Voitinskii. While early histories of the CCP claimed that Chen had been a commited communist since 1918, his interest in federalism during 1919 prove that he actually turned to communism for good only after meeting Voitinskii.[40] According to Robert C. North, Chen made this fateful decision when he realized that the "real victory had not been won by Woodrow Wilson . . . but by Lenin, Trotsky and Marx."[41] As a result, Chen soon formed China's first communist cell. Thereafter, in May 1920, he organized a "provisional Central Committee for the new Communist Party."[42]

Li Dazhao and Chen Duxiu's experience as authors, editors, and professors meant that they had a wide range of contacts throughout China. Many of the Chinese intellectuals who turned to communism at this time had formerly been Li's and Chen's students. Among this number were such famous communist leaders as Zhou Enlai and Mao Zedong. According to Han Suyin, it was Li Dazhao who recognized Zhou's organizational skills and helped him to study in Europe.[43] Mao Zedong was also Li's student, and Edward E. Rice has concluded that it was Chen Duxiu who "undoubtedly asked Mao Zedong to set up a [Marxist] cell in Hunan."[44]

The Karakhan Manifesto and Voitinskii's timely arrival in China had a crucial impact on Li Dazhao and Chen Duxiu. Although Chen felt betrayed by Versailles, only after meeting Voitinskii did he turn resolutely against the United States and its policies, such as democracy and capitalism. As summarized by Lee Feigon, Chen thought that he saw in the Soviet model an "instrument for fostering the development of China in a way that would avoid the evils of Western society."[45] Therefore, according to Ssu-yu Teng and John Fairbank: "By 1921 he [Chen] had become a convinced Marxist and took part in the founding of the Chinese Communist Party, of which he was the leader and general secretary until 1927."[46]

## Shandong and the Founding of the Chinese Communist Party

The shock of the Shandong resolution not only radicalized Chinese intellectuals, but it also led to the formation of the Chinese Communist Party. There is a general concensus among China scholars that: "By the middle of 1920 Chen [Duxiu] was totally committed to the new revolutionary social science of Marxism."[47] But Versailles alone was not enough to convince Chinese intellectuals to create a communist party. According to Victor A. Yakhontoff: "Another important factor was the so-called declaration of Karakhan . . . which naturally played a conspicuous role in enlisting Chinese sympathizers and paving the road for Communism."[48] The active intervention of Comintern operatives also helped bring about this Bolshevik goal.

As discussed above, in addition to converting Chen Duxiu to communism, Voitinskii also promoted the formation of Marxist study groups as a predecessor to founding a communist party. At least a half dozen study groups were started all over China during 1920. One early communist party member, Chen Gongbo, wrote in 1924 that a total of seven "sections" were represented at the first party congress in July 1921: "Guangzhou, Beijing, Hunan, Shanghai, Shandong, Tianjin, [and] Hankou."[49]

It is important that the organizational complexity of these small groups not be exaggerated. Chinese intellectuals in the post–May Fourth era had at best a limited knowledge of Leninism prior to Voitinskii's arrival in China. The full adoption of the Leninist party structure, i.e. a small, secret party of professional revolutionaries acting as the vanguard of the proletariat, appeared in China only after years of political and ideological training at the hands of the Comintern advisers. Benjamin Schwartz has even commented that at this early stage Chen was virtually "unaware of the role of the party in the Leninist scheme."[50]

The Comintern representatives' primary task, therefore, was to teach the Chinese the basics of communism. Their training was described in great detail by a contemporary Korean socialist, who wrote in August 1920 that it was the duty of Soviet Russia and the Comintern to give the Chinese revolution both "moral and material assistance," such as providing "the Chinese intellectuals-revolutionaries with clear instructions on proletariat tactics for internal ideological-political struggle."[51]

The almost total lack of information about communism was prevalent among Chinese intellectuals. For example, in late 1920 a Comintern representative soundly criticized the Wuhan study group for changing its name between 7 November and 21 November: "It is characteristic that the members of the study groups one time call themselves socialist study group—Socmol, and then another time call themselves communist—Komsomol." The membership of these small groups was also not highly selective, and the Wuhan group included among its prospective members students, workers, peasants, ricksha coolies, railway workers, transportation workers, shop-assistants, soldiers, and then, finally, "all sympathizers, who were supported by a majority of the study group members."[52]

Even given these limitations, Voitinskii had already made significant progress in setting up a pro-Soviet revolutionary movement in China by the summer and fall of 1920. Voitinskii saw his primary duty as collecting all of the radical Chinese intellectuals into communist cells, and then promoting greater organization within these groups. In order to oppose anarchist thinking and to train the Chinese communists in Leninist organizational techniques, the Comintern even funded the publication of a Chinese-language magazine, and on 7 November 1920 the first issue of *The Communist* was circulated.

Voitinskii's continued influence over Chen Duxiu was most clearly shown in *The Communist's* opening declaration, in which Chen made a strong appeal to China's anarchists to renounce anarchism and join the communists:

> Gentlemen anarchists! You originally also opposed capitalism and the system of private property, so we ask you not to falsely give up your precious freedom to the capitalists. All tools of production should be turned over to the workers; all power should be turned over to the workers to manage, this is our creed. If you are not happy at conniving with the evil deeds of capitalists who do not engage in work, then this ought to also be your creed.

Chen publicly supported "methods of class struggle" in order to destroy capitalism. He also advocated a "dictatorship of the proletariat" to put all political power into the hands of the proletariat, so they could form a workers' state. Chen directed his criticism against the United States and the Western European powers, by predicting the early "collapse" of capitalism in these countries, after which all countries would turn to the "socialist production" of Soviet Russia.[53]

Voitinskii's ultimate goal was to organize a Chinese Communist Party along lines set by the Bolsheviks. It was probably not a coincidence, therefore, that an article in the very first issue of *The Communist* discussed how to organize a true communist party. This article first explained that the Soviet state was now surrounded by imperialist armies and that it was the duty of all communists, including the Chinese communists, to protect Soviet Russia so that it could "awake the proletariat of Western Europe," and when the fire of the revolution struck, it would "reduce to ashes all of the world's capitalists."[54]

This prediction of capitalism's ultimate destruction was to prove particularly attractive to those Chinese intellectuals who had felt humiliated by Versailles. According to Marilyn Levine, Cai Hesen was a good example, since he was "disillusioned by the Versailles Conference, [and] Cai thought that Wilsonian democracy was a bankrupt alternative and only succeeded in exacerbating the current repression in the world. Only the organization of a disciplined Communist Party could overcome Capitalist oppression."[55]

An important new stage in the development of the party was reached with the arrival in China of the Dutch Comintern representative, Henk Sneevliet (Maring), during April 1921. After spending some time in Beijing, Maring traveled to Shanghai on 3 June 1921.[56] According to one memoir, it was Maring who first suggested that a party congress be held.[57] Another described how Maring took charge on the first day of the congress with an opening speech lasting five hours.[58] Even though all of Maring's remarks had to be translated into Chinese, other participants described Maring as the "central actor" at the congress.[59] There can be little doubt of the enormous impact of the Comintern representative.

While Maring apparently had little trouble getting most of his organizational changes accepted by the congress, he ran into stiff opposition when he suggested working more closely with other political parties.[60] In particular, Maring vocally supported a United Front policy of working with Sun Yat-sen's Nationalist Party, even announcing at one point that it was not a matter of whether the bourgeoisie and the revolutionaries worked together, but of how to work together.[61] This suggestion prompted an acrimonious debate over the question of working with other parties. According to some reports, Maring had to take the unusual stance of opposing the more "orthodox Marxists" when he tried to talk them out of their opposition to the Nationalist Party.[62]

The decision to issue an official congress manifesto was left up to the Central Executive Committee, with Chen Duxiu as the party secretary. One interpretation of why a manifesto was never published was that Maring thought that it was too critical of Sun Yat-sen. As a result, the manifesto was never distributed and its existence is known to scholars only through secondary sources. In an account by Chen Gongbo, a delegate at the first congress, he claims that the manuscript criticized both the Beijing government and the southern government under Sun Yat-sen as being equally evil.[63]

The decision to join the Comintern was deferred, but the CCP did agree to join the following year. In addition to making monthly reports to the Comintern headquarters in Moscow, all communist parties affiliated with the Comintern had first to agree to respect all of its organizational rules, the most important being that all member parties had to follow the orders sent to them by the Executive Committee of the Comintern. By joining the Comintern, therefore, each and every communist party member was considered to be only a part of the larger organization.

As a result of joining the Comintern, the CCP had to pattern its party organization on the Bolshevik Party, and "iron discipline" had to be maintained within the party. According to Dov Bing, it was Maring who talked the Chinese communists into joining the Comintern, a decision which he later said gave "the Kremlin a new channel through which to enter China."[64] This decision also gave Moscow the authority to order the CCP to form a United Front with the Nationalist Party led by Sun Yat-sen. This event is widely seen as a crucial stage on the CCP's road to power.

## Shandong and the United Front Strategy

Similar to the early Chinese communists, the Shandong resolution had as important an impact on Sun Yat-sen, the nationalist leader of China's opposition government in Guangzhou. In 1922, the Soviet Union ordered the Chinese Communist Party to join with Sun Yat-sen's Nationalist Party in an anti-imperialist United Front. Under the auspices of the United Front, Soviet advisers came to China to reorganize the Nationalist Party and modernize its army.[65] Once again, an essential element underlying the Bolsheviks' success was the Comintern's criticism of Wilson and the Paris Peace Conference for granting the Shandong concession to Japan.

Ever since 1918, the Bolsheviks had been working behind the scenes to form an alliance with Sun Yat-sen's Guangzhou government. It was Chinese disillusionment with the West that allowed the Comintern to establish the CCP in June 1921. Almost immediately afterward, Maring also began promoting the formation of a United Front between the CCP and Sun Yat-sen's Nationalist Party, the Guomindang. In Maring's discussions with Sun, the Shandong resolution once again proved to be a mighty lever, since Maring could claim that the decisions made by the Paris Peace Conference proved that China was being treated as a colony by the "big Powers," and urged Sun to work closely with the CCP to oppose foreign imperialism.[66]

Although Maring strongly supported a political alliance with Sun, most of the founding members of the Communist Party opposed it. But once Maring convinced the Chinese communists to join the Comintern, which the party did in July 1922, the Comintern ordered them to ally with Sun Yat-sen in August 1922. In articles written in Chinese under a Chinese pen name, Maring openly denounced the Paris Peace Conference for its "oppression" of China, and for allowing China's "power" to be "captured by the great powers."[67] Elsewhere, he wrote that "during the days of the Versailles negotiations . . . China was deceived again by the allies who had driven China into the war."[68]

China's warm reception for the Karakhan Manifesto also helped pave the way for an alliance between the Soviet-supported CCP and Sun's Nationalist Party. During November 1922, immediately before meeting with Soviet representatives, Sun told Japanese reporters that: "If Japan actually wants Asia's fate to be decided by Asiatics, she must settle her relations with Russia. The Russians are also Asiatics. The blood of Asiatics circulates in their veins. Together with Russia, Japan must defend the common cause against Anglo-Saxon supremacy."[69]

On 23 January 1923, the Soviet envoy Adolf Joffe and Sun Yat-sen signed an agreement that formally inaugurated the United Front policy. Comintern advisers arrived in China soon afterwards, and Sun gave them permission to reorganize the Nationalist Party along Bolshevik lines. Following Lenin's death in early 1924, Sun even delivered a eulogy in which he called Lenin a "great man," and further claimed: "I wish to proceed along the path pointed out by you."[70]

Disappointment over Shandong was a major reason why Sun and his Nationalist followers decided to turn to Russia. That Shandong was ultimately at the root of the United Front was perhaps best shown on 9 March 1924, when the Nationalists sponsored a memorial in Guangzhou to honor the recently deceased Lenin. Liao Zhongkai, a high-ranking Nationalist official and adviser to Sun Yat-sen, compared Lenin directly to President Wilson. After pointing out that Lenin had succeeded while Wilson had failed, Liao explained that while the Paris Peace Conference had declined to carry through Wilson's objectives, Lenin's worldwide struggle was continuing and China would eventually be "liberated" from imperialist oppression.[71]

The history of the United Front has been discussed at great length elsewhere.[72] However, for our purposes here it is important to emphasize that the formation of the United Front was an all-important stepping-stone in the Chinese communists' twenty-eight year struggle to take power in China. Chinese anger over the Shandong resolution was an important reason why both the Chinese communists and the Nationalists turned to Soviet Russia. According to C. Martin Wilbur, the decisions of the Versailles Peace Conference "had a radicalizing effect on educated Chinese youth and was one of the immediate antecedents of the Chinese communist movement. It also stimulated Sun Yat-sen and a few close colleagues to revivify the Guomindang. In short, the war and its immediate aftermath greatly stimulated Chinese nationalism and also led to a growing interest in Soviet Russia."[73]

If there had not been widespread and virulent resentment in China against the Shandong resolution, it is highly improbable that the Chinese Communist Party would have been formed in 1921. It is also unlikely that the Soviet Union would have been able to ally with Sun Yat-sen and the Nationalists. Chinese history would have been very different if these two events had never taken place.

## Conclusions

China's disappointment at Paris opened the door for Bolshevik propaganda. This led to the 1921 creation of the Chinese Communist Party and to the 1923 formation of the Communist–Nationalist United Front. These two events were to have an enormous impact on twentieth-century Chinese history. Had they not occurred, it is extremely doubtful that China would have gone down the path leading to communism.

It was the Chinese public's misguided belief that the Shandong resolution entailed an enormous "loss of face" for China, coupled with the general perception that the Soviet Union had given China "face" by means of the Karakhan Manifesto, that were integral to China's eventual decision to follow the USSR instead of the West. As discussed by Franz Schurmann and Orville Schell: "One of the wellsprings of Chinese Communism was the May Fourth Movement. The student-led demonstrations and the great general strike in Shanghai, organized by students in response to their Beijing comrades, convinced many Chinese intellectuals that alliance with the masses was the only road to revolution and regeneration. Students began to go forth from the universities into factories and villages, much as Russian students had done several decades earlier."[74]

The Soviet government took advantage of this timely and largely unexpected opportunity to spread communism into China. Generous promises of equal treatment convinced many Chinese intellectuals to adopt the Soviet model of development. This ploy would not have been successful without the widespread dissatisfaction with the Shandong decision. Thus, it was the Versailles Peace Treaty's perceived mistreatment of China that turned many Chinese intellectuals away from the United States and toward the Soviet Union.

The importance of the Versailles decision was acknowledged by official Communist histories. According to an early Communist document entitled *A Brief History of the Chinese Communist Party*:[75]

> The imperialist nations at the peace conference had very little sympathy or concern for enslaved China; their major concern was the protection of their own respective interests. It was a great humiliation for China! Although this was not China's first taste of humiliation, its impact was singularly profound, and it will never be forgotten by the progressive masses of the Chinese people, especially the urban masses. The development of the working class and the moral and spiritual humiliation of Versailles were special phenomena of China in 1919. These two forces were of unusual significance and were properly utilized by tthe true revolutionaries who joined the Communist movement as individuals for the purpose of organizing an embryo for the future Communist Party.

According to another account by Hugh Deane, the May Fourth turmoil resulting from the Shandong decisions "led to a succession of revolutionary advances: the formation of the Communist Party in 1921; the Guomindang–Communist alliance forged by Sun Yat-sen; the reorganization of the Guomindang."[76]

China's post-Versailles disappointment with Wilson and the decision of many Chinese intellectuals to turn to Bolshevism was to have a profound impact on modern Chinese history. Ishwar C. Ojha shows how the failure of the Western powers to "protect" China from Japanese demands in Shandong became a "principal instrument of disillusionment." Following Japan's unchecked invasion of Manchuria in the 1930s, Ojha concludes that with "this view of betrayal as their immediate historical heritage, the Chinese Communists came to power."[77]

Without a doubt, the Shandong resolution played a pivotal role in the success of the Soviet Union's propaganda in China. It was largely this event that allowed the Comintern to: first, make contact with Li Dazhao and Chen Duxiu; second, organize Marxist study groups and found the Chinese Communist Party; and third, order the Chinese Communist Party to join with the Nationalists in an anti-imperialist United Front. As summarized by John E. Schrecker: "In 1921, Li Dazhao and Chen Duxiu took the lead in organizing the Chinese Communist Party, and in the following decades Marxism became the preeminent outlook of

Chinese thinkers and revolutionaries. Not everyone adopted the philosophy, of course, but it became the central focus of social analysis and controversy even for those who did not, and, in one way or another, almost all political activists came under its influence."[78]

Even more importantly, the leaders of the Chinese Communist Party were convinced by the Karakhan Manifesto and by Soviet propaganda that the USSR intended to treat China fairly. Mao Zedong even rewrote the cause-and-effect relationship between Versailles' Shandong decision and the origins of China's interest in communism when he stated in his famous tract *New Democracy* that the May Fourth Movement had been summoned by "the Russian revolution, and at the call of Lenin."[79]

Without a doubt, these Chinese leaders lived and died without ever realizing that the story of Wilson's betrayal was a myth. Also, only after Mao and the other Chinese communist leaders came to power in 1949 did they have access to the Beijing government's diplomatic records and learn for the first time the truth behind Moscow's false promises to treat China equally. This topic will be addressed more fully in the next chapter.

## Notes

1. The Soviet government's French-language telegram to the Beijing government, dated 26 March 1920, containing the original 25 July 1919 version of the Karakhan Manifesto, Foreign Ministry Archives, Institute for Modern History, Academia Sinica, Nangang, Taiwan, 外交檔案 (*Waijiao Dangan,* or WJDA below), 03-32, Volume 463(1).

2. "Cablegram from Tumulty to President Wilson," 31 December 1918, WWP Microfilm Reel 388.

3. Zhang Yongjin, 95.

4. Bruce Elleman, "Sun Yat-sen and the Soviet Modernity Model," *Journal of the Southwest Conference on Asian Studies,* Vol. 2 (2000), 21-34.

5. For more information on this aspect of Sino-Soviet relations, see Bruce Elleman, *Diplomacy and Deception: The Secret History of Sino-Soviet Diplomatic Relations, 1917-1927* (Armonk, NY: M.E. Sharpe, 1997), especially Chapter 8.

6. Chow, 171.

7. S. A Korff, "Russia in the Far East," *The American Journal of International Law,* Vol. 17 (1923), 252-284.

8. Germaine Hoston, *Marxism and the Crisis of Development in Prewar Japan* (Princeton, NJ: Princeton University Press, 1986), 24.

9. John K. Fairbank, ed., *The Cambridge History of China,* Vol 12, Part 1 (New York: Cambridge University Press, 1983), 506.

10. One of the first Chinese journals to discuss the October Revolution during 1918 referred to the Bolshevik form of government as "anarcho-communism." Arif Dirlik, *The Origins of Chinese Communism* (New York: Oxford University Press, 1989), 27.

11. Hsueh Chun-tu, *Revolutionary Leaders of Modern China* (New York: Oxford University Press, 1971), 375; Dirlik, 25.

12. Li Dazhao (李大钊), "Bolshevism的勝利" (The Victory of Bolshevism), 新青年 (*New Youth*), Volume 5, # 5, 15 November 1918, 442-448; Interestingly, the term "Bolshevism" was so new to Chinese that Li chose to use the English term.

13. Li Dazhao (李大钊), "庶民的勝利" (The Victory of the Masses), 新青年 (*New Youth*), Volume 5, # 5, 15 November 1918, 436-438.

14. Chen Duxiu (陈独秀), 陈独秀文章选编 (*Collection of Articles by Chen Duxiu*), (Beijing, 1984), 373.

15. Dirlik, 37.

16. John King Fairbank, *The United States and China*, 3rd ed. (Cambridge, MA: Harvard University Press, 1971), 206; that Fairbank continued to hold this view throughout his long career is shown by the fact that this line appears unchanged in: John King Fairbank, *China: A New History* (Cambridge, MA: The Belknap Press, 1992), 267.

17. John Israel, *Student Nationalism in China, 1927-1937* (Stanford, CA: Hoover Institution Press, 1966), 3.

18. Noel H. Pugach, "American Friendship for China and the Shantung Question at the Washington Conference," *The Journal of American History*, Vol. LXIX, No. 1 (June 1977), 67-86.

19. Robert C. North, *Chinese Communism* (New York: McGraw-Hill Book Company, 1966), 36.

20. Lucien Bianco, *Origins of the Chinese Revolution, 1915-1949* (Stanford, CA: Stanford University Press, 1971), 32.

21. Marilyn A. Levine, *The Found Generation: Chinese Communists in Europe during the Twenties* (Seattle, WA: University of Washington Press, 1993), 15.

22. Vladimir Vilenskii (Владимир Виленский), Китай и Советская Россия (*China and Soviet Russia*), (Moscow, 1919), 3.

23. Tony Saich, *The Origins of the First United Front in China: The Role of Sneevliet (Alias Maring)*, (New York: E. J. Brill, 1991), Vol. 1, 27-28.

24. George Moseley, *China Since 1911* (New York: Harper & Row, 1968), 42.

25. "Letter from Secretary of State Robert Lansing to President Woodrow Wilson," 7 August 1919, Robert Lansing collection, Box 3.

26. Allen S. Whiting, *Soviet Policies in China, 1917-1924* (New York: Columbia University Press, 1954), 37-38.

27. This meeting was described in a 15 March 1925 *Pravda* article that Gregorii Voitinskii wrote soon after Sun Yat-sen's death.

28. Meisner, 95-97.

29. Feigon, 74, 99, 105.

30. *Ibid.*, 110.

31. Lao Xiuchao (Лау Сиу-Джау), "Представитель Китая о III Интернационале" (The Chinese Representative about the Third International). *Izvestiia*, 6 March 1919.

32. 北洋政府檔案 (Beiyang Zhengfu Archive), Document # 1001, 3483, Nanjing Number Two Historical Archive, Volume 15, 469-474. According to a Beijing government report dated 30 July 1920, the American embassy in Shanghai sent letters on 2 February and 26 March reporting these materials. The Beijing government further reported that six Germans and five Russians were suspected of distributing these propaganda materials and openly blamed the "Russian-Lenin government" for sponsoring their activities. According to this

report, the six Germans were: 1. Friedrich Saphra; 2. W. Beuschel; 3. Hugo Gerisch; 4. Richard Ledermann; 5. W. Peruger; 6. Kurt Henke; and the five Russians were: 1. N. Vralonaskij; 2. Finon Sutrina; 3. Ksaverin Trlcinski; 4. Simon Martiejan; 5. Vladimir Lebedev.

33. Voitinskii actually arrived in China during April with his wife, M. F. Kuznetsova, his interpreter, Yang Ming-chai, and then I. K. Mamaev and his wife. C. Martin Wilbur and Julie Lien-ying Now, *Missionaries of Revolution: Soviet Advisers and Nationalist China, 1920-1927* (Cambridge, MA: Harvard University Press, 1989), 23.

34. 新青年 (*New Youth*), Volume 7, # 6, appendix. During May 1920, the magazine *New Youth* published a copy of the Karakhan Manifesto and also published positive responses from fifteen societies and dozens of newspapers to this manifesto.

35. One account says that Li Dazhao's first contact with Bolsheviks took place during the summer of 1919, when he met with N. Burtman in Tianjin, and later in September with A. A. Muller. Lydia Holubnychy, *Borodin and the Chinese Revolution, 1923-1925* (New York: Columbia East Asian Institute, 1979), 142.

36. According to Feigon, two other Comintern representatives, M. Kuznetsobai and M. Sakh'ianova also accompanied Voitinskii, Feigon, 165.

37. Thomas C. Kuo, *Ch'en Tu-hsiu (1879-1942) and the Chinese Communist Movement* (South Orange, NJ: Seton Hall University Press, 1975), 79-80.

38. Chen Duxiu (陳獨秀), "實行民治的基礎" (The Basis of Putting Democracy into Practice), 新青年 (*New Youth*), Volume 7, # 1, 13-21.

39. Urban George Whitaker, "Americans and Chinese Political Problems, 1912-1923," University of Washington Dissertation, 1954.

40. Wilbur, *Missionaries*, 449.

41. North, *Chinese Communism*, 37.

42. Feigon, 164.

43. Han Suyin, *Eldest Son: Zhou Enlai and the Making of Modern China, 1898-1976* (New York: Hill and Wang, 1994), 48.

44. Edward E. Rice, *Mao's Way* (Berkeley, CA: University of California Press, 1972), 23.

45. Feigon, 165.

46. Ssu-yu Teng and John K. Fairbank, *China's Response to the West: A Documentary Survey, 1839-1923* (Cambridge, MA: Harvard University Press, 1954), 240.

47. Charlotte Furth, "Intellectual Change: From the Reform Movement to the May Fourth Movement, 1895-1920," John K. Fairbank, ed., *The Cambridge History of China*, Volume XII (New York: Cambridge University Press, 1983), 402.

48. Victor A. Yakhontoff, *The Chinese Soviets* (New York: Coward-McCann, Inc., 1934), 70.

49. Chen Gongbo, *The Communist Movement in China: An Essay Written in 1924* (New York: Octagon Books, 1966), 81. Tony Saich has argued that only six small groups were formed by July 1921, and his list does not include Tianjin. Tony Saich, "Through the Past Darkly," *International Review of Social History*, Volume XXX, 1985, part 2, 169. However, in March 1921, B. Shumianskii referred to a Tianjin study group's charter. Бюллетени Дальне-восточного Секретариата Коминтерна (*Bulletins of the Far Eastern Secretariat of the Comintern*), Irkutsk, # 2 (20 March 1921), 3.

50. Benjamin I. Schwartz, *Chinese Communism and the Rise of Mao* (Cambridge, MA: Harvard University Press, 1979), 31.

51. Signed Р. (R.) "Член Корейской Социалистической Партии" (Member of the Korean Socialist Party), "Положение в Восточной Азии" (The Situation in East Asia), Коммунистический Интернационал (Communist International), # 13, August 1920, 2553-2562.
52. Shumianskii, 3.
53. Chen Duxiu (陳獨秀), "端言" (Declaration), 共產黨員 (*The Communist*), 7 November 1920, #1, 1.
54. Li Mu, "共產黨的組織" (The Organization of a Communist Party), 共產黨員 (*The Communist,*) 7 November 1920, #1, 15-25.
55. Levine, 143.
56. Tony Saich, "Henk Sneevliet and the Origins of the First United Front (1921-1923)," *Issues and Studies,* August 1986, 124.
57. Dov Bing (道夫宾), "斯内夫利特和初期的中国共产党," (Sneevliet and the Early Days of the Chinese Communist Party," 马林在中国的关于资料 (*Documents on Maring in China*), (Beijing, 1980), 34.
58. Bao Huiseng (包惠僧), "回忆马林" (Memories of Maring), *Ibid.*, 95.
59. Dov Mu, *Ibid.*, 35; as confirmed again by Bao Huiseng, 97.
60. Chen Gongbo, 84.
61. Allen Whiting, *Soviet Policies in China, 1917-1924* (New York: Columbia University Press, 1954), 53.
62. Dov Bing, 马林, 35.
63. Chen Gongbo, 84.
64. Dov Bing, 马林, 36.
65. For more on the formation of the Nationalist army, see Bruce A. Elleman, *Modern Chinese Warfare, 1795-1989* (New York: Routledge Press, 2001), 149-177.
66. Saich, *The Origins,* Vol. 1, 230.
67. *Ibid.,* Vol. 2, 780-781.
68. *Ibid.* Vol. 2, 810.
69. B. Nicolaevsky, "Russia, Japan, and the Pan-Asiatic Movement to 1925," *The Far Eastern Quarterly,* Vol. VIII, No. 3 (May 1949), 259-295: 276.
70. Dan N. Jacobs, *Borodin, Stalin's Man in China* (Cambridge, MA: Harvard University Press, 1981), 132.
71. Published copy of Liao Zhongkai's speech at the Guangzhou Lenin memorial, 9 March 1924, 中國國民黨週刊 (*Chinese Guomindang Weekly*), Archives of the Historical Commission of the Central Committee of the Guomindang Party, Document 433-32.
72. Elleman, *Diplomacy and Deception,* 55-84.
73. Wilbur, *Missionaries,* 19.
74. Franz Schurmann and Orville Schell, *Republican China: Nationalism, War, and the Rise of Communism, 1911-1949* (New York: Vintage Books, 1967), 87.
75. Wilbur, *Missionaries,* 446.
76. Hugh Deane, *Good Deeds & Gunboats: Two Centuries of American-Chinese Encounters* (San Francisco, CA: China Books & Periodicals, 1990), 17.
77. Ishwar C. Ojha, *Chinese Foreign Policy In An Age of Transition: The Diplomacy of Cultural Despair* (Boston, MA: Beacon Press, 1969), 56-57.
78. John E. Schrecker, *The Chinese Revolution in Historical Perspective* (New York: Greenwood Press, 1991), 147.
79. North, *Chinese Communism,* 37.

# 8
# The Myth of Soviet Equal Treatment of China

> Both the Central Government in Beijing and the local authorities along the borders readily capitalized on the situation in Russia, and in spite of the opposition from other treaty Powers, took initiatives to shake off the treaty limitations on China's sovereign rights in an attempt to assert China's independence and sovereignty. They achieved a certain degree of success. This constituted an important part of China's consistent efforts to break down the structure of foreign rights and privileges and to recover its lost sovereign rights from the treaty Powers whenever and wherever possible.[1]
>
> Zhang Yongjin, Chinese historian (1991)

Disappointment over the Shandong resolution had a direct and immediate impact on Chinese foreign policy. Beijing, believing that Soviet Russia would treat China more fairly than the Versailles powers, shifted toward Moscow. This policy brought immediate success. One Chinese historian has argued: "By the end of 1920, most Russian treaty rights in China were suspended and China had put itself on a *de facto* equal footing with Russia."[2] This chapter will show that Chinese officials consciously tried to make use of the Bolshevik threat to exert pressure on the Western powers and Japan to eliminate the so-called unequal treaties. This strategy eventually led to Beijing's recognition of the Soviet government in 1924, which made China one of the first nations in Asia to open relations with the Soviet Union. But the price that China paid in return for this strategy was high, since the USSR was able to use its new position of strength to reopen relations with Japan. In the process these two countries once again divided China into competing spheres of influence.

Wellington Koo and C. T. Wang, two of the most outspoken Chinese delegates in Paris, played a crucial role in opening diplomatic relations with the USSR. During September–December 1922 Koo directed Sino-Soviet negotiations with Adolf Joffe, the first full Soviet envoy to China. Soon afterward, in March 1923, Wang was named director-general of the Commission for Sino-Russian Affairs, a position that put him in daily contact with Soviet diplomats. Later, when Koo was made China's minister of foreign affairs from April 1923 through September 1924, he worked closely with Joffe's successor, Lev Karakhan. On 31 May 1924 diplomatic relations between China and the USSR were opened when these two men signed the first Sino-Soviet treaty.³ Finally, Wang, after replacing Koo as foreign minister in the fall of 1924, for a time assumed responsibility for directing China's relations with the USSR.⁴

Although many scholars have asserted that the Bolsheviks' declarations promising to treat China as an equal were actually carried out during the 1920s, Beijing's diplomatic records have since revealed that Soviet diplomats resorted to secret diplomacy to retain the unequal terms of the former Tsarist treaties. Thereafter, in a 1925 treaty with Japan the USSR's Ambassador to China, Lev Karakhan, recognized the Twenty-one Demands; by doing so the USSR reaffirmed Japan's imperialist holdings in Manchuria and Shandong.

In sharp contrast to the United States, therefore, which consistently refused to recognize the Twenty-one Demands and worked hard to convince Japan to return its territorial concessions to China, the Soviet Union secretly supported Japanese imperialism. This chapter will show that it was the Chinese public's misunderstanding of these two diplomatic events—the first concerning the United State's role in the Shandong question and the second concerning the Soviet Union's true relations with China—that ultimately helped thrust the Chinese people down the path toward communism.

**Shandong and the Diplomatic Legacy of Versailles**

Just as Chinese intellectuals were tempted to increase ties with the Bolshevik Party, Beijing officials sought to do the same with the Soviet government. The Karakhan Manifesto's key enticements were the Soviet promises to abolish all former "unequal" Sino-Russian treaties and to return the Chinese Eastern Railway without compensation. On paper these Soviet offers were much more generous than anything being discussed by Japan or the Western nations. In particular, the Soviet government appeared to be offering Beijing the chance to obtain the very renunciation of special rights and privileges from Russia that the other—capitalist—nations had so recently rejected at the Paris Peace Conference.

Even prior to the Paris Peace Conference's announcement of the Shandong resolution, Beijing tried to use the Bolsheviks as a threat against the Versailles powers. For example, on 8 April 1919, Koo warned the Western powers: "The brightest future of China lies along the path of intimate cooperation with America and Europe as well as with her neighbor [Japan] in Asia. They are now at the crossroads. If they are unable to win support for their just cause this time, the consequences of a change of attitude on their part vis-à-vis the Occident, once it is affected, may endure for decades before they can be checked or removed."⁵

Three days later, on 11 April 1919, the Chinese delegation proclaimed to the world that Soviet Russia would undoubtedly return all of Tsarist Russia's concessions to China: "[That] the Republic of Russia, once internal peace has been re-established, will not fail to satisfy the legitimate aspirations of her neighbor is today confidently believed."⁶ Clearly, the Chinese delegates hoped to prompt just such a Soviet offer so as to apply diplomatic pressure on the other powers to agree to China's proposals. By and large, this tactic was ignored during spring 1919. But, once Soviet Russia issued the Karakhan Manifesto in July 1919, the Western powers had little choice but to sit up and take note.

The Soviet offers in the Karakhan Manifesto actually appeared in the same order and were divided into the exact same categories as China's opening proposals at Paris: territorial integrity, political rights, and economic questions. Specifically, Karakhan promised to return tsarist Russia's territorial concessions, abolish all unequal treaties, renounce all of Russia's extraterritorial rights in China, and cancel the Boxer indemnity.

In sharp contrast to Japan's attempts to retain control over the Shandong railway, Karakhan's most important promise was to return the Chinese Eastern Railway to China free of charge. This Soviet offer promised to be a diplomatic boon to Beijing, since it challenged and undermined Japan's insistence that the Shandong railway be run as a joint Sino-Japanese venture. Chinese control of the Chinese Eastern Railway would also allow Beijing to limit Japan's influence in Manchuria, which would be a major step toward regaining control over the Japanese-managed South Manchurian Railway. Obtaining both of these goals would allow China to decrease Japan's presence in China and negate the impact of this "pincer movement" on Beijing. As if to emphasize this point, Karakhan told China that its main allies in the struggle for liberty from imperialism—notably Japanese imperialism—were the "Russian worker and peasant and the Red Army of Russia."[7]

A 1919 Soviet propaganda pamphlet published by Vladimir Vilenskii reprinted the Karakhan Manifesto in full. The chapter entitled "China and the Lesson of Versailles" shows that the manifesto was intended to capitalize on China's failure at Paris (see Document 19). In this section, Vilenskii made a harsh comparison between the Soviet government's friendly offers to China and the poor treatment of China at the Paris Conference by "America, Great Britain, and France." The pamphlet then proposed that China redeem herself through anti-imperialist revolution. The Bolsheviks offered the Russian proletariat's help in urging "forward and accelerating the beginning of revolutionary movements in the Far East."[8]

The Bolsheviks hoped to tap into the enormous Chinese dissatisfaction with Versailles' resolution of the Shandong question. This event soon became the focus of Bolshevik propaganda. It also led to a major reorientation of the Soviet regime's grand strategy. On 5 August 1919, Trotsky explained in a secret report to the Central Committee that supporting the growth of Asian nationalist movements might prove to be the key to the Bolsheviks' revolutionary goals.[9]

But the Karakhan Manifesto was much more than just a propaganda document. It was also the first step in opening diplomatic negotiations with Beijing. By promising to grant Beijing the very concessions that had been denied so recently by the Western nations at Paris, the Soviet government was also offering to serve as a diplomatic lever against the West and Japan; in this regard Moscow was apparently accepting Beijing's request, mentioned above, to satisfy the "legitimate aspirations of her neighbor."

Interest in opening relations with Soviet Russia increased even more after the Karakhan Manifesto was widely published throughout China during Spring 1920. In August 1920, Ignatii Iurin, chief of the Far Eastern Republic's Mission to China, arrived in Beijing. The Siberian-based Far Eastern Republic was a Soviet puppet state and so the Chinese Ministry of Foreign Affairs was eager to discuss the Karakhan Manifesto with Iurin. In fact, a 2 September 1920 meeting of the "Committee for the Study of Russian Treaties" was convened specifically to examine the rights and interests which Soviet Russia had renounced.

Soon after Iurin arrived, Beijing unilaterally suspended all extraterritorial rights of so-called "White" Russians living in China—Russians who had fled to China after the October Revolution and who were generally hostile to the Bolshevik government—and also ordered all diplomatic and consular representatives of the former Russian provisional government to leave China. This action threatened the extraterritoriality and concession rights of other foreigners in China. Many foreign legations in Beijing protested, accusing Beijing of trying to take advantage of the Karakhan Manifesto to open diplomatic relations with the Bolsheviks.

Thereafter, on 2 October 1920, Karakhan met in Moscow with a Chinese military mission headed by General Zhang Silin. Zhang reported to Beijing that "the Soviet Government felt honored that of all the nations [of Asia], China was the first to send its representative to Moscow."[10] At this time, Karakhan presented China with the so-called second Karakhan Manifesto. This declaration repeated the earlier Soviet promises to abolish all former Sino-Russian treaties, return to China without compensation all Russian concession areas, revoke extraterritoriality for Russians living in China, and renounce the Boxer indemnity.

But, unlike the original Karakhan Manifesto, the promise to return the Chinese Eastern Railway without compensation was no longer included. It soon became clear that the Bolsheviks did not actually intend to give up the Tsarist Russian concessions, but used their promises for diplomatic leverage. They were also waiting to see what Japan would do with its railway concession in Shandong.

During 1921, Moscow tried to convince Beijing to sign new treaties validating these Tsarist terms over the Chinese Eastern Railway. In December 1921 the first official Soviet envoy, Aleksandr Paikes, arrived in Beijing. On 26 April 1922, Paikes accused a Beijing official of misunderstanding the Karakhan Manifesto: "[Y]our government mistakenly thought that the 1919 manifesto unconditionally . . . said that . . . the Chinese Eastern Railway was already returned to China's control. On these matters your government is mistaken."[11]

The Soviet government's goal was to retain the railway on the same terms as the former unequal treaties. On 3 August 1922, Paikes further explained that Tsarist Russia's holdings in China were still valid, since the former treaties have "not yet been revised."[12] This meant that Soviet Russia continued to claim in secret the very same unequal rights and privileges from China that it publicly accused the other powers of not renouncing.

When Beijing would not agree to renew the terms of the former Sino-Russian treaties, Moscow sent Adolf Joffe to China during the fall of 1922. In his

## Китай и урок Версаля.

Китай, как южный, так и северный, имеет все основания оставаться недовольным результатами и решениями Версальской конференции.

В преддверии к этой, с позволения сказать, «мирной» конференции Китаю многое обещалось. Не без влияния этих обещаний революционный южный Китай пошел на временное соглашение с реакционным северным Китаем и послал в Версаль объединенную делегацию под руководством Лу-Чен-Хсианга.

Программа Китая на мирной конференции очерчивалась следующими пунктами:

1) Цзиндао должно быть возвращено Японии.
2) Немецкие владения Квантунской области переходят к Китаю, а не к Японии.
3) Россия должна передать Восточно-Китайскую жел. дор. непосредственно Китаю, вмешательство Японии или другой какой-нибудь державы в этом вопросе недопустимо.
4) Экстерриториальность в Китае отменяется.
5) Все иностранные гарнизоны должны быть удалены из пределов Китая.
6) Китай имеет право выполнять свои долговые обязательства, устанавливать и взимать налоги без вмешательства иностранных держав.
7) Аннулирование всех тайных договоров и соглашений, заключенных между китайскими империалистами, с одной стороны, и японскими капиталистами—с другой, безразлично, были ли эти договоры заключены с ведома токийского правительства или без оного.
8) Иностранцам разрешается жить во внутренних городах Китая и вне предоставленных концессий или сфер влияния.
9) Одинаковые для всех права торговли в пределах Китайской республики.
10) Пересмотр всех старых договоров и соглашений с иностранцами, потому что все они были подписаны Китаем под давлением вооруженной силы или под угрозой иностранного нашествия тогда, когда правительство Китая не было еще в курсе современной дипломатии».

**Document 19**: "China and the Lesson of Versailles" from the Vilenskii Pamphlet, which also included the 25 July 1919 Karakhan Manifesto confidential talks with Koo, Joffe swore that Soviet Russia had never promised to return the Chinese Eastern Railway, denying that this promise was "contained either in the authentic text of the Declaration of 25th July, 1919."[13] Instead, Joffe referred to a second abridged version that did not include this promise.

It was now becoming clear to Beijing officials that the Soviet government did not actually intend to fulfill the Karakhan Manifesto. However, Beijing kept this situation a closely guarded secret, since any hint of the truth would undermine their political leverage against Tokyo. During lengthy Sino-Japanese talks conducted in Washington, the Chinese were intent on playing the "Soviet card" to convince the Japanese to agree to return the Shandong concession to China and to sell the railway to the Beijing government.

Beijing cleverly used the threat of improving Sino-Soviet relations to reclaim its lost rights from the West. One historian has accurately linked Beijing's new policy to China's failure at Paris, noting that by opening relations with Soviet Russia, the Beijing government hoped to eliminate the "foreign usurpation of China's sovereignty."[14] Another has discussed how China used its relations with the Bolsheviks to enter "international society," not by accepting unequal international standards, but by orchestrating a "revolt against the regime Europe introduced to regulate its relations with the non-European world."[15] Finally, a third has concluded: "When China failed to recover its Shandong concessions at the peace conference in Paris, the Chinese revolution took on a new front of struggle against foreign encroachment."[16] In short, Beijing was able to use the Karakhan Manifesto to begin the task of implementing its failed proposals at the Paris Peace Conference. The next stage of this lengthy process took place in Washington during late 1921 through early 1922.

**The 1921-1922 Washington Conference**

The Shandong concession's transfer was negotiated at the 1921-1922 Washington Conference.[17] Although the Chinese had opposed Wilson's Shandong resolution in public, in private Koo confided to Frank L. Polk on 18 November 1919 that: "he thought the Chinese government would in the case of direct negotiation with Japan have to take as basis the Shandong settlement made by the Supreme Council, with the object of improving upon it. China would not base her negotiations upon the agreements and notes of 1915 and 1918, [which was] based upon and growing out of the twenty-one demands, as China had on more than one occasion made it clear that she intended to have them annulled."[18] Therefore, even though Koo criticized Wilson in public, in private he admitted that Wilson's compromise was superior to China's own treaties with Japan. To avoid a deadlock over face, a "face-saving formula" was adopted whereby the Sino-Japanese meetings "were termed 'conversations,' rather than negotiations, and they did not assume the legality of Japan's status in Shandong."[19]

At the Washington Conference, Japan's opening statement of 7 September 1921 proposed that the Shandong railway become a joint Sino-Japanese enterprise "in point of capital and management both in name and in fact." As for new railways in China, Japan suggested opening these activities up to the International Financial Consortium, of which Japan would be a member but by no means an exclusive member. Finally, Japan agreed to give up Germany's former right of having first option on the supply of men, capital, and material, which many thought would turn Shandong into an exclusive "sphere of influence" for Japan.[20]

Wellington Koo, China's main delegate to the Washington Conference, used the Karakhan Manifesto's promises—to return the Chinese Eastern Railway without compensation and to abolish all Sino-Russian unequal treaties—to protest even these vastly improved terms and to demand the immediate return of the Shandong railway. In what was described by the organizers of the conference as "the most acute question . . . [and] the most difficult to settle satisfactorily,"[21] the Chinese and Japanese delegates met a total of thirty-six times with American negotiators from 1 December 1921 to 31 January 1922 to discuss the railway.

At America's urging Japan finally agreed to sell the Shandong railway outright to China. The date of transfer was within nine months after the signing of the treaty.[22] However, in the meantime China would pay for the railway by issuing fifteen-year treasury notes to Japan, with the option of immediate redemption after five years; for reasons of face, a Chinese managing director would be in charge, with a Japanese traffic manager selected by Beijing to run the railway.[23]

On 4 February 1922, a final treaty between China and Japan was concluded in Washington, D.C., entitled "For the Settlement of Outstanding Questions Relating to Shandong." Its first article stated: "Japan shall restore to China the former German Leased Territory of Jiaozhou" and all Japanese troops and gendarmes would be withdrawn from Shandong no later than six months from the signing. Japan agreed to turn over to China all "public properties including land, buildings, works or establishments in the former German Leased Territory of Jiaozhou" in exchange for "a fair and equitable proportion of the expenses" that it had incurred during reconstruction; meanwhile all the original German public property was handed over to China free of charge. In addition to this transfer, the Qingdao-Jinan railway was sold to China outright, for which China agreed to pay Japan 53,406,141 gold marks. Finally, Japan agreed to give up its preferential economic rights over the railway lines, coal and iron mines, and salt fields.[24]

In addition to resolving the Shandong question, the participants at the Washington Conference considered China's opening proposals to the Paris Peace Conference. On 6 February 1922 a general agreement entitled the "Nine Power Treaty" was signed, which outlined the principles of the nine nations'—including, most importantly, Japan's—relations with China: "1) to respect the sovereignty, independence, and territorial and administrative inviolability of China; 2) to grant China completely and without constraint the opportunity to develop and to support its capable and stable government; 3) to utilize their influence for the purpose of truly establishing and supporting the principle of equal opportunity for trade and industry of all nations in all the territory of China; 4) to abstain, at the present time in the Chinese theater, from striving for special rights and advantages, detrimental to the rights of the subjects or citizens of friendly nations, or the support of activities hostile to the security of these nations." The signatories also promised not to sign agreements that might establish "superior rights in relation to mercantile or economic development in any particular region of China," "monopolies or preferences," or "spheres of influence."[25] Finally, the Washington Conference immediately raised China's tariff rate and set up two commissions to study ways of revising China's tariff system to make it independent and to find a way to help China adopt legislation and judicial reforms that would allow for the gradual relinquishing of extraterritoriality rights.[26]

The 1922 Sino-Japanese treaty on Shandong not only fulfilled but exceeded in many ways all of Japan's 1919 promises to China at Paris. Meanwhile, the Nine-Power Treaty promised to respect China's sovereignty and territorial integrity in line with the Open Door Policy. These conditions exactly fulfilled Wilson's 1919 goals of inducing Japan to recognize the "Open Door Policy in China" and to "compel Japan to give up an exclusive sphere of influence."[27] As a result, one historian has concluded that the Shandong settlement proved that "American friendship for China did shape official United States policy."[28]

The Washington Conference's transfer of the Shandong concession to China and its promises to reform gradually the tariff system and extraterritoriality belied all earlier criticism of Wilson's mistreatment of China. These criticisms were harsh, and could be heard from Chinese, Soviet, and Western sources; for example, on 11 September 1919 the then Senator Warren G. Harding inaccurately described Versailles' treatment of China as "the rape of the first great democracy of the Orient."[29] But although Japan exactly fulfilled its promises to Wilson, and Wilson achieved his goal of enforcing the Open Door Policy in China, the myth that he had somehow betrayed China lived on; ironically, President Warren Harding was later credited with achieving the resolution of the Shandong question at the Washington Conference instead of the bed-ridden Wilson.

Other scholars disagree about Washington's intentions, arguing instead that it was a "victory for Japan," since the "Chinese were unable to redeem the railroad, which remained in Japanese control until after the Second World War."[30] According to one critic, the biggest problem was that: "The Washington Conference formulated high ideals but provided no way to enforce them."[31] Because of domestic turmoil which soon engulfed China, the final transfer of the Shandong railway was delayed time and time again.[32] But as the next section will show, Washington's plans failed because they were actively undermined by Moscow.

**Soviet Diplomacy and the United Front Strategy**

The Soviet Union's generous sounding promises undoubtedly helped the Chinese to leave Washington victorious. But in private Soviet diplomats informed the Chinese that their abolition of all former Sino-Russian treaties did not mean new terms had been negotiated; rather, so long as new terms were not negotiated, the old terms remained in effect. Over time it became clear that Moscow expected to assert control over the Chinese Eastern Railway, to regain its territorial concessions, and to retain Russia's special territorial position, such as in Outer Mongolia. When Beijing balked, Moscow turned to the Chinese Communist Party and ordered it to join with Sun Yat-sen's Nationalist Party in the United Front. The United Front then exerted pressure on Beijing to agree to Moscow's terms, terms that in fact reaffirmed the former unequal treaties. Once again, perhaps the most essential element underlying the success of this complicated strategy was the Comintern's criticism of Wilson and the Shandong resolution.

Anger at Versailles and the warm Chinese reception for the Karakhan Manifesto helped pave the way for an alliance between the Soviet Union and Sun Yat-sen. This alliance has most often been described in terms of Wilson's failure to secure China's right to self-determination:[33]

> The Chinese nationalists of the 1920s launched a movement to fight for national sovereignty and self-determination. They denounced all treaties previously concluded with foreign nations as "unequal." Thanks to the influence of Marxism-Leninism, Chinese nationalism gained an overtone of anti-colonialism and anti-imperialism. To the Chinese leaders who were concerned with the dismemberment of China, "national salvation" required a campaign against foreign political intervention and economic exploitation.

Moscow hoped to use this new alliance to manipulate public opinion in China. As discussed in great detail by Koo's biographer, Pao-chin Chu, public opinion took on a new meaning after the Paris Peace Conference: "Throughout the period of warlord China, public opinion, which was dominated by intelligentsia such as professors and college students in Beijing and professional journalists, probably exerted more pressure on the Government than at any period of Chinese history since the unification of the Warring States by Qin in 221 B.C. The intellectuals and professional journalists, due to their control over the news media, became a factor in the policy-making of the Beijing Government."[34]

When Adolf Joffe could not persuade Wellington Koo to renew the joint Sino-Soviet management of the Chinese Eastern Railway, he turned instead to Sun Yat-sen. In return for Joffe's promises of Soviet financial and military support, Sun agreed to support in public the Soviet railway proposal. On 26 January 1923, Joffe and Sun signed an agreement in which Sun publicly called for the joint Sino-Soviet management of the Chinese Eastern Railway, which exactly paralleled the Sino-Japanese management of the Shandong Railway. But instead of being satisfied with equal management, it later turned out that the USSR hoped to regain a majority of the seats on the railway's board of directors, giving it complete control. Sun also helped them to carry out this policy.[35]

In the end, Soviet Russia's promise to return the railway to China without compensation was merely a ploy to open diplomatic relations with Beijing.

When Beijing proved unwilling to accept the Soviet terms, Joffe turned to Sun Yat-sen, who quickly agreed. Thereafter, Soviet diplomats periodically threatened Beijing that they might open official diplomatic relations with Guangzhou if Beijing did not cooperate. This threat, when joined with the public pressure that the Chinese communists and Nationalists could direct against Beijing, eventually allowed the Soviet diplomats to convince the Beijing government to accept joint management of the Chinese Eastern Railway. This Soviet ploy would not have been successful without the public outcry surrounding the Shandong question.

In the end, the Soviet government's United Front tactic exerted tremendous pressure on Koo and Wang to back down and accept Moscow's terms. Even though it soon became apparent that Moscow did not intend to carry through on its generous promises, Beijing officials never released transcripts of their confidential meetings with Soviet officials nor did they denounce the Bolsheviks' intentions. By keeping this information secret, Koo and Wang helped create the myth that the Soviet Union was actually treating China equally. Beijing diplomats tried, but ultimately failed, to use this myth to pressure Japan to hand over its concessions, including the Shandong railway.

**Lev Karakhan's Secret Diplomacy and the CER**

When Beijing refused to renew the terms of the former Sino-Russian treaties, Moscow turned to secret diplomacy. While continuing to announce in public that the USSR had abolished all former Sino-Russian treaties, Lev Karakhan, Moscow's new envoy to China, signed a secret protocol with Beijing stating that these treaties still existed even though not enforced. Beijing's recognition of the unequal treaties meant that Moscow could adhere to the old terms until new treaties were negotiated, an eventuality that was delayed time and time again when Karakhan refused to meet to negotiate them. By signing additional secret agreements with the Manchurian warlord Zhang Zuolin and with Japan, Karakhan was able to regain control over the Chinese Eastern Railway, over many of Russia's territorial concessions throughout China, and over Outer Mongolia.

When Karakhan first arrived in Beijing, he publicly announced on 4 September 1923 that his generous manifestos from 1919 and 1920 were still in force and would be the foundation for his future negotiations with China. During intensive negotiations with Chinese officials, Karakhan stated that Moscow was still willing to return the railway to China, to give up its concessions, and to recognize that Outer Mongolia was Chinese territory, but he soon resorted to secret diplomacy to retain these privileges. In a secret protocol negotiated by Karakhan and Wang, the two agreed that all former Sino-Russian treaties would not be enforced during the interim as new treaties were being negotiated.[36]

To force Beijing to sign the draft treaty as written, including this secret protocol, Karakhan issued a three-day ultimatum. In particular, he exerted public pressure on Koo and Wang by means of the United Front between the Chinese Communists and Sun Yat-sen. By arranging to have the contents of the Sino-Soviet draft treaty published in the local Chinese press—minus the crucial secret protocol—Karakhan deluded the Chinese public into thinking that China had received everything from the USSR that the Paris Peace Conference had denied it. As a result, Koo and Wang were subjected to enormous public pressure as groups in Shanghai, Beijing, and other cities demonstrated to sign the treaty.[37]

On 31 May 1924, the final Sino-Soviet Treaty was signed by Karakhan and Koo. When the President of the Republic of China issued Koo complete powers to sign the agreement in the name of China, his order included the secret protocol negotiated by Karakhan and Wang. By signing this secret protocol, both China and the Soviet Union officially agreed that all former Sino-Russian agreements were not to be enforced after 31 May 1924. Although this protocol seemed to satisfy China's desires to abolish the unequal treaties, until new agreements were negotiated the secret protocol actually recognized that all former Sino-Russian treaties still existed, albeit unenforced. To Moscow this meant that all it had to do was delay signing new treaties to retain the terms of the old ones.

According to the 31 May 1924 agreement, a Sino-Soviet conference had to convene within one month to begin negotiating new treaties. By delaying the Sino-Soviet conference, Moscow continued to enjoy the benefits of the former Sino-Russian treaties even though it had publicly renounced them. This solution was perfect both for the Soviet government, which did not want to give up control over these assets, and for Bolshevik propaganda, which wanted to make it appear that the USSR was treating China better than the capitalist nations.

Since the method by which Moscow was able to retain these concessions remained completely secret, the Chinese public was easily persuaded that the Soviet Union had really abolished its unequal treaties with China. This belief added to the myth surrounding the USSR's generosity and, by contrast, made Wilson's apparent betrayal of China look even more despicable.

To regain majority control over the Chinese Eastern Railway, Karakhan turned to the autonomous Manchurian warlord Zhang Zuolin. On 20 September 1924, Moscow signed a supplemental agreement with Zhang that outlined how the railway should be jointly managed. A secret protocol attached to this agreement transferred to Zhang the power to choose which Chinese officials would represent China in the joint commission that managed the railway. This protocol actually transferred the Chinese share of the joint authority over the railway away from Beijing and to Zhang Zuolin.[38] Next, to outwit Zhang, Karakhan turned to Japan.

**The 1925 Restoration of Soviet-Japanese Diplomatic Relations**

After several abortive attempts to open diplomatic relations—at Soviet-Japanese conferences at Dalian, Changchun, and then in Tokyo—serious diplomatic talks leading to formal relations between the USSR and Japan opened in Beijing during 1924. In its negotiations with the USSR, Japan's goals included renewing the former Russo-Japanese treaties, and especially the Portsmouth Peace Treaty. As for Japan's other treaties with Tsarist Russia, Tokyo hoped to retain all of its territorial and economic gains from these former treaties. Japan succeeded in achieving this goal when the Japanese and Soviet negotiators recognized all former treaties, but acknowledged that they could be changed at a future conference; so long as this conference was never held, however, the terms of all of the former Russo-Japanese treaties remained valid.

Before Kenkichi Yoshizawa opened talks with Karakhan in late March 1924, the Japanese Foreign Ministry discussed its goals with regard to the former Russo-Japanese treaties. On 14 March 1924, a list of treaties that Japan hoped to retain included the 1875 Treaty of St. Petersburg, the 1905 Portsmouth Peace Treaty, the 1907 Fishing Convention, and the 1907 Secret Treaty.[39] By contrast, Lev Karakhan's goal seemed to be to abolish all former Russo-Japanese treaties: upon his arrival in Beijing in September 1923, Karakhan gave a speech in which he reiterated that in his 1919 declaration the Soviet government had abolished "all the agreements with Japan from 1901 to 1916."[40]

Thereafter, Karakhan opened negotiations with Yoshizawa on 15 May 1924 by insisting that all of the former Soviet-Japanese treaties be abolished. The Soviet goals included negotiating new treaties with Japan without ever recognizing the validity of the former agreements. Therefore, in this early Soviet draft not only was there no attempt to reaffirm the former treaties, but point three specifically suggested concluding a Soviet-Japanese Commercial Agreement, point five suggested signing a Fishing Convention, while point seven suggested that all treaties with third parties aimed against the other should be abolished.[41]

In reply, Yoshizawa proposed on 17 May 1924 the following article: "Treaty of Peace of 1905 shall remain in force in its entirety. Other treaties and agreements concluded between Japan and Russia shall be replaced by new treaties and agreements so as to conform to new situation, it being understood that all rights and interests secured through old treaties and agreements to the High Contracting Parties and respective nationals shall be respected."[42]

In sharp contrast to the Soviet approach, Japan hoped to retain the old treaties so that it would not lose control over its "rights and interests" in Korea, Manchuria, and Inner Mongolia. Later, Yoshizawa changed his proposal on 25 May 1924 to make it clear that the *status quo* should not be affected: "As regards the other treaties and agreements concluded between the Imperial Japanese Government and the former Russian Government, that is to say, the Imperial Russian Government and the Provisional Russian Government which succeeded, the Governments of the two Contracting Parties agree to revise them at a future conference in a manner corresponding to the altered circumstances, on the basis that the rights and interests enjoyed by the respective governments, citizens or subjects of the two countries by virtue of these instruments shall be fully respected, and that accomplished facts accruing from them shall not be affected."[43] As late as 24 May 1924, however, Karakhan repeated yet again that the Soviet position was to first "open diplomatic relations" and only later negotiate new treaties.[44]

In addition to insisting that the Portsmouth Peace Treaty be recognized, Yoshizawa also made two further proposals intended to guarantee Japan's sphere of influence in China. The first was a denunciation by both sides of any "military alliance, . . . any secret agreement of military alliance, . . . [or] any secret agreement entered into with any third party," which was "calculated to infringe upon the sovereignty or territorial rights of or to menace the safety of the other."[45] The second was that neither party should conclude any "treaty or agreement with any third party looking to the cession, transfer or lease of any portion of their territories adjacent to the territory of the other, which is likely to be used in a manner affecting the security or vital interests of that other."[46]

Clearly, both of these points, if adopted, would have had the effect of halting the USSR from returning its Manchurian railway or its Outer Mongolian protectorate to China. In fact, as shown by the Paikes mission, Tokyo's reluctance to see the *status quo* altered suited Moscow quite well. Soon after Karakhan signed the Sino-Soviet treaty on 31 May 1924, recognizing all former Russo-Chinese treaties, albeit unenforced, he agreed to recognize the former Russo-Japanese treaties as well. In a manner that closely paralleled how the USSR and China had approached the same problem of what to do with their old treaties, Karakhan and Yoshizawa agreed to recognize the former treaties while promising to convene a conference to renegotiate them; in fact, this solution guaranteed that Soviet-Japanese relations remained the same as before World War I.

In July 1924, an early form of this article was presented. It read: "It is agreed that the Treaties, Conventions and Agreements, other than the said Treaty of Portsmouth, which were concluded between Japan and Russia prior to November 7, 1917, shall be re-examined at a Conference to be subsequently held between the Governments of the High Contracting Parties and are liable to revision and amendment as altered circumstances may require." This wording made it too clear that the former Russo-Japanese treaties would continue unchanged, however, and so in a 21 July 1924 draft the term "amendment" was changed to "annulment."[47]

By 30 October 1924, a final draft appeared that remained in the 20 January 1925 Convention: "It is agreed that the Treaties, Conventions and Agreements, other than the said Treaty of Portsmouth, which were concluded between Japan and Russia prior to November 7, 1917, shall be re-examined at a Conference to be subsequently held between the Governments of the High Contracting Parties and are liable to revision and annulment as altered circumstances may require."[48]

Although this article may seem harmless enough, in fact the negotiating records make clear that the underlying intent was to once again recognize the former Russo-Japanese treaties, and in particular the secret agreements from 1907-1916 and the 5 March 1917 Russo-Japanese treaty on Shandong. By this action, Moscow and Tokyo formally recreated the Russo-Japanese spheres of influence that divided China. Japan retained unhampered control over Korea, Southern Manchuria, eastern Inner Mongolia, and the railway in Shandong, while the USSR received Japanese assurances that its claims over Outer Mongolia, northern Manchuria, and western Inner Mongolia would not be challenged by Japan. As a result, this article had an immediate effect on Soviet-Japanese relations in East Asia, and so also impacted the USSR's relations with China.

## Lev Karakhan and the Twenty-one Demands

Although the Soviet-Japanese Convention agreed that all treaties signed before 7 November 1917 had to be reviewed by a special joint conference, it reaffirmed the validity of the Portsmouth Peace Treaty of 5 September 1905.[49] By upholding this treaty, Japan acknowledged the USSR's control over the Chinese Eastern Railway, while Moscow likewise reaffirmed Japan's over the South Manchurian Railway. In essence, the pre-war imperialist treaties dividing China had been recreated. Thus: "The 1925 renewal of the Russo-Japanese secret agreements once again divided China into competing Soviet and Japanese spheres of influence."[50] In the process, Karakhan supported Japan by recognizing the Twenty-one Demands, a decision that Wilson consistently refused to make at Paris.

The Soviet agreement with Japan was a renunciation—albeit a secret one—of the Bolshevik propaganda that opposed foreign imperialism in China. After Shen Ruilin replaced Wang as foreign minister, Shen secretly protested this Soviet-Japanese Convention on 11 February 1925. He accused the USSR of violating the sovereign rights of China. In response, Karakhan sent Shen a letter on 26 February 1925 (see Document 20). In this letter, Karakhan accused Shen of "fully ignoring those acts which the Chinese Government has itself concluded with Japan." He pointed in particular to China's agreements with Japan signed in 1905 and 1915, both of which reaffirmed the Portsmouth agreement.[51]

In Moscow, the Chinese minister immediately protested directly to Commissar of Foreign Affairs Georgii Chicherin that the reference to a 1915 treaty with Japan was none other than the Twenty-one Demands, an agreement that China had publicly denounced on numerous occasions and the terms of which Wilson had helped to alter at Versailles. Beijing's protest proved futile, however, and the Soviet Union and Japan continued to cooperate in controlling the largest foreign concessions in China.

By January 1925, therefore, it was becoming clear that the USSR's real policy in Asia was to uphold its own power; in the process, Moscow helped Tokyo do the same. In the meantime, the Comintern's propaganda denouncing imperialism helped undermine the Nine Power Treaty, even while increasing Soviet influence.

It is important to recall that as early as 11 May 1915, President Wilson had condemned the Twenty-one Demands, accusing Japan of threatening the "territorial integrity of the Republic of China."[52] Later, at Paris, Wilson succeeded in negotiating new and improved terms for Shandong. However, because Wilson's assistance to China remained largely unknown, Chinese intellectuals and officials accused Wilson of betraying and sacrificing China. Chinese disillusionment with Wilson led to a major reaction against Western democracy and capitalism.

Meanwhile, the publication of the Karakhan Manifesto gave the Chinese people false hope that one country at least—Soviet Russia—would treat China fairly. Karakhan's subsequent public diplomacy appeared to reaffirm that the Soviet Union was true to its word, while only in his secret dealings did he uphold the validity of Japan's infamous Twenty-one Demands. Six years after the Karakhan

February 26, 1925.

Monsieur le Ministre,

I have the honour to acknowledge the receipt of Your Excellency's Note of the 11th inst., protesting against the recognition, according to the Soviet-Japanese agreement of January 20th,1925, of the validity of the Treaty of Portsmouth of 1905, as violating the sovereign rights and interests of China.

Your Excellency's protest would have been quite timely and have had perfectly reasonable grounds twenty years ago, ..,1915, on the strength of an agreement concluded between China and Japan directly and without any reference to the Treaty of Portsmouth, the rights which, twenty years ago, have been ceded to Japan by the Tsarist Government, were established on a new formal basis. I may be permitted here to invite Your Excellency's kind attention to the fact that those rights which have now apparently caused the protest on Your Excellency's part were fixed in 1915 for terms many times longer than those which were granted by China to the former Russian Imperial Government.

I wish to assure Your Excellency that neither in its part referring to the Treaty of Portsmouth, nor, for that matter, in any other part of the Soviet-Japanese Convention of January 20th, 1925, or the documents apposed thereto, can there be found any stipulation violating the interests of China, and that the said agreement does not even embody any question in whatever way affecting the sovereign rights and interests of the Chinese people.

I take this opportunity to renew to Your Excellency, Monsieur le Ministre, the assurances of my highest consideration.

L. Karakhan.

a Excellency
Shen Jui lin,
Minister of
reign Affairs of
ae Republic of
C h i n a,
to..etc.,etc...

**Document 20**: Excerpts from Ambassador Lev Karakhan's 26 February 1925 Letter to Minister of Foreign Affairs Shen Ruilin

Manifesto was first announced, therefore, the Soviet government was in fact once again basing its foreign policy in China on unequal treaties, the very same unequal treaties that it had formerly claimed to have rejected.

In the end, the USSR's supposedly equal treatment of China proved illusory. Although Koo and Wang could have exposed Moscow's duplicity and sought Western help, to admit that their secret diplomacy with the USSR had backfired would have constituted an enormous loss of face. Public knowledge of the Soviet Union's secret diplomacy with China would also undermine Beijing's wavering domestic authority and tarnish China's international image. Therefore, unbeknownst to the average Chinese citizen, the United States remained alone among the major nations in refusing to recognize the Twenty-one Demands.

**Conclusions**

China's disappointment with Versailles' solution to the Shandong question allowed the Bolsheviks to increase their diplomatic and political influence in China. On the surface, China's attempt to overthrow the unequal treaties seemed to be successful; Zhang Yongjin, for example, falsely concluded that by 1920: "The Russian treaty structure had been been practically dismantled, only to be legalized in the Sino-Soviet Friendship Treaty in 1924."[53] But, Soviet diplomats, instead of carrying through on their public promises to treat China equally, actually based their relations with Beijing on the unequal terms of prior Sino-Russian treaties.[54] In the end, China's misguided anger over the Shandong question opened the door for an even greater danger, the continuation and expansion of the Soviet-Japanese competition to divide and conquer China.

Archival documents prove that the USSR used secret diplomacy to regain its special rights and privileges in China. This tactic allowed the USSR to retain control over the Chinese Eastern Railway, Russia's territorial concessions in China, and Outer Mongolia. Most importantly, in January 1925 the Soviet Ambassador to China secretly recognized Japan's Twenty-one Demands. All of these actions were in opposition to Wilson's efforts to halt territorial imperialism in China, and they threatened to renew the division of China into competing spheres of influence.

Conversely, widespread misunderstanding of the Shandong resolution was one of the factors that had dissuaded the United States from joining the League of Nations; without American participation in the League, this organization later proved ineffectual in halting the spread of Japanese territorial imperialism during the 1930s.[55] China's secret dealings with the Soviet Union also undermined the effectiveness of the Nine Power Treaty. These two setbacks were to have a catastrophic impact on balance-of-power relations throughout Asia. Without America to stand by its side, China was to face one disaster after another.

In retrospect, China's decision to turn away from the West and embrace the Soviet model of development was based on two powerful myths. Just as the truth behind the myth that Wilson betrayed China at Paris remained virtually unknown to the Chinese public, the truth behind the myth that the USSR treated China as an equal was also hidden. This deadly combination was to have enormous long-range repercussions in China.

In the end, the Chinese public's perception that America's solution to the Shandong question entailed an enormous "loss of face," together with their perception that the Soviet Union had given China "face," were integral to China's decision to follow the USSR instead of the West. Arguably, it was this unique alignment of factors that allowed the Soviet Union to have such an enormous impact on the Far East. To this day, China has not yet fully reversed the ill effects of this decision. Therefore, it is of great contemporary importance to set the record straight: contrary to popular belief the United States did not betray China, but the Soviet Union did.

**Notes**

1. Zhang Yongjin, 149.
2. *Ibid.*
3. *The China Yearbook* 1925/26 "Who's Who," 1248.
4. *Ibid.*, 1282a.
5. Memorandum, 8 April 1919, V. K. Wellington Koo papers, Box 1.
6. "Peking Government's Official Communiqué *China's Reply to Japan,*" 11 April 1919, SKH Papers, Box 328; reprinted from the *North-China Herald*, 19 April 1919, 144.
7. "Original French-language telegram from Soviet government to Peking Government," 26 March 1920, *WJDA*, 03-32, 463(1).
8. Vladimir Vilenskii (Владимир Виленский), Китай и Советская Россия (*China and Soviet Russia*), (Moscow, 1919), 12.
9. Document 2956, Leon Trotsky Archives, Houghton Library, Harvard University.
10. Zhang Yongjin, 172.
11. "Chinese-language Minutes of Paikes' Meeting with Waichiaopu Officials," 26 April 1922, *WJDA*, 03-32, 200(3).
12. "English-language letter from Paikes," 3 August 1922, *WJDA*, 03-32, 207(1).
13. *New Russia*, Volume 1, #10, 6 January 1923, 305.
14. Li Jianmin (李健民), "顏惠慶與停止舊俄使領待遇" (Yen Huiching and the End of the Tsarist Officials' Special Privileges), 近代史研究所集刊 (*Journal of the Modern History Institute, Taiwan*), #6, 1977, 123-143.
15. Zhang Yongjin, 196.
16. Odoric Y. K. Wou, "The Military and Nationalism: The Political Thinking of Wu P'ei-fu," F. Gilbert Chan and Thomas H. Etzold, eds., *China in the 1920s: Nationalism and Revolution* (New York: New Viewpoints, 1976), 111.
17. Erik Goldstein and John Maurer, eds., *The Washington Conference, 1921-22: Naval Rivalry, East Asian Stability and the Road to Pearl Harbor* (Portland, OR: Frank Cass, 1994).
18. "Memorandum of a Conversation Between V.K. Wellington Koo and Frank L.

Polk," 18 November 1919, V. K. Wellington Koo papers, Box 1; this admission by Koo is especially important since in his personal memoirs, written 30-40 years later, he accuses Wilson of not being sympathetic to China and of recognizing the Twenty-one Demands. This clear contradiction shows the dangers inherent in relying on memoir literature.

19. Noel Pugach, 77.

20. "Japan's Proposals on the Shantung Question," 7 September 1921, Edward T. Williams Papers, Bancroft Library, University of California, Berkeley.

21. Charles E. Hughes, Henry Cabot Lodge, Oscar W. Underwood, Elihu Root, "Conference on the Limitation of Armament: Report of the American Delegation, February 9, 1922," *The American Journal of International Law*, Vol. 16 (1922), 159-233.

22. Department of State, *Conversations between the Chinese and Japanese...*, 386-387.

23. Godshall, 414.

24. "Treaty Between China and Japan For the Settlement of Outstanding Questions Relation to Shantung—with an Agreement Supplementary Thereto," 4 February 1922, SKH Papers, Box 383.

25. "Постановления Вашингтонской Конференции 1921/22" (Resolutions of the Washington Conference 1921/22), Е. D. Grimm (Е. Д. Гримм), Сборник договоров и других документов по истории мЕждународных отношений на Дальнем Востоке (1842-1925) (*Collection of Treaties and Other Documents on the History of International Relations in the Far East [1842-1925]*), (Moscow, 1927), 204-209.

26. Akira Iriye, *After Imperialism: The Search for a New Order in the Far East, 1921-1931* (Cambridge, MA: Harvard University Press, 1965), 21.

27. "Unpublished diary of Vance C. McCormick," 5 July 1919 entry 119, Vance C. McCormick Papers, Hoover Institution Archives.

28. Noel Pugach, 69.

29. Raymond Leslie Buell, *The Washington Conference* (New York: Russell & Russell, 1922), 255.

30. Granat Stanley Jerome, *Chinese Participation at the Washington Conference* Ph.D. Dissertation, 1969, 355.

31. Fairbank and Feuerwerker, eds., *The Cambridge History...*, 106.

32. During mid-March 1923, C. T. Wang, acting Foreign Minister, unilaterally announced that the Shandong railway was China's, but Japan protested. Exactly one year later, Wang and Lev Karakhan, the Soviet envoy, announced a draft Sino-Soviet treaty that seemed to hand over the Chinese Eastern Railway to China. Clearly, Beijing timed this event to put diplomatic pressure on Japan to give up the Shandong railway. This plan backfired, since it instead prompted Japan and the USSR to open negotiations that eventually allowed both countries to retain their railway concessions.

33. Buell, 255.

34. Chu, 296.

35. Saich, Vol. 2, 545.

36. "Draft Treaty," 14 March 1924, *WJDA*, 03-32, 506(5).

37. According to Chu, Beijing's Teachers' University, Engineering University, Teachers' Colleges for Girls, and the College of Fine Arts sponsored pro-treaty demonstrations.

38. Two signed copies of this secret protocol are now available to scholars, one copy in the PRC and the other in Taiwan (Nanjing, File 1039, #99; *WJDA*, 03-32, 491(2)).

39. Gaimushō, 2.5.1-106-5-9.

40. Gaimushō, B100 C/R1(1); 6 September 1923, *Peking Daily News*.
41. Gaimushō, 2.5.1-106-5.4.
42. *Ibid.*
43. Gaimushō, 2.5.1-106-5.5.
44. *Ibid.*
45. Gaimushō, 2.5.1-106-5.6.
46. *Ibid.*
47. Gaimushō, 2.5.1-106-5.8.
48. Gaimushō, 2.5.1-106-5.11.
49. Grimm, 213-218.
50. Bruce A. Elleman, "The 1907-1916 Russo-Japanese Secret Treaties: A Reconsideration," *Asian Cultural Studies*, Vol. 25 (30 March 1999), 29-44.
51. "English-language letter to Shen Ruilin, signed by Lev Karakhan," 26 February 1925, *WJDA*, 03-32, 497(2).
52. Richard C. DeAngelis, "Jacob Gould Schurman and American Policy Towards China, 1921-1925," St. John's University Ph.D. Dissertation, 1975, 83-84.
53. Zhang Yongjin, 187.
54. Elleman, *Diplomacy and Deception*, especially chapter 3.
55. There is a certain amount of irony in the fact that the anti-Japanese mood in America during 1919-22, when Japan was trying to cooperate with Washington, ultimately stopped the U.S from joining the League and thus from being able to exert pressure on Tokyo during the 1930s, when Japan was not trying to cooperate. According to one scholar it was: "a violent anti-Japanese mood [that] swept over the country, and the question of Shantung became one of the most powerful arguments in the Republican arsenal against Wilson and his League of Nations." Jan Willem Schulte Nordholt, *Woodrow Wilson: A Life for World Peace* (Berkeley, CA: University of California Press, 1991), 352. Because of wide-spread misunderstanding of what Wilson was trying to do with China, even pro-China progressives, like John Dewey, urged the Senate to reject the League. Nemai Sadham Bose, *American Attitude and Policy to the Nationalist Movement in China (1911-1921)* (Bombay: Orient Longmans, 1970). When it came time to vote, therefore, all but one Republican and a total of five Democrats voted for proposed reservations to be attached to the League charter, including overthrowing the Shandong resolution. This 53-41 vote against the League of Nations doomed the United States to remain outside of the one multinational security organization that might have been able to halt Japanese expansion during the 1930s. Leon H. Canfield, *The Presidency of Woodrow Wilson: Prelude to a World in Crisis* (Rutherford, N.J.: Fairleight Dickinson University Press, 1966). A second historical irony is that by not cooperating more closely with the United States at Paris, Great Britain later found that the very magnitude of the Japanese threat to its empire in Asia made it more difficult for Britain to stand up to Hitler and Mussolini. Margaret Lamb and Nicholas Tarling, *From Versailles to Pearl Harbor: The Origins of the Second World War in Europe and Asia* (New York: Palgrave Press, 2001).

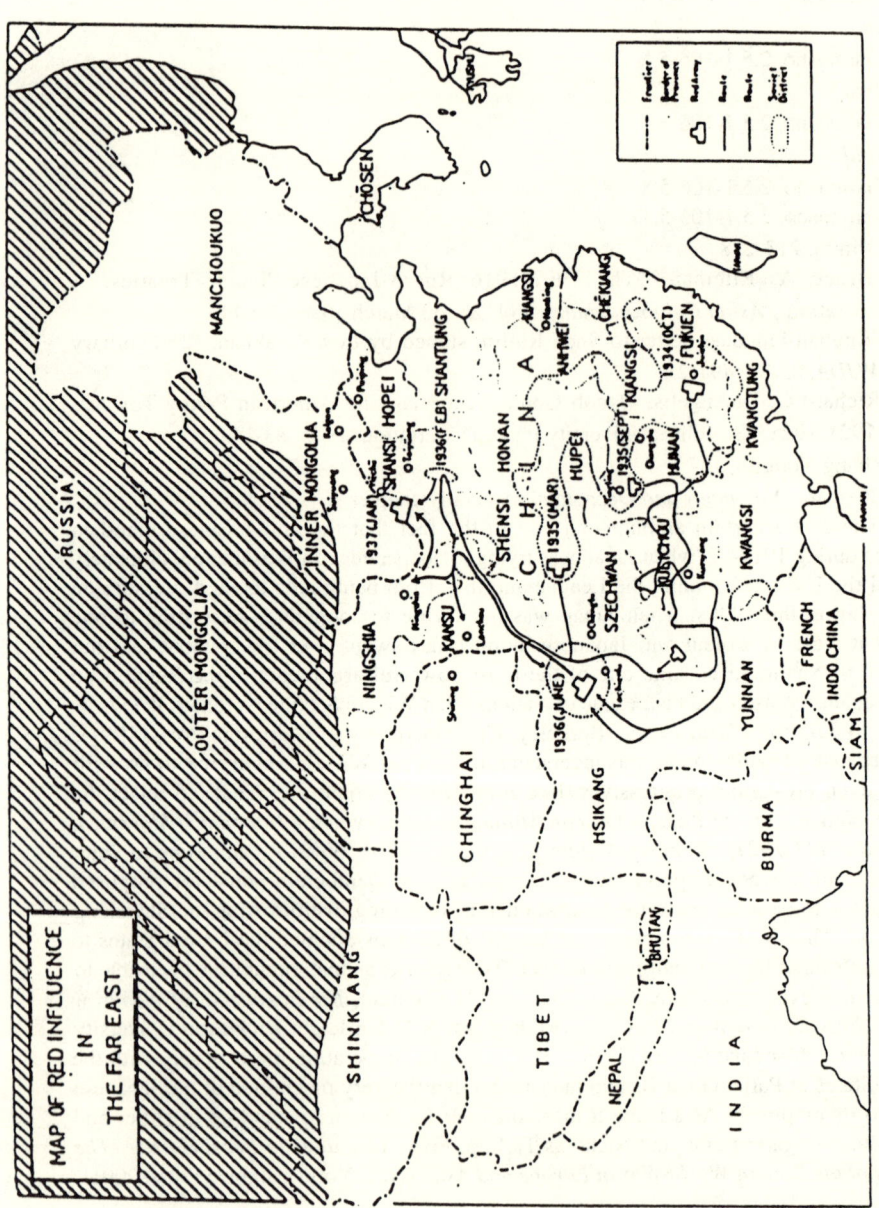

**Map 3.** Japanese Map of the USSR's "Red Influence" in China ("The Present Situation of the Red Activities in China and Manchuria," *Contemporary Manchuria*, Volume 1, No. 1, April 1937, 73-96)

# *Epilogue: The Impact of the Shandong Question*

> It is unfortunate that the real issues involved have been very largely misunderstood in the popular mind. The term "Shandong question," is itself a misnomer. The question is not one which affects the whole Province of Shandong. The important points now awaiting adjustment relate only to the manner of restoring to China an area of territory, less than one-half of 1 per cent of the Shandong Province, and also the disposition of a railway 290 miles long, and its appurtenant mines, formerly under exclusive possession and management of the Germans.[1]
>
> Baron T. Kato, Japanese diplomat (1 December 1921)

On 10 December 1922, Japan transferred the Shandong concession to China and by the end of the month all remaining Japanese troops had been withdrawn from Jiaozhou bay; meanwhile, the railway remained under joint Sino-Japanese control. The Shandong question, which had been the primary focal point of the May Fourth Movement and the spark that led to the creation of the Chinese Communist Party, died away without any fanfare. As one surprised foreign journalist commented: "Hardly one prominent Chinese, other than the members of the Rendition Commission, was present to witness the consummation of what had been represented at Versailles and Washington as the passionate desire of the whole Chinese nation."[2] In fact, by the end of 1922 the damage had already been done, since there was a thriving communist movement in China that was on the verge of joining forces with a surging nationalist movement. Both were determined to make the West pay for the humiliation that China had been forced to suffer at Versailles.

As this book has tried to show, Wilson's role in resolving the Shandong question at the Paris Peace Conference was misrepresented by the American press, which largely misunderstood and sensationalized these events; by the Chinese delegation, which blamed Wilson for its own failings; and by the Chinese reformers of the May Fourth Movement, who were outraged that China had apparently not received equal treatment and justice at Paris. Most importantly, Soviet Russia used the turmoil and dissatisfaction associated with the Shandong question to gain a foothold in China. As a result, the Soviet Union won and the United States lost the battle for the hearts and minds of the Chinese people.

In sharp contrast to the general condemnation of Wilson, the Bolsheviks were generally given far greater credit than they deserved. Although the USSR promised to treat China equally, Moscow's decision to use secret diplomacy actually allowed it to regain most of Tsarist Russia's special concessions, rights, and privileges. By the time the Chinese people began to suspect that their victory over Western imperialism was a pyrrhic one, it was too late. As one Chinese scholar put it, China's plight could be compared to the old proverb: " 'Drips of water may, if unplugged, flow like a river.' Indeed, had the Japanese delegates in Paris given heed to Koo's appeal for a concrete proof of friendship from Japan, and had the two Far Eastern countries been able to work together in a genuine spirit of mutual understanding, the pages of history might have been re-written."[3]

\*     \*     \*

As this work has shown, China rejected American attempts to form a multinational security structure in Asia, and instead attempted to use supposedly equal relations with the Soviet Union as a lever against Japan. This plan backfired. Beginning in 1924, the Soviet Union and Japan opened diplomatic negotiations that led in 1925 to the founding of Soviet-Japanese relations based on Japan's former treaties with Tsarist Russia; previous accounts of these relations have mistakenly concluded that the 1907-17 Russo-Japanese secret treaties, which divided China into Russian and Japanese spheres of influence, were abolished either during, or soon after, the Bolshevik Revolution of October 1917.[4] With the renewal of the secret treaties, however, the former spheres of influence were also revived, which in turn initiated an interwar Soviet-Japanese competition for control over China.

When the 1925 Soviet-Japanese Convention once again recognized the former Russo-Japanese secret treaties, they largely remained in force through 1945. The revival of the Russo-Japanese secret treaties of 1907-17 had an enormous and lasting impact throughout East Asia. Although largely unseen, when the USSR and Japan successfully renewed political and economic relations on 20 January 1925, they also renewed the former Russo-Japanese spheres of influence, including Korea, Manchuria, Inner and Outer Mongolia, and Shandong; later, the USSR also used these treaties to expand into Xinjiang.

The Soviet-Japanese Convention had an immediate impact on China. For example, by reaffirming the validity of the Portsmouth Peace Treaty, Tokyo tacitly acknowledged the USSR's control over the Chinese Eastern Railway, while Moscow likewise reaffirmed Japan's control of the South Manchurian Railway. Beijing's hopes of regaining these foreign concessions were soon dashed. Unlike the public outpouring that had met the Versailles decision, however, foreign attention paid to the Soviet-Japanese Convention was relatively slight, probably because the most important decisions remained secret. Soon after this convention was signed, one newspaper did warn that it was "tantamount to a league of the East facing an unleagued West across the Pacific."[5] Another linked the Soviet-Japanese Convention with the USSR's treaties with Germany, warning that this agreement was actually the final brick in a "Far Eastern 'bloc' " between Russia, Japan, and Germany.[6] But when this alliance did not immediately form, interest in the 1925 convention diminished; only in spring 1941 was this triple bloc temporarily achieved, when the USSR signed non-aggression pacts with both Germany and Japan.

Ever since the October Revolution, Japan had been concerned that the Soviet government might attempt to regain full control over the Tsarist concessions in China. Although Japan had supported America's Open Door Policy at the Washington Conference in 1921-22, and it agreed to return its own Shandong concession to China, Tokyo made it quite clear that if changes in China directly threatened its economic interests, then Japan was prepared to "protect to the utmost her legitimate and important rights and interests in China through reasonable means."[7] Once Moscow succeeded in using secret diplomacy to regain the Tsarist concessions in China, then Tokyo felt that it had little choice but to adopt similar policies. In the process, Japan ignored its promises at the Washington Conference not to create spheres of influence in China. In doing so, Japan helped undermine the validity of the Open Door Policy.

Knowledge of these diplomatic agreements helps to explain the competition that characterized Soviet-Japanese relations during the interwar period. According to some scholars, this competition was rooted in the 1894-5 Sino-Japanese War: "The [Sino-Japanese] war would be the first act of a protracted struggle between Japan and Russia to establish spheres of influence in the Far East, a struggle which would continue unabated from the Russo-Japanese War (1904-5) until it culminated in a general Asian war in the 1930s and 1940s."[8]

The Soviet-Japanese secret diplomacy during the 1930s demands further study. However, it is clear that Moscow's and Tokyo's goals continued to be to divide East Asia into exclusive Soviet and Japanese spheres of influence. The United States opposed these efforts, advocating instead the Open Door Policy's goal of promoting free trade in order to eliminate the need for specific spheres of influence. With the renewal of the Portsmouth Peace Treaty and the Russo-Japanese secret treaties of 1907-17, however, the USSR and Japan directly challenged the validity of the Open Door Policy. As a result, both countries were eventually put on an East Asian collision course with the United States.

\*       \*       \*

The Shandong question had an unexpected impact on the origins of World War II in East Asia. Throughout the interwar period, China continually tried to play the USSR and Japan against each other to its own advantage. This policy was especially clear during May 1929, when the Chinese government in Nanjing tried to regain control over the Chinese Eastern Railway by demanding the Soviet government sell the railway to China, as it had promised to do in 1924. Tensions increased until an undeclared state of war existed. On 3 December 1929, China's foreign minister, C. T. Wang, sent a note to the Japanese Chargé d'Affaires accusing the USSR of reverting to force to resolve the dispute.[9] China was clearly hoping that Japan would intervene, but Japan, upholding its 1925 Convention with the USSR, remained neutral.

Although the Bolsheviks profited from Japan's neutrality in 1929, the 1925 convention worked to Japan's advantage in 1931 following the Manchurian Incident. In fact, one Japanese historian has discussed this period in terms of a "hidden crisis" between the Soviet Union and Japan, and has shown how the Japanese Kwantung Army was initially "apprehensive and cautious about invading the Soviet sphere of influence" and only later became bolder once it became clear that the USSR was "exercising a policy of general retreat."[10]

Specialists on Soviet-Japanese diplomacy have never before been able to explain how Japan obtained the "neutrality of the USSR during the Manchurian Incident."[11] Some have even commented on the strange nature of this relationship, since when the Soviet government proposed that the two countries sign a non-aggression pact, the "Japanese declined, stating that there was no need for a nonaggression pact"; one historian, not knowing about the 1925 renewal of the pre-1917 Russo-Japanese alliance system, has even mistakenly assumed that Japan's attitude was actually in line the Briand-Kellogg Pact outlawing war.[12]

The truth was much less benign, however, and soon after sponsoring the formation of Manchukuo in 1932, Tokyo and Moscow agreed to convene a conference to discuss the status of the Chinese Eastern Railway. During 1935, Moscow sold the railway to Japan, which was an enormous boon to Japan's expansionist plans. Following the sale of the railway, a 1937 secret Japanese Foreign Ministry publication reprinted the 1907-17 treaties as if they were still operative. The 1907 secret treaty was substantially altered, however, since a crucial section on the Chinese Eastern Railway was completely eliminated. The presence of this alteration in 1937 is a final reconfirmation that the 1925 Convention had indeed renewed all of the former Russo-Japanese secret treaties.

The Soviet-Japanese Convention should not be misconstrued as meaning that Soviet-Japanese relations were particularly friendly. According to one diplomatic historian, the 1925 Convention "did not bring about any change in the basic Japanese attitude of distrust, suspicion, and hostility towards the Soviet Union."[13] Thereafter, Japan, in opposition to the USSR, continued to make inroads further into China. Tokyo even justified its 1937 invasion into central China as necessary to oppose Moscow's parallel efforts in Xinjiang.

Throughout the 1930s and early 1940s the Soviet-Japanese struggle to divide China continued unabated. This struggle eventually led to a Soviet-Japanese stalemate, as Tokyo opposed the USSR's so-called "Red Influence" (see Map 3). Japanese fear of the unchecked spread of communism led to numerous border conflicts between Japan and the Soviet Union, particularly in 1939 at Nomonhan along the Mongolian-Manchurian border.

In 1941 this stalemate was broken when the USSR and Japan began negotiating a non-aggression pact that divided almost the whole of northern China between the two countries. The existence of the 1907-17 treaties made this new Soviet-Japanese pact more likely. On 13 April 1941, the USSR and Japan signed a non-aggression pact that secured Japan's strategic rear. Soon afterward, Japan invaded southward into China and Indochina, a military policy that quickly brought Japan into conflict with the United States. In sharp contrast to being a break with earlier Japanese foreign policy, as many authors have suggested, the origins of the World War II in Asia can perhaps best be seen as the end result of the 1925 Soviet-Japanese Convention's renewal of the Tsarist-Japanese secret treaties.[14] Japan's increasing tensions with the United States over the Open Door Policy inevitably led Tokyo to consider Washington as its prime enemy.

\*      \*      \*

After World War II, the long-term impact of the Shandong question can be seen in the origins of the cold war in Asia. In fact, much of the Far Eastern geopolitical framework in post-war Asia can be traced back to the Tsarist-Japanese secret agreements, and to their subsequent renewal and alterations by the USSR and Japan in 1925, 1935, and 1941. The fact that these treaties were never abolished following the October Revolution, despite Soviet propaganda claims to the contrary, is of enormous importance for a fuller understanding of the still murky events leading up to the cold war struggle over Asia during the late 1940s, 1950s, and beyond.

The Soviet Union hoped to be the big winner in Asia if Japan and the United States went to war over China. This Soviet desire did not completely escape American diplomats' notice. William C. Bullitt, the American ambassador to Moscow, even warned in a 19 July 1935 dispatch to Washington that the USSR's real goal was to promote a war between the United States and Japan, and that if this happened, the Soviet Union would try to "avoid becoming an ally until Japan had been thoroughly defeated and would then merely use the opportunity to acquire Manchuria and Sovietize China."[15]

Bullitt's warning proved to be little short of prophetic, as Moscow's non-aggression pact with Tokyo in 1941 allowed the Japanese military forces to divert troops from Siberia to exert their full strength against the United States. After America defeated Japan, the USSR was virtually unopposed when it moved into the East Asian vacuum caused by Japan's defeat.

Although Washington's support for the Open Door Policy once again intensified during World War II, it was unable to marshal sufficient power to enforce this policy. In negotiations leading up to the 11 February 1945 Yalta agreement, Stalin appeared to support the Open Door Policy; he even acknowledged that after Japan's defeat the Manchurian port of Dalian should be made an international port open to all countries. In exchange for American Lend-Lease aid, Stalin promised Ambassador Averell Harriman that the USSR would adhere to this policy. But on 18 July 1945, Harriman warned Truman that if Stalin succeeded in gaining exclusive control over the Manchurian railways and the port city of Dalian, then "such control would violate the established [Open Door] policy and principles which the United States has held for a long period of time."[16]

Archival records of Stalin's summer 1945 negotiations with T. V. Soong, Chiang Kai-shek's brother-in-law and the Chinese envoy to Moscow during the Sino-Soviet talks, show that Stalin obtained just such power over Manchuria. In fact, Stalin insisted that Yalta's resolution giving the USSR "preeminent interests" along the Manchurian railways actually meant that the USSR's rights throughout Manchuria would be greater than "China and other countries."[17] Once Stalin forced Soong to adopt this interpretation, Soong and Stalin signed a secret protocol on 14 August 1945 which stated that not only would the USSR have predominant control over the Manchurian railways, but the port of Dalian would "be leased free of charge to Russia."[18]

This secret Sino-Soviet agreement violated the Open Door Policy, since it gave the USSR special rights and privileges in Manchuria. As a result, Moscow was later able to provide the Chinese Communist Party with a base in Manchuria from which it could expand its power throughout all of northern, central, and eventually southern China. Soviet military supplies arrived via the Manchurian railways, which also gave the Chinese Communist Party a crucial advantage in its on-going civil war with the Nationalist Party. By 1949 the communists were able to consolidate power throughout most of continental China. With the beginning of the Korean War the following year, East Asia quickly became the most active theater in the evolving cold war.

\*     \*     \*

The short-, middle-, and long-term impact of Versailles' resolution of the Shandong question was much greater than anyone could have predicted at the time. Arguably, it was the overlapping and combining of two myths—Wilson's betrayal and the Bolsheviks' equal treatment—that proved so important in determining China's future course; one myth alone probably would not have been sufficient to impel the Chinese people to abandon the United States and follow the USSR.

China's fateful decision to reject Western democracy and capitalism in favor of the socialist model was clearly a decision rooted in the 1919 Paris Peace Conference. The misunderstandings and misperceptions surrounding the Shandong question were instrumental in helping to send China down the path toward communism, a journey that ultimately included decades of civil war, the Chinese Communist Party's 1949 victory, and then many more decades of even more destructive domestic turmoil, including the Cultural Revolution. Only during the 1980s did the Chinese government begin to rectify the enormous physical and human damage that China's decision to follow the Soviet path had inflicted on twentieth-century China.

The Paris Peace Conference's decision to transfer Shandong to Japan proved to be a major twentieth-century crossroads for China. Without this event, the USSR would have undoubtedly experienced greater difficulties in cultivating intellectual and diplomatic ties with the Chinese people and the Beijing government. President Woodrow Wilson helped to negotiate this agreement.

## THE SHANDONG QUESTION 181

Although Wilson attempted to assist China, to ignore Japan's legal case would have called into question the sanctity of treaties and undermined the very legal tradition on which Western democracy and capitalism was based. This Wilson could not do. But in making his fateful decision, Wilson unwittingly helped push China ever farther away from those very values that he so admired. Ironically, Wilson's solution to the Shandong question helped to create in China what Wilson had fought so hard to defeat at Paris.

**Notes**

1. *Conversations between the Chinese and Japanese Representatives in Regard to the Shantung Question* (Washington, D.C.: Government Printing Office, 1922), 2.

2. Yamato Ichihashi, *The Washington Conference and After* (New York: AMS Press, 1969), 288; quoting from H. G. W. Woodhead, *North China Herald*, 23 December 1922.

3. Wunsz King, "Woodrow Wilson, Wellington Koo and the China Question at the Paris Peace Conference," unpublished manuscript (dated 13 March 1959), Koo Papers, Columbia University.

4. For example, Rajendra Jain stated that the secret Russo-Japanese treaties were "nullified by the Russian Revolution of 1917." Rajendra Kumar Jain, *The USSR and Japan, 1945-1980* (New Delhi: Radiant Publishers, 1981), 5-6. Also see George Alexander Lensen, *Japanese Recognition of the U.S.S.R. Soviet-Japanese Relations, 1921-1930* (Tokyo: Sophia University Press, 1970), 365; Savitri Vishwanathan, *Normalization of Japanese-Soviet Relations, 1945-1970* (Tallahassee, Florida: The Diplomatic Press, 1973), 7. After World War II, the Japanese Foreign Ministry even collected and published in 1951 a list of all of Japan's pre-war treaties with various countries. Under the heading Russia/USSR, the secret treaties of 1907, 1910, 1912, 1916 were not listed. This publication noted that in 1925 the Soviet and Japanese governments agreed that all treaties "prior to Nov. 7, 1917, shall be re-examined at a conference to be subsequently held between the two governments," but then added that "no such conference was held between Japan and the USSR nor was any measure taken by either party to revise or denounce these treaties." Although admitting that a Soviet-Japanese conference had never revised these earlier agreements, this publication then falsely concluded that the four secret Russo-Japanese treaties had been "deemed void under obvious circumstances."

5. 23 January 1925, "Is it East Against West?" *Oregon Journal*.

6. 8 April 1925, "Viscount Goto's Proposal," *Honolulu Star-Bulletin*.

7. Chinliang Lawrence Huang, "Japan's China Policy Under the Premier Tanaka, 1927-1929," New York University Ph.D. Dissertation, 1968, 31.

8. S.C.M. Paine, "The Impact of the Sino-Japanese War (1894-5) on Russian Foreign Policy," *Asian Cultural Studies*, Vol. 25 (30 March 1999), 13-28.

9. Gaimushō, F 192.5-4-4. In this document, C. T. Wang urges Japan to oppose the Soviet "armed invasion" of Manchuria.

10. Ikuhiko Hata, *Reality and Illusion: The Hidden Crisis Between Japan and the U.S.S.R., 1932-1934* (New York: Columbia University Press, 1967), 4.

11. Viswanathan, 7.

12. George Alexander Lensen, *The Strange Neutrality: Soviet-Japanese Relations during the Second World War, 1941-1945* (Tallahassee, Florida: The Diplomatic Press, 1972), 1.

13. Jain, 6-7.

14. Foreign Minister Georgii Chicherin also predicted in 1925 that these tensions would result in Japan's "coming war" with America. Lensen, *Japanese Recognition*, preface.

15. Hoover Institution Archives, Loy W. Henderson Collection, Volume Five, 978-980; also quoted in: George W. Baer, ed., *A Question of Trust–The Origins of U.S.-Soviet Diplomatic Relations: The Memoirs of Loy W. Henderson* (Stanford: Hoover Institution Press, 1986), 469.

16. Library of Congress, Manuscript Division, W. Averell Harriman collection, Box 181: "Yalta Agreement Affecting China," 8-9; this document was declassified in 1986, but only became available in the Library of Congress during 1990 due to restrictions on the Harriman collection.

17. 2 July 1945–14 August 1945, "Notes taken at Sino-Soviet Conferences," 76 pages, Hoover Institution Archives, Victor Hoo collection, Box 7, 4.

18. 14 August 1945, "Meeting between Dr. Soong and Mr. Molotov," 3 pages, Hoover Institution Archives, Victor Hoo collection, Box 7, 3.

# Appendix A:
# 27 January 1919 Notes

(THIS DOCUMENT IS THE PROPERTY OF HIS BRITANNIC MAJESTY'S GOV'T.)

SECRET.

DECLASSIFIED

I.C.122.   Secretary's Note of a Conversation held in Pichon's Room at the Quai d'Orsay, Paris, on Monday, January 27th, 1919, at 15.00 hrs.

PRESENT

| AMERICA | BRITISH EMPIRE | FRANCE |
|---|---|---|
| President Wilson | The Rt.Hon.D.Lloyd George,M.P. | M. Clemenceau |
| Mr. R. Lansing | The Rt.Hon.A.J.Smuts, M.P. | M. Pichon |
| Dr. G. J. Beer | The RT.Hon.Sir R.L.Borden,G.C.M.G. | M. Dutasta |
| Prof. E.T.Williams | The RT.Hon.W.M.Hughes | M. Borthelot |
| Mr. A. H. Frazier | Gen.The Rt.Hon.L.Botha | Capt. Portier |
| Mr. L. Harrison | The Rt.Hon.W.F.Massey | |
| Col. U.S.Grant | Lt.-Col.Sir M.P.A.Hankey,K.C.P. | |
| | Major A.M.Caccia, M.V.θ. | |
| | Mr. H. Norman | |

| ITALY | JAPAN | CHINA |
|---|---|---|
| M. Orlando | Baron Makino | Dr. C. Thomas Wang |
| M. Sonnino | H.E.M.Matsui | Dr. V.K.Wellington Koo |
| Count Aldrovandi | M.Saburi | Mr. W. P. Wei |
| Major A. Jones | | |

Interpreter -------------------- Professor P. J. Mantoux.

183

M. Clemenceau having declared the meeting opened, said that he would call on the Japanese representatives, Baron Makino to put forward the views of the Japanese Government on the question of the Pacific, with special reference to the German Pacific Islands. It had been decided to take into consideration the question of Kiaochow at a subsequent meeting.

Baron Makino then read the following statement:-

"The Japanese Government feel justified in claiming from the German Government the unconditional cession of:

(a) The leased territory of Kiaochow together with the railways, and other rights possessed by Germany in respect of Shantung province.

(b) All of the Islands in German possession in the Pacific Ocean North of the Equator together with the rights and properties in connection therewith.

At the outbreak of the war, the German military and naval base at Kiaochow constituted a serious menace to the international trade and shipping, jeopardising the peace in the Extreme Orient. The Japanese Government in consultation with the British Government conformably with the agreement of 1911, gave notice to the German Government to surrender the leased territory of Kiaochow with a view to its restoration to China. The German Government failing to make reply within the specific time limit, no other course was left to Japan but to proceed to reduce the German base by recourse to arms. The Japanese forces have, in conjunction with the British contingents, succeeded in taking the leased territory as well as the railway line connecting Tsingtao with Chinanfu, which the Germans used for military purposes. Japan had since continued in possession of the rights then enjoyed by Germany. By the reduction of the German stronghold, the base of her military as well as political offensive in the Extreme Orient has been completely destroyed, thereby re-establishing the uninterrupted course of trade, commerce, and communication in these regions.

Now that the primary object for which Japan entered the war and which was clearly set forth in her Declaration of war against Germany,

has

has been successfully achieved, Japan cannot view with equinimity anything that may tend to revive German activities in the Far East to the undoing of all that has been achieved at no small sacrifice, and is compelled to advance the claims under item A.

Subsequently to the fall of Kiaochow it became a matter of urgent necessity to clear the Indian and Pacific Oceans, including the Australian routes, of the enemy ships and to keep these waters free and secure from enemy raids; and for carrying out this object, the Japanese navy extended its sphere of activities in cooperation with those of the British navy. The enemy ships had been planning to escape from the superior Japanese and British naval forces, and the Japanese squadron, upon arrival at Panope, of the East Caroline group, found that they had just left. From the objects and materials left behind, it was abundently claer that a full preparation for further raids was being made, using the harbour as their naval base. The circumstances demanded that the German South Sea Islands should forthwith be taken possession of in order to defeat the enemy's object, and the German possessions North of the Equator have since remained under Japanese occupation and control. The inhabitants of these Islands are being given employment so as to endure livelihood for them, besides being provided with schools for their instruction, and they are fully contented under the present regime. The total area of these Islands is about two thousand five hundred square kilèmeters with the population of some fifty thousands in all, composed of many different tribes. These tribes have each its own peculiar language, unable to understand one another without resorting to the medium of interpretations; and being on the whole still in a primitive state, they are not in a position to organize themselves politically, economically, or socially, in the modern sense. Japan being in actual possession and having regard to the circumstances which led to such occupation and to the present conditions above alluded to, and further, in view of the public opinion of Japan which is unanimous in this conncetion, she claims the definite possession of these Islands where she may continue to protect the inhabitants and to endeavour to

better better

better their conditions.

In conclusion, it may be stated that, in view of the extent of their efforts and achievements in destroying German base in the Extreme Orient and the South Seas, and in safeguarding the important routes on the Pacific and Indian Oceans and the Mediterranean waters, to say nothing of their contribution in other respects, the Japanese Government feel confident that the claims above advanced would be regarded as only just and fair."

Baron Makino added that a documentary statement setting forth the Japanese claims in full would be handed in by him at a later date.

Dr. Koo said that the question was of such vital interest to China that he hoped the Great Powers would reserve decision until the views of China had been heard.

(This was agreed to)


(The discussion passed to the principle of mandatory system.)

# Appendix B:
# 28 January 1919 Notes

(After the discussion of the mandatory system)

(THIS DOCUMENT IS THE PROPERTY OF HIS BRITANNIC MAJESTY'S GOVERNMENT.)

SECRET.

I.C.123.  SECRETARY'S NOTES OF A CONVERSATION
         HELD IN M. PICHON'S ROOM AT THE
REVISE). QUAI D'ORSAY, PARIS, ON TUESDAY,
         JANUARY 28th, 1919, at 11 hrs.

| AMERICA | BRITISH EMPIRE | FRANCE |
|---|---|---|
| President Wilson | The Rt.Hon.D.Lloyd George,M.P. | M.Clemenceau |
| Mr. R. Lansing | The Rt.Hon.A.J.Balfour,M.P. | M. Pichon |
| Mr. A.H.Frazier | The Rt.Hon.Sir R.L.Borden | M.Dutasta |
| Mr. L. Harrison | The Rt.Hon.W.M.Hughes | M. Berthelot |
| Col. Williams | Gen.The Rt.Hon.L.Botha | Capt. Portier |
| Dr. L. Beer | The Rt.Hon.W.P.Massey | |
| Prof.E.T.Williams | Lt.-Col.Sir M.P.A.Hankey | |
| | Captain E.Abraham | |
| | Mr. E. Philipps. | |

| ITALY | JAPAN | CHINA |
|---|---|---|
| M. Orlando | Baron Makino | Dr. C. Thomas Wang |
| M. Sonnino | H.E.M.Matsui | Dr. V. K. Wellington Koo |
| Count Aldrovandi | Viscount Chinda | Mr. Chuan Chao |
| Major Jones | General Nava | |
| | M. Yamakawa | |
| | M. Saburi | |

Interpreter ---------- Professor P. J. Mantoux.

187

## APPENDIX B

(After the discussion of the Mandatory System)

M. Clemenceau said that this part of the discussion was now adjourned. The Council would proceed to discuss the question of the German possessions in the Far East, together with the Chinese Delegates.

2. German leasehold rights in China.

Mr. Koo said that he was very glad, on behalf of China, to have the opportunity of putting the case of his country before the Conference. He had heard with interest the Dominion speakers, who spoke on behalf of a few million people. He felt his own responsibility was enhanced by the fact that he was the spokesman of 400 million people, one quarter of the human race.

The Chinese Delegation would ask the Peace Conference for the restoration to China of the leased territory of Kiaochow, the railway in Shantung, and all other rights Germany possessed in that Province before the war. He would confine himself to broad principles in order not to employ too much of the Council's time. Technical details would be explained in full in a memorandum which he proposed to submit.

The territories in question were an integral part of China. They were part of a province containing 36 million inhabitants, of Chinese in race, language and religion. The history of the lease to Germany was doubtless familiar to all. The lease had been wrung out of China by force. The German fleet had occupied the coast of Shantung and landing parties had penetrated into the interior. The lease had been extorted as a price for the withdrawal of the expedition. The pretext for this proceeding was the accidental killing of two missionaries in the interior of the country in a manner quite beyond the control of the Chinese Government. On the principle of nationality and of territorial integrity principles accepted by the Conference, China had a right to the restoration of these territories. The Chinese Delegation would feel that this was one of the conditions of a just peace. If, on the other hand, the Congress were to take a different view and were to transfer these territories to any other Power, it would, in the eyes of the Chinese Delegation, be adding one wrong to another.

The Shantung Province, in which Kiaochow and the railway to Chinanfu

Chinanfu were situated, was the cradle of Chinese civilization, the birthplace of Confucius and Mencius and a Holy Land for the Chinese. All eyes of the people in China were centered on this province which had always taken an important part in the development of China.

Economically, it was a densely populated country, with 36 million people in an area of only 35,000 square miles. The density of the population produced an intense competition and rendered the country quite unsuitable for colonization. The introduction of a Foreign Power could only lead to the exploitation of the inhabitants, and not to genuine colonization.

Strategically, Kiaochow commanded one of the main gateways of North China. It controlled one of the shortest approaches from the sea to Peking, namely the railway to Chinanfu which, at its junction with the railway from Tientsin, led straight to the capital. In the interest of Chinese national defence which in time would be organised, the Chinese Delegation would be unable to admit that any Foreign Power had claims to so vital a point.

China was fully cognisant of the service rendered to her by the heroic Army and Navy of Japan in rooting out German power from Shantung. China was also deeply indebted to Great Britain for helping in this task at a time of great peril to herself in Europe. China was also not forgetful of the services rendered to her by the troops of the other Allies in Europe, which had held in check an enemy who might otherwise have easily sent reinforcements to the Far East and thereby prolonged hostilities there. China appreciated these services all the more because her people in Shantung had also suffered and sacrificed in connection with the military operations for the capture of Kiaochow, especially in regard to requisitions for labour and supplies of all kinds.

But, grateful as they were, the Chinese Delegation felt that they would be false to their duty to China and to the world if they did not object to paying their debts of gratitude by selling the birthright of their countrymen, and thereby sowing seeds of discord, for

the

the future. The Chinese Delegation therefore trusted that the Conference, in considering the disposal of the leased territory and other rights held by Germany in Shantung, would give full weight to the fundamental and transcendant rights of China, the rights of political sovereignty and territorial integrity, as well as to her earnest desire to serve the cause of universal peace.

Baron Makino said that he had listened with great attention to what had fallen from his Chinese colleague concerning the direct restitution of Kiaochow to China. In the statement put forward on the previous day, he had explained the reason for which the Japanese Government had undertaken the reduction of this German stronghold.

As the question of restitution of the fortress had been raised, he thought it useful to read the words of the Japanese ultimatum to Germany because it had a bearing on the purpose in hand:-

"Considering it highly important and necessary in the present situation to take measures to remove all causes of disturbance to the peace of the Far East, and to safeguard the general intercourse contemplated by the agreement of the Alliance between Japan and Great Britain, in order to secure a firm and enduring peace in Eastern Asia, the establishment of which is the aim of the said agreement - the Imperial Japanese Government sincerely believe it their duty to give advice to the Imperial German Government to carry out the following two propositions:

(1) To withdraw immediately from Japanese and Chinese waters German men-of-war and armed vessels of all kinds, and to disarm at once those which cannot be withdrawn.

(2) To deliver on a date not later than the 15th September, 1914, to the Imperial Japanese authorities without condition and compensation the entire leased territory of Kiaochow, with a view to eventual restoration of the same to China."

Since the occupation of Kiaochow, Japan had been in actual possession. In view of all that had passed between the Governments of China and Japan, Baron Makino thought that China fully realised the import of Japanese occupation. The friendly interchange of views on this subject had been entered into and Japan had agreed to restore Kiaochow

Kiaochow as soon as Japan had free disposal of the place. Agreements had also been reached with regard to the leased railways.

As notes had been exchanged, he thought that a statement of these engagements might be worth the consideration of the members of the Council.

President Wilson asked Baron Makino whether he proposed to lay these notes before the Council.

Baron Makino said that he did not think the Japanese Government would raise any objection, but as the request was an unexpected one, he would be compelled to ask its permission.

President Wilson asked on behalf of China if Mr. Koo would do likewise.

Mr. Koo said that the Chinese Government had no objection to raise.

M. Clemenceau asked both the Japanese and Chinese Delegates to state whether they would make known to the Council the conditions of the restoration agreed between them.

Baron Makino said that he would do so, provided his Government would make no objection. He did not think it would, If it were within his own power, he would produce these documents as soon as possible. There was however, one point he wished to make clear. Japan was in actual possession of the territory under consideration. It had taken it by conquest from Germany. Before disposing of it to a third party it was necessary that Japan should obtain the right of free disposal from Germany.

President Wilson pointed out that the Council was dealing with territories and cessions previously German without consulting Germany at all.

Baron Makino said that the work now in hand was one of preparation for the presentment of the case to Germany. It followed therefore that the cession of Kiaochow would have to be agreed upon by Germany before it was carried out. What should take place thereafter had already been the subject of an intercourse of views with China.

Mr. Koo

Mr. Koo said that China did not hold quite the same view as Baron Makino regarding the restoration of Kiaochow. He was far from desiring, in his statement of China's case, even to intimate that Japan, after obtaining the leased territory and other rights in Shantung from Germany, would not return them to China. In fact, he added, China had every confidence in Japan's assurances to her and the world that she, Japan, would not retain them, herself; and he was particularly glad to hear Baron Makino confirm theses assurances before the Conference. But there was a choice between direct and indirect restitution. Of the two China would prefer the first. It was always easier to take one step than two if it had led to the same place.

As to the arrangements referred to by the Plenipotentiary from Japan, Mr. Koo presumed that reference was to the treaties and notes made in consequence of the negotiations on the twenty-one demands in 1915. It was not necessary to describe in detail the circumstances which were, to say the least, disconcerting to the Chinese Government, as the latter was constrained to agree to them only after an ultimatum from Japan. Quite apart from the circumstances of their making, however, they were at best, in the view of the Chinese Government, only provisional and temporary arrangements subject to the final review of this Conference, because they were questions arisen from the war.

Furthermore, even if the treaties and notes had been entirely valid, the fact of China's declaration of war on Germany had altered the situation in such a way that on the principle of rebus stantibus they could not be transferred enforced to-day. China had been made to g agree that she would give full assent to whatever arrangements Japan might agree with Germany on the disposition of Germany's rights, privileges and Concessions in Shantung. But the provision did not preclude China's joining the war nor did it prevent China from participating in this Conference as a belligerent; nor could it therefore preclude her from demanding from Germany direct restitution of her rights.

Moreover, in her Declaration of War against Germany, China expressly stated that all treaties and conventions concluded between China and Germany should be considered as nullified by the state of

-6-

war between them. If then the leased conventions had been so terminated the leased territory of Kiaochow and such other rights and privileges enjoyed by Germany in Shantung had all reverted to China as the territorial sovereign.

Even if the lease had not been terminated by China's declaration of war, Germany would be incompetent to transfer it to any other power than China because of an express provision therein against transfer to another Power.

(The Meeting then adjourned)

Villa Majestic, Paris.
January 28th, 1919.

Interpreter ............ Professor ...........

# Appendix C:
# 22 April 1919 Notes

SECRET

DECLASSIFIED

NOTES OF A MEETING WHICH TOOK PLACE AT
PRESIDENT WILSON'S HOUSE, PLACE DES ETATS-UNIS, PARIS,
ON TUESDAY, APRIL 22nd, 1919, at 4.30 p.m.

PRESENT

United States of America
President Wilson

British Empire
The Right Hon. D. Lloyd George, M.P

China
Mr. Lou Tseng Tsiang.
Mr. V. K. Wellington Koo.

Accompanied by:

Mr. Chuan Chao.
Mr. William Hsieh.

France
M. Georges Clemenceau

Secretary,    Sir M.P.A. Hankey, K.C.B.
Interpreter,  Professor P. J. Mantoux.

Kiauchau and Shantung

The Chinese Case

1. President Wilson said that the Chinese Plenipotentiaries know the interest he felt in the Kiauchau-Shantung settlement. On the previous day he had a Conference with the Japanese representatives, and this morning they had come to confer. M. Orlando, unfortunately, could not be present. Since he had last seen Mr. Koo, he had carefully read the documents, from which he gathered the following was the chain of events.

Before China entered into the war, there had been an exchange of Notes. He thought in 1915 (Mr. Koo said it was the 25th May). In that exchange of notes, the Japanese Government had said that when the German rights in

-2-

Kiauchau were transferred after the war to Japan, Japan would return them to China. The Chinese Government had taken note of this. Subsequently, there had been a further exchange of notes, and he believed, also a Treaty although he had only seen Notes, in which the Japanese Government laid down certain conditions. The Chinese Government had accepted these conditions. Great Britain and France (Mr. Lloyd George said that this had occured between the two exchanges of Notes between China and Japan) had entered into a similar but not identical agreement with Japan to the effect that they would support the claims of the Japanese Government on the Continent and in the island North of the Equator. In the case of the British Government it had been on the understanding that Japan supported her claim to German islands South of the Equator. Hence, Great Britain and France were in much the same position in the matter.

Mr. Lloyd George explained that at that time the submarine campaign had become very formidable. Most of the British torpedo-boat-destroyers were in the North Sea, and there was a shortage of those craft in the Mediterranean. Japanese help was urgently required, and Japan had asked for the arrangement to be made. We had been very hard pressed, and had agreed.

President Wilson then read extracts from the exchange of Notes printed on page 62 of the Official Claim of China for direct restitution to herself of the leased territory of Kiauchau, etc., circulated by the Chinese Delegation:-

"When, after the termination of the present War, the leased territory of Kiauchau Bay is completely left to the free disposal of Japan, the Japanese Government will restore the said leased territory to China under the following conditions".

-3-

He then read the following reply of the Chinese Foreign Minister, in which, after rehearsing the whole of the Japanese Notes, he had said "In reply, I beg to state that I have taken note of this declaration". He then read an extract from page 82, namely, exchange of Notes dated September 24, 1918.

> "The Japanese Government, mindful of the amiable relations between our two countries and out of a spirit of friendly cooperation, propose to adjust all the questions relating to Shantung in accordance with the following articles:
> 1. Japanese troops along the Kiaochow-Chinan railway, except a contingent of them to be stationed at Chinanfu, shall be withdrawn to Tsingtao.
> 2. The Chinese Government may organise a Police Force to undertake the policing of the Kiaochow-Chinan railway.
> 3. The Kiaochow-Chinan Railway is to provide a reasonable amount to defray the expense for the maintenance of the above-mentioned Police Force.
> 4. Japanese are to be employed at the Headquarter of the above-mentioned Police Force, at the principal railway stations, and at the Police Training School.
> 5. Chinese citizens shall be employed by the Kiaochow-Chinan Railway Administration as part of its staff.
> 6. The Kiaochow-Chinan Railway, after its ownership is definitely determined, is to be made a Chino-Japanese joint enterprise.
> 7. The Civil Administration established by Japan and existing now is to be abolished.
> The Japanese Government desires to be advised of the attitude of your Government regarding the above-mentioned proposal."

To this the Chinese Minister had replied:-

> "In reply I have the honour to state that the Chinese Government are pleased to agree to the above articles proposed by the Japanese Government."

The Chinese Delegation would see, President Wilson continued, the embarrassing position which had been reached. Mr. Lloyd George and M. Clemenceau were bound to support the claims of Japan. Alongside of them the Chinese had their exchange of notes with Japan. He reminded Mr. Koo that when urging his case before the Council of Ten at the Quai d'Orsay, he had maintained that the war cancelled the agreement with the German Government.

It did not, however, cancel the agreement between China and the Japanese Government, which had been made before the war. What he had himself urged upon the Japanese was that, as in the case of the Pacific Islands, the leased territory of Kiaochow should be settled by putting it into the hands of the Five Powers as Trustees. He did not suggest that Treaties should be broken, but that it might be possible, in Conference, to bring about an agreement by modifying the Treaty. He also proposed to them that all Governments should renounce the special rights they had acquired in China, so as to put China in a position free from the special limitations which had been imposed upon her. The Japanese were not willing to have Kiaochow handed over to the Five Powers, and the British and French Governments were embarrassed by their Treaties. When he pressed the Japanese for explanations of the meaning of their agreement, they had replied that the exploitation of two coal-mines and one iron-mine had not proved a successful venture, and were now bound up with the railway. They stated, however, that they would withdraw the civil administration; that they would maintain troops only on the termini of the railway; and that if a general agreement was reached, they would withdraw their extra-territoriality. They urged that they wanted a community of interest with the Chinese in the railway, and the only reserve they made was for a residential district in Kiaochow.

Mr. Koo said that the Treaties of 1915 and the subsequent exchange of Notes were the outcome of the 21 demands which Japan had made on China and were all part and parcel of one transaction. He hoped he had made this clear before the Council of Ten. He felt that the Treaties and Notes which had been exchanged after Japan had delivered an ultimatum stood outside of the regular procedure and course of Treaties. They dealt with matters arising out of the war.

Mr. Lloyd George asked what ultimatum he referred to.

President Wilson asked if Mr. Lloyd George had never heard of the twenty-one points.

Mr. Lloyd George said he had not.

Mr. Koo said that in January 1915 after the capture of Kiaochow that port had been opened up to trade; China then asked Japan to withdraw her troops from the interior of the Province. The Japanese took occasion to treat this note as though it were an unfriendly act and shortly after sprung on China twenty-one demands divided into five groups - for example, that China should accept Japanese advisers; that they should give up railway concessions in which Western Powers were concerned, and he would draw Mr. Lloyd George's attention to the fact that Great Britain was concerned. China was put in an extremely embarrassing position. She resisted and resisted and only gave up when she was absolutely compelled to. On the 7th, May the Japanese sent China an ultimatum in regard to the majority of demands giving China only 48 hours within which to accept; otherwise Japan would consider herself free to take such steps as she thought fit to enforce them. This caused absolute consternation to the Chinese Government which eventually had to submit to force majaeure.

Mr. Lloyd George asked if they had not appealed to the United States of America.

President Wilson said they had and the United States had intervened in regard to the infringement of sovereignty and political independence. The whole transaction, however, had been kept extremely secret and the United States only learnt of it in a roundabout way.

Mr. Koo said that secrecy had been imposed upon China by Japan upon severe penalties. It had been said that Japan had informed the Allied Governments and the United States Government that there had been only 11 Demands; but actually 21 Demands had been made on China. The Chinese Government felt that the Treaties and Notes exchanged as a result of these demands followed by an ultimatum were on a different footing from the ordinary. China had always endeavored to carry out to the letter to engagements made in good faith. These, however, had been made against China's free will, and the same applied to the notes exchanged in the previous year. For the last four years since they had captured Kiaochow, Japanese troops had penetrated far into the Province of Shantung, where there was a population of 36,000,000 people. This had been very uncomfortable for the general population, and the results had been disturbance and trouble. The Chinese Government had protested and asked Japan to withdraw her troops who were stationed 250 miles up the railway, but they had refused and had established civil administration bureaux in the interior of Shantung and extended their control even over the Chinese people by levying taxes on Chinese people and asserting judicial power over them. The feelings of the Chinese people against the extension of Japanese control were so strong that the Chinese Government felt constrained to take some immediate step to induce Japan to withdraw her troops and remove the civil administration bureaux, the object being to relieve the tense situation until the question could be finally settled at the Peace Conference.

Mr. Lloyd George said that it looked that by the Treaty with China, the Japanese Government would get more than the Germans had had. He asked Mr. Koo which he would prefer:- the Treaty with Japan, or the transference to Japan of the German rights?

Mr. Koo said that the situation was so difficult that he felt he must speak very frankly. The Japanese position was so close to China; especially in Manchuria, where they occupied a railway which was connected with Pekin; that merely to transfer German rights would create a very serious situation. With the Japanese on the Manchurian railway, and the Shantung railway, Pekin would be - as it were - in a pincers.

President Wilson pointed out that the Japanese claimed that the administration of the Shantung railway would be a joint one, and they proposed to withdraw the Japanese administration.

Mr. Lloyd George said that Mr. Koo had not quite answered his point. Supposing the Great Powers had to decide (and this really was his position since he was bound by a Treaty) between Japan inheriting Germany's rights in Shantung or exercising the rights under the treaty with Japan, which would China prefer? He pointed out that Great Britain was only bound by the rights which Japan inherited from Germany.

President Wilson said that if Japan inherited the German rights, it would involve her retaining the leased territory. He thought Mr. Lloyd George's point was that possibly Japan was claiming greater rights than Germany had exercised. As the British and French Governments had to support the Japanese claim to what Germany had had, they wanted to know whether China would be better off according as Japan could exercise the rights that Germany had or those that she obtained by her Treaty.

Mr. Lloyd George agreed that this was the point, and said the real question was whether the Treaty with Japan was better for China than Germany's rights.

(At this point there was an interval to permit the Chinese plenipotentiaries to confer).

Mr. Koo said that he had now consulted his colleague. He could make no choice, because both alternatives were unacceptable; he would merely compare them. The Treaty and Notes with Japan provided for restoration of the leased territory to China on certain conditions, but such restoration would be only nominal. Between the two, he thought that the German rights were more limited than the rights claimed by Japan under her Treaty and Notes with China. Even mere succession to the German rights, however, would create a grave situation for China's future. In claiming direct restitution of German rights, he was not asking for any compensation or remuneration for China as a result of her entry into the war, but only for what was necessary for peace in the Far East. The experience of the last three years made it so clear what the Chinese position would be if Japan was allowed either to succeed to the German rights in Shantung or to retain the rights she claimed under her treaty with China. It was an uncomfortable position both to the Chinese people and the Government. He was

-9-

not in the least exaggerating, but only saying what was necessary to explain the situation.

President Wilson said that M. Clemenceau and Mr. Lloyd George would bear witness that he had put the Chinese case as well as he could to the Japanese Delegation in the morning. He had emphasised the great need of trust and friendship between Japan and China, which he regarded as essential to peace in the Far East. He had urged that China should be free and unfettered to carry out her development. What he asked now was only a means of getting out of a position that was extremely difficult. In this Conference the United States of America was the only power that was entirely unbound. Great Britain, France, China and Japan were all bound by Treaties. They were bound to keep these treaties because the war had largely been fought for the purpose of showing that Treaties could not be violated.

Mr. Lloyd George suggested that in the exchange of notes of September 1918, China might have stood out.

Mr. Koo said that the exchange of notes in 1918 was the result of the Shantung Treaty, made in consequence of the 21 Demands. It was part of the same transaction.

President Wilson said that the exchange of notes had grown out of the previous agreement. He looked for the Shantung Treaty.

Mr. Koo said that it was on page 59 of China's Claim for Direct Restitution of Kiaochow, etc.

President Wilson read the following extracts from the Treaty and said that China had then had to accept and had had no other choice:

"Art. 1- The Chinese Government agrees to give full assent to all matters upon which the Japanese Government may hereafter agree with the German Government relating to the disposition of all rights, interests and concessions which Germany, by virtue of treaties or otherwise, possesses in relation to the Province of Shantung,

"Art. 2- The Chinese Government agrees that as regards the railway to be built by China herself from Chefoo or Lungkow to connect with the Kiaochow-Chinanfu railway, if Germany abandons the privilege of financing the Chefoo-Weihsien line China will approach Japanese capitalists to negotiate for a loan."

Mr. Lloyd George said he would like to have the two positions examined by British, French and American experts, and to learn their views as to which course would be best for China.

M. Clemenceau said he had no objection.

Mr. Lloyd George said that it was also only fair that China should be given more time to consider this question. This seemed to be the only alternative there was to acquiescing in the Treaties between China and Japan. Great Britain and France, however, were not bound by this latter Treaty, but only by their own arrangements with Japan.

President Wilson then read the following extracts from the 21 Demands on page 52 and 53 of the Chinese Document:

Group IV.

The Chinese Government engages not to cede or lease to a third Power any harbour or bay or island along the coast of China.

Group V.

Art. 1.- The Chinese Central Government shall employ influential Japanese advisers in political, financial, and military affairs.

Art. 3.- Inasmuch as the Japanese Government and the Chinese Government have had many cases of dispute between Japanese and Chinese police which caused no little misunderstanding, it is for this reason necessary that the police departments of important places (in China) shall be jointly administered by Japanese and Chinese or that the police department of these places shall employ numerous Japanese, so that they may at the same time help to plan for the improvement of the Chinese Police Service.

Art.4.- China shall purchase from Japan a fixed amount of munitions of war (say 50% or more of what is needed by the Chinese Government) or that there shall be established in China a Sino-Japanese jointly worked arsenal. Japanese technical experts are to be employed and Japanese material to be purchased."

-11-

President Wilson recalled that there were other demands designed to exclude other Powers from the commercial and industrial development;
(Mr. Koo said, on page 52.).

President Wilson read Article 1 of Group III as follows:

"The two Contracting parties mutually agree that when the opportune moment arrives the Hanyehping Company shall be made a joint concern of the two nations and they further agree that without the previous consent of Japan, China shall not by her act dispose of the rights and property of whatever nature of the said Company nor cause the said Company to dispose freely of the same."

Mr. Koo pointed out that the Hanyehping Company was the largest coal and iron mining Company of China, situated in the Yantze Valley. He requested the reading of Article 2 which, he said, was even more serious.

President Wilson read the following:

"Art. 2- The Chinese Government agrees that all mines in the neighbourhood of those owned by the Henyehping Company shall not be permitted, without the consent of the said Company, to be worked by other persons outside the said Company; and further agrees that if it is desired to carry out any undertaking which, it is apprehended, may directly or indirectly affect the interests of the said Company, the consent of the said Company shall first be obtained."

Mr. Lloyd George asked whether China had agreed to this Article.

Mr. Koo said that the Chinese Government had had to accept most of the 21 Demands with slight modifications. That was why China was seeking some redress.

President Wilson asked if the following point of view would make any appeal to the Chinese Plenipotentiaries? Hereafter whatever arrangements were made both Japan and China would be members of the League of Nations, which would guarantee their territorial integrity and political independence. That is to say, that these matters would become the concern of the League and China would receive a kind of protection that she had never had before to intervene. Before, it had been, comparatively speaking, none of our business to interfere in these matters. The Covenant, however, laid down that whatever affected the peace of the world was a matter of concern to the League of Nations and to call attention to such was not an hostile but a friendly act. He, himself, was prepared to advocate at the Council of the League and at the body of Delegates that the special positions occupied by the various nations in China should be abandoned. Japan declared that she was ready to support this. There would be a forum for advocating those matters. The interests of China could not then be overlooked. He was stating this as an element of security for China in the future if the Powers were unable to give her what she wanted now, and he asked the Chinese Delegates to think the matter over. While there was doubt as to the Treaty and Notes between China and Japan, there was no doubt whatsoever as to the agreements entered into by France and Great Britain. Hence, even if the agreements between them and Japan were abandoned, these two Governments were bound to support Japan in getting whatever rights in Shantung Germany had had. Hence, the question which the Chinese Plenipotentiaries had to consider was, would they prefer to retain the rights which Japan had secured in their treaty with her or would they prefer that Japan should inherit the German rights in Shantung.

Mr. Koo said that he could not lay too much emphasis on the fact that the Chinese people were now at the parting of the ways. The policy of the Chinese Government was cooperation with

Europe and the United States as well as Japan. If however, they did not get justice, China might be driven into the arms of Japan. There was a small section in China which believed in Asia for the Asiatics and wanted the closest cooperation with Japan. The position of the Government, however, was that they believed in the justice of the West and that their future lay there. If they failed to get justice there, the consequential reaction might be very great. Further, he wished to suggest that the validity of the arrangements was questionable owing to the following fact (1) They arose out of the War; (2) China had subsequently come into the war herself; (3) New principles had now been adopted by all the nations as the basis of the peace and the agreements with Japan appeared to be in conflict with them. Consequently, in thanking the Supreme Council for hearing the views of the Chinese Delegation, he wished to state the great importance of attaining a peace which could be relied on to endure for 50 years instead of a peace so unjust that it would only sow the seeds of early discord.

President Wilson said that these were serious considerations, but he would not like Mr. Koo even personally to entertain the idea that there was injustice in an arrangement that was based on Treaties which Japan had entered into. The sacredness of treaties had been one of the motives of the war. It had been necessary to show that treaties were not mere scraps of paper. If treaties were inconsistent with the principle on which the peace was being formed, nevertheless we could not undo past obligations. If that principle were accepted, we should have to go back and France would have the treaty of 1815 and there would be no end to it. He would not like to feel that because we were embarrassed by a treaty we were disregardful of justice. Moreover, the unjust treatment of China in the past had not be any means been confined to Japan. He hoped that the quandary in which the Powers were would be stated to the Chinese people. He hoped that it would be shown to them that the undoing of the trouble depended on China uniting in reality with other nations, including the Western nations. He felt absolute confidence that the opinion of the world had the greatest sympathy for the realm of China. The heart of the world went out to her 400 million people. Any statemen who ignore their fortunes were playing a dangerous game. But it would not do to identify justice with unfortunate engagements that ha d been entered into.

Mr. Koo said he believed prevention to be better than cure. He thought that it would be better to undo unfortunate engagements now, if they endangered the permanence of the future peace.

Mr. Lloyd George said the object of the war was not that. The war had been fought as much for the East as for the West. China also had been protected by the victory that had been won. If Germany had won the war and had desired Shantung or Pekin, she could have had them. The very doctrine of the mailed fist had been propounded in relation to China. The engagements that had been entered into with Japan had been contracted at a time when the support of that country was urgently needed. He would not say that the war could not have been won without this support. But he could say that Kiaochow could not have been captured without Japanese support. It was a solemn treaty and Great Britain could not turn round to Japan now and say "All right, thank you very much. When we wanted your help, you gave it, but now we think that

-15-

the treaty was a bad one and should not be carried out." Within the treaties he would go to the utmost limits to protect the position of China. On the League of Nations he would always be prepared to stand up for China against oppression, if there was oppression. China was a nation with a very great past and, he believed, with a still greater future. It would however, be of no service to her to regard treaties as Bethmann von Hollweg had regarded them, as mere scraps of paper to be turned down when they were not wanted.

M. Clemenceau said that Mr. Koo could take every word that Mr. Lloyd George had said as his also.

President Wilson asked whether assuming for the sake of argument that the engagements were unfortunate nevertheless they had been entered into for the salvation of China, because they had been entered into for the salvation of the world, of which China was a part. In fact, it would be said that the very engagements was instrumental for the salvation of China.

Mr. Koo said they had been designed apparently to meet a situation in Europe and not in the Far East.

Mr. Lloyd George pointed out that if Germany had won the war in Europe, she would have won it in the Far East also. The world would have been at her feet.

President Wilson pointed ou that the German project was not only domination from Hamburg to Bagdad but also the control of the East. Germany knew China to be rich. Her objects were mostly material. The Kaiser had been the great exponent of what was called the "Yellow Peril". He wanted to get to France and Great Britain out of the way and afterwards to get everything else he could.

-16-

One result of the war undoubtedly had been to save the Far East in particular, since that was as unexploited part of the world.

Mr. Lloyd George said that he wished to consider the question further before arriving at a decision.

President Wilson asked the Chinese Delegates also to give further consideration to the question and hoped that it could be taken up again.

(The Chinese Representatives then withdrew.)

Villa Majestic, Paris,
23rd April 1919.

# *Bibliography*

## MANUSCRIPT SOURCES

Bliss, Tasker, Papers, Library of Congress, Washington, D.C.
Department of State, Records, National Archives, Washington, D.C.
Foreign Ministry, Beijing Government, Records, Taipei, Taiwan.
Number Two Historical Archives, Nanjing, PRC.
Foreign Ministry, Japan, Records, Tokyo, Japan.
Hornbeck, Stanley K., Papers, Hoover Archives, Stanford University.
Koo, V. K. Wellington, Papers, Rare Book Library, Columbia University.
Lansing, Robert, Papers, Mudd Archives, Princeton University.
MacMurray, John V. A., Papers, Mudd Archives, Princeton University.
McCormick, Vance, Papers, Hoover Archives, Stanford University.
Trotsky, Leon, Papers, Houghton Library, Harvard University.
White, Henry, Papers, Library of Congress, Washington, D.C.
Williams, Edward T., Papers, Bancroft Library, University of California, Berkeley.
Wilson, Woodrow, Papers, Mudd Archives, Princeton University.
Wilson, Woodrow, Presidential Papers Microfilm Series, Washington, D.C.

## PUBLISHED CONTEMPORARY SOURCES

Baker, Ray Stannard. *What Wilson Did At Paris* (New York: Doubleday, Page & Company, 1919).
_____. *Woodrow Wilson and World Settlement* (Gloucester, MA: Peter Smith, 1960), Two Volumes.
_____. "How Japan Forced Shantung Clause," *New York Times*, 17 August 1919.
Buell, Raymond Leslie. *The Washington Conference* (New York: Russell & Russell, 1922).
Chen Gongbo. *The Communist Movement in China: An Essay Written in 1924* (New York: Octagon Books, 1966).
Daniels, Josephus. *The Life of Woodrow Wilson, 1956-1924* (Philadelphia, PA: John C. Winston Company, 1924).
Department of State. *Conversations Between the Chinese and Japanese Representatives in Regard to the Shantung Question* (Washington, D.C., 1922).
_____. *The Treaty of Versailles and After* (Washington, D.C., 1947).
Dillon, Emile Joseph. *The Inside Story of the Peace Conference* (New York: Harper & Brothers Publisher, 1920).
Dodd, William Edward. *Woodrow Wilson and His Work* (Garden City, NY: Doubleday, Page & Company, 1922).

Gouin, Gustave. *Why China Did Not Sign the Peace Treaty* (Paris: "La Vérité," 1919).

Grimm, E.D. (Гримм, Е. Д.), Сборник договоров и других документов по истории международных отношений на Дальнем Востоке *(1842-1925)* (*Collection of Treaties and Other Documents on the History of International Relations in the Far East [1842-1925]*), (Moscow, 1927).

House, Edward Mandell, and Seymour, Charles, eds. *What Really Happened at Paris* (New York: Charles Scribner's Sons, 1921).

Iyenaga, Toyokichi. "Iyenaga Decries Shantung Charge," *New York Times*, 1 August 1919.

Lansing, Robert. *The Peace Negotiations: A Personal Narrative*. (New York: Houghton Mifflin Company, 1921).

Liang Qichao. "China and the Shantung Settlement," *Manchester Guardian*, 16 June 1919.

_____. "Causes of China's Defeat at the Peace Conference," *Millard's Review*, 19 July 1919.

McMaster, John Bach. *The United States in the World War* (New York: D. Appleton and Company, 1920).

MacMurray, John V. A., ed. *Treaties and Agreements with and Concerning China, 1894-1919* (New York: Oxford University Press, 1921), Volume II.

Reinsch, Paul S. *An American Diplomat in China* (New York: Doubleday, Page & Company, 1922).

Robinson, Edgar Eugene. *The Foreign Policy of Woodrow Wilson, 1913-1917* (New York: The MacMillan Company, 1917).

State Department, *Official Documents Concerning Shantung* (Washington, D.C.: Press of National Publishing Co., 1922)

Sun Yat-sen. *The Vital Problem of China* (Taipei: China Cultural Service, 1953).

Tumulty, Joseph P. *Woodrow Wilson as I Know Him* (New York: Doubleday, Page & Company, 1921).

Vilenskii, Vladimir. Китай и Советская Россиия (*China and Soviet Russia* ), (Moscow, 1919).

Wilson, Woodrow. *Selected Addresses and Papers of Woodrow Wilson* (New York: Review of Review Corporation, 1924).

Wood, G. Zay. *The Shantung Question A Study in Diplomacy and World Politics* (New York: Fleming H. Revell Company, 1922).

中外舊約章彙編 (*A Collection of Chinese-Foreign Treaties*), (Beijing: Xinhua Publishers, 1982), Volume 1.

SECONDARY SOURCES

Ambrosius, Lloyd E. *Woodrow Wilson and the American Tradition: The Treaty Fight in Perspective* (New York: Cambridge University Press, 1987).

Baer, George W., ed. *A Question of Trust–The Origins of U.S.-Soviet Diplomatic Relations: The Memoirs of Loy W. Henderson* (Stanford, CA: Hoover Institution Press, 1986).

Bailey, Thomas A. *Wilson and the Peacemakers* (New York: The Macmillan Company, 1947).

———. *Woodrow Wilson And The Great Betrayal* (New York: The MacMillan Company, 1945).

Beers, Burton F. *Vain Endeavor: Robert Lansing's Attempts to End the American-Japanese Rivalry* (Durham, NC: Duke University Press, 1962).

Bianco, Lucien. *Origins of the Chinese Revolution, 1915-1949.* (Stanford, CA: Stanford University Press, 1967).

Black, Harold Garnet. *The True Woodrow Wilson: Crusader for Democracy* (New York: Fleming H. Revell Company, 1946).

Blum, John Morton. *Woodrow Wilson and the Politics of Morality* (Boston, MA: Little, Brown and Company, 1956).

Bose, Nemai Sadhan. *American Attitude and Policy to the Nationalist Movement in China (1911-1921) (Bombay: Orient Longmans, 1970).*

Canfield, Leon H. *The Presidency of Woodrow Wilson: Prelude to a World in Crisis* (Rutherford, NJ: Fairleigh Dickinson University Press, 1966).

Chan, F. Gilbert, and Etzold, Thomas H., eds. *China in the 1920s: Nationalism and Revolution* (New York: New Viewpoints, 1976).

Chen Duxiu (陈独秀), 陈独秀文章选编 (*Collection of Articles by Chen Duxiu*), (Beijing, 1984).

Chow Tse-Tsung. *The May 4th Movement–Intellectual Revolution in Modern China* (Cambridge, MA: Harvard University Press, 1980).

Chu Pao-chin. *V. K. Wellington Koo: A Case Study of China's Diplomat and Diplomacy of Nationalism* (Hong Kong: Chinese University Press, 1981).

Clements, Kendrick A. *Woodrow Wilson: World Statesman* (Boston: Twayne Publisher, 1987).

*A Collection of Chinese-Foreign Treaties* (Beijing: Xinhua Publishers, 1982), Volume 1.

Conyne, G.R. *Woodrow Wilson: British Perspective, 1912-21* (London: MacMillan Academic and Professional Ltd., 1992).

Cooper, John Milton Jr. *Breaking the Heart of the World: Woodrow Wilson and the Fight for the League of Nations* (New York: Cambridge University Press, 2001).

Cronon, E. David, ed. *The Political Thought of Woodrow Wilson* (New York: The Bobbs-Merrill Company Inc., 1965).

Curry, Roy Watson. *Woodrow Wilson and Far Eastern Policy, 1913-1921* (New York: Bookman Associates, 1957).

Day, Donald. *Woodrow Wilson's Own Story* (Boston, MA: Little, Brown and Compancy, 1952).

Deane, Hugh. *Good Deeds & Gunboats: Two Centuries of American-Chinese Encounters* (San Francisco, CA: China Books & Periodicals, 1990).

## BIBLIOGRAPHY

Degras, Jane. *Soviet Documents on Foreign Policy* (New York: Oxford University Press, 1952), Volume 1.

Dickinson, Frederick R. *War and National Reinvention: Japan in the Great War, 1914-1919* (Cambridge, MA: Harvard University Press, 1999).

Dirlik, Arif. *The Origins of Chinese Communism* (New York: Oxford University Press, 1989).

Dockrill, Michael L. & J. Douglas Goold. *Peace Without Promise: Britain and the Peace Conferences, 1919-23* (London: Batsford Academic and Educational Ltd, 1981).

Dos Passos, John. *Mr. Wilson's War* (Garden City, NY: Doubleday & Company, Inc, 1962).

Eiland, Murray L. III. *Woodrow Wilson: Architect of World War II* (New York: Peter Lang, 1991).

Elleman, Bruce A. *Diplomacy and Deception: The Secret History of Sino-Soviet Diplomatic Relations, 1917-1927* (Armonk, NY: M.E. Sharpe, 1997).

_____. *Modern Chinese Warfare, 1795-1989* (New York: Routledge Press, 2001).

Fairbank, John King. *The United States and China*. 3rd edition (Cambridge, MA: Harvard University Press, 1971).

_____. *China: A New History* (Cambridge, MA: The Belknap Press, 1992).

_____, and Feuerwerker, Albert, eds., *The Cambridge History of China*. Volume 13, Part 2 (New York: Cambridge University Press, 1986).

_____. *The Cambridge History of China*. Volume 12, Part 1 (New York: Cambridge University Press, 1983).

Feigon, Lee. *Chen Duxiu: Founder of the Chinese Communist Party* (Princeton, NJ: Princeton University Press, 1983).

Ferrell, Robert H. *Woodrow Wilson and World War I: 1917-1921* (New York: Harper & Row Publishers, 1985).

Fifield, Russell H. *Woodrow Wilson and the Far East* (New York: Thomas Y. Crowell Company, 1952).

Floto, Inga. *Colonel House in Paris* (Princeton, NJ: Princeton University Press, 1973).

Freud, Sigmund, and Bullitt, William C. *Thomas Woodrow Wilson: Twenty-eighth President of the United States* (Boston, MA: Houghton Mifflin Company, 1967).

Gardner, Lloyd C. *Wilson and Revolutions: 1913-1921* (Philadelphia, PA: J.B. Lippincott Company, 1976).

Godshall, Wilson Leon. "The International Aspects of the Shantung Question," University of Pennsylvania Ph.D. Dissertation, 1923.

_____. *Tsingtau Under Three Flags* (Shanghai, China: The Commercial Press, Ltd., 1929).

Goldstein, Erik, and Maurer, John, eds. *The Washington Conference, 1921-22: Naval Rivalry, East Asian Stability and the Road to Pearl Harbor* (Portland, OR: Frank Cass, 1994).

Han Suyin. *Eldest Son: Zhou Enlai and the Making of Modern China, 1898-1976* (New York: Hill and Wang, 1994).

Hatch, Alden. *Edith Bolling Wilson: First Lady Extraordinary* (New York: Dodd, Mead & Company, 1961).

Heater, Derek. *National Self-Determination: Woodrow Wilson and His Legacy* (New York: St. Martin's Press, 1994).

Heckscher, August. *Woodrow Wilson* (New York: Charles Scribners Sons, 1991).

Holubnychy, Lydia. *Borodin and the Chinese Revolution, 1923-1925* (New York: Columbia East Asian Institute, 1979).

Hoston, Germaine. *Marxism and the Crisis of Development in Prewar Japan* (Princeton, NJ: Princeton University Press, 1986).

Houston, David F. *Eight Years With Wilson's Cabinet, 1913 to 1920: With a Personal Estimate of the President.* Volume 2 (New York: Doubleday, Page & Company, 1926).

Hsu, Immanuel C. Y. *The Rise of Modern China* (New York: Oxford University Press, 2000).

Hsueh Chun-tu, ed. *Revolutionary Leaders of Modern China* (New York: Oxford University Press, 1971).

Huang, Chinliang Lawrence. "Japan's China Policy Under the Premier Tanaka, 1927-1929," New York University Ph.D. Dissertation, 1968.

Hunt, Michael H. *The Genesis of Chinese Communist Foreign Policy* (New York: Columbia University Press, 1996).

_____, and Niu Jun, eds. *Toward a History of Chinese Communist Foreign Relations, 1920-1960s* (Washington, D.C.: Woodrow Wilson Center Asia Program, 1992).

Iriye, Akira. *After Imperialism: The Search for a New Order in the Far East, 1921-1931* (Cambridge, MA: Harvard University Press, 1965).

Isaacs, Harold R. *The Tragedy of the Chinese Revolution* (Stanford, CA: Stanford University Press, 1961).

Israel, John. *Student Nationalism in China, 1927-1937* (Stanford, CA: Hoover Institution Press, 1966).

Jacobs, Dan N. *Borodin, Stalin's Man in China* (Cambridge, MA: Harvard University Press, 1981).

Jain, Rajendra Kumar. *The USSR and Japan, 1945-1980* (New Delhi: Radiant Publishers, 1981).

Kajima, Morinosuke. *The Diplomacy of Japan, 1884-1922* (Tokyo: Kajima Institute of International Peace, 1980).

Kawamura, Noriko. *Turbulence in the Pacific: Japanese-U.S. Relations During World War I* (Westport, CT: Praeger Press, 2000).

Kerney, James. *The Political Education of Woodrow Wilson* (New York: The Century Co., 1926).

King, Wunsz. *Woodrow Wilson, Wellington Koo and the China Question at the Paris Peace Conference* (Leyden: A. W. Sythoff, 1959).

_____. *China at the Paris Peace Conference in 1919* (New York: St. John's University Press, 1961).
Knock, Thomas J. *To End All Wars: Woodrow Wilson and the Quest for a New World Order* (New York: Oxford University Press, 1992).
Kuo, Thomas C. *Ch'en Tu-hsiu (1879-1942) and the Chinese Communist Movement* (South Orange, NJ: Seton Hall University Press, 1975).
Lamb, Margaret and Tarling, Nicholas. *From Versailles to Pearl Harbor: The Origins of the Second World War in Europe and Asia* (New York: Palgrave, 2001).
Latham, Earl. *The Philosophy and Policies of Woodrow Wilson* (Chicago, IL: The University of Chicago Press, 1958).
Lensen, George Alexander. *Japanese Recognition of the U.S.S.R. Soviet-Japanese Relations, 1921-1930* (Tokyo: Sophia University Press, 1970).
Leong, Sow-theng. *Sino-Soviet Diplomatic Relations, 1917-1926* (Honolulu, HI: University Press of Hawaii, 1976).
Levenson, Joseph R. *Liang Ch'i-ch'ao and the Mind of Modern China* (Berkeley, CA: University of California Press, 1959).
Levine, Marilyn A. *The Found Generation: Chinese Communists in Europe during the Twenties* (Seattle, WA: University of Washington Press, 1993).
Li Zhisui. *The Private Life of Chairman Mao* (New York: Random House, 1994).
Li, Tien-yi. *Woodrow Wilson's China Policy* (New York: University of Kansas City Press–Twayne Publishers, 1952).
Link, Arthur S. *Wilson the Diplomatists: A Look At His Major Foreign Policies* Baltimore, MD: The Johns Hopkins Press, 1957).
_____. *Woodrow Wilson and a Revolutionary World, 1913-1921* (Chapel Hill, N.C.: University of North Carolina Press, 1982).
_____. ed. *The Deliberations of the Council of Four (March 24-June 28, 1919) Notes of the Official Interpreter Paul Mantoux* (Princeton, NJ: Princeton University Press, 1992).
Loth, David. *Woodrow Wilson–The Fifteenth Point* (New York: J.B Lippincott Company, 1941).
MacMillan, Margaret. *Peacemakers: The Paris Conference of 1919 and its Attempt to End War* (London: John Murray, 2001).
Mao Zedong. *The May 4th Movement* (Beijing: Foreign Languages Press, 1969).
_____. *Selected Works of Mao Tse-tun.g* Volume Two (Beijing: Foreign Languages Press, 1965).
Marks, Sally. *The Illusion of Peace: International Relations in Europe, 1918-1933* (London: The MacMillan Press Ltd, 1976).
Mee, Charles L. Jr. *The End of Order: Versailles 1919* (New York: E.P. Dutton, 1980).
Meisner, Maurice. *Li Ta-chao and the Origins of Chinese Marxism* (Cambridge, MA: Harvard University Press, 1967).
Moseley, George. *China Since 1911* (New York: Harper & Row, 1968).

Nathan, Andrew J. *Peking Politics, 1918-1923: Factionalism and the Failure of Constitutionalism* (Berkeley, CA: University of California Press, 1976).

_____, and Link, Perry, eds. *The Tiananmen Papers: The Chinese Leadership's Decision to Use Force Against Their Own People—In Their Own Words* (New York: Public Affairs, 2001).

Nicolson, Harold. *Peacemaking 1919* (Gloucester, MA: Peter Smith, 1984).

Ninkovich, Frank. *Wilsonian Century: U.S. Foreign Policy since 1900* (Chicago, IL: The University of Chicago Press, 1999).

Noggle, Burl. *Into the Twenties: The United States From Armistice to Normalcy* (Chicago, IL: University of Illinois Press, 1974).

Nordholt, Jan Willem Schulte. *Woodrow Wilson: A Life For World Peace* (Berkeley, CA: University of California Press, 1991).

North, Robert C. *Moscow and the Chinese Communists* (Stanford, CA: Stanford University Press, 1963).

_____. *Chinese Communism* (New York: McGraw-Hill Book Company, 1966).

_____, and Eudin, Xenia Joukoff. *Soviet Russia and the East, 1920-1927* (Stanford, CA: Stanford University Press, 1957).

Notter, Harley. *The Origins of the Foreign Policy of Woodrow Wilson* (Baltimore, MD: The Johns Hopkins Press, 1937).

Ojha, Ishwar C. *Chinese Foreign Policy In An Age of Transition: The Diplomacy of Cultural Despair* (Boston, MA: Beacon Press, 1969).

Paine, S. C. M. *Imperial Rivals: China, Russia, and Their Disputed Frontier* (Armonk, NY: M.E. Sharpe, 1996).

_____. *The Sino-Japanese War, 1894-5: Perceptions, Power, and Primacy* (New York: Cambridge University Press, 2002).

Paxson, Frederic L. *Postwar Years: Normalcy, 1918-1923* (Berkeley, CA: University of California Press, 1948).

Parsons, Edward B. *Wilsonian Diplomacy: Allied-American Rivalries in War and Peace* (St. Louis, MO: Forum Press, 1978).

Pisney, Raymond F. *Woodrow Wilson in Retrospect* (Verona, VA: McClure Printing Company Inc., 1978).

Price, Ernest Batson. *The Russo-Japanese Treaties of 1907-1916 Concerning Manchuria and Mongolia* (Baltimore, MD: The Johns Hopkins Press, 1933).

Pugach, Noel H. *Paul S. Reinsch: Open Door Diplomat in Action* (Millwood, NY: KTO Press, 1979).

Restarick, Henry Bond. *Sun Yat-sen: Liberator of China* (New Haven, CT: Yale University Press, 1931).

Rice, Edward E. *Mao's Way* (Berkeley, CA: University of California Press, 1972).

Robertson, James Oliver. *No Third Choice: Progressives in Republican Politics, 1916-1921* (New York: Garland Publishing, Inc, 1983).

Rummel, R. J. *China's Bloody Century* (New Brunswick, NJ: Transaction Publishers, 1991).

Safford, Jeffrey J. *Wilsonian Maritime Diplomacy, 1913-1921* (New Brunswick, NJ: Rutgers University Press, 1978).
Saich, Tony. *The Origins of the First United Front in China: The Role of Sneevliet (Alias Maring)* (New York: E. J. Brill, 1991).
Saunders, Robert M. *In Search of Woodrow Wilson: Beliefs and Behavior* (Westport, CN: Greenwood Press, 1998).
Schrecker, John E. *The Chinese Revolution in Historical Perspective* (New York: Greenwood Press, 1991).
Schurmann, Franz, and Schell, Orville. *Republican China: Nationalism, War, and the Rise of Communism, 1911-1949* (New York: Vintage Books, 1967).
Schwartz, Benjamin I. *Chinese Communism and the Rise of Mao* (Cambridge, MA: Harvard University Press, 1979).
Seymour, Charles. *Woodrow Wilson and the World War: A Chronicle of Our Own Times* (New Haven, CT: Yale University Press, 1921).
_____. *The Intimate Papers of Colonel House: The Ending of the War* (New York: Houghton Mifflin Company, 1928).
Sharp, Alan. *The Versailles Settlement: Peacemaking in Paris, 1919* (London: MacMillan Education, Ltd., 1991).
Sheridan, James E. *China in Disintegration: The Republican Era in Chinese History, 1912-1949* (New York: Free Press, 1975).
Smith, Gene. *When the Cheering Stopped: The Last Years of Woodrow Wilson* (New York: William Morrow and Company, 1964).
Spence, Jonathan. *The Search for Modern China* (New York: W. W. Norton & Company, 1990).
Steigerwald, David. *Wilsonian Idealism in America* (Ithaca, NY: Cornell University Press, 1994).
Teng Ssu-yu, and Fairbank, John K. *China's Response to the West: A Documentary Survey, 1839-1923* (Cambridge, MA: Harvard University Press, 1954).
Tung, William L. *V. K. Wellington Koo and China's Wartime Diplomacy* (New York: St. John's University, 1977).
Whiting, Allen. *Soviet Policies in China, 1917-1924* (New York: Columbia University Press, 1954).
Wilbur, C. Martin, and Hoq, Julie Lien-ying. *Missionaries of Revolution: Soviet Advisers and Nationalist China, 1920-1927* (Cambridge, MA: Harvard University Press, 1989).
_____, ed., Chen Gongbo. *The Communist Movement in China* (New York: Columbia University East Asian Institute, 1960).
Wu Xiangxiang (吳相湘). 俄帝侵略中國史 (*The History of Imperial Russia's Aggression in China*), (1954; reprint, Taiwan, 1968).
Xu Guoqi. "The Age of Innocence: The First World War and China's Quest for National Identity," Harvard University Ph.D. Dissertation, 1999.
Yakhontoff, Victor A. *The Chinese Soviets* (New York: Coward-McCann, Inc., 1934).

Vishwanathan, Savitri. *Normalization of Japanese-Soviet Relations, 1945-1970* (Tallahassee, FL: The Diplomatic Press, 1973).

Walworth, Arthur. *America's Moment: 1918, American Diplomacy at the End of World War I* (New York: W.W.Norton & Company, Inc, 1977).

_____. *Woodrow Wilson* (New York: W.W. Norton & Company, 1978).

White, Wm. Allen. *Woodrow Wilson: The Man, His Times And His Task* (New York: Houghton-Mifflin, 1924).

Wilson, Edith Bolling. *My Memoir* (New York: The Bobbs-Merrill Company, 1939).

Yamato Ichihashi. *The Washington Conference and After* (New York: AMS Press, 1969).

Zhang Yongjin. *China in the International System, 1918-20: The Middle Kingdom at the Periphery* (London: Macmillan, 1991).

# *Index*

American Chamber of Commerce 21, 31*n*.41, 113
April 1919 Communiqué 44, 156
Asia. *See* Far East
August 14, 1945 Sino-Soviet Treaty of Friendship and Alliance.
 *See* Treaties, 14 August 1945 Sino-Soviet Treaty of Friendship and Alliance.
Australia 53
Austria 21-22, 24, 28-29, 33-34, 39-40, 44, 94, 96, 130
Autonomous Three Eastern Provinces. *See* Zhang Zuolin

Baker, Ray Stannard 2, 5, 124, 133*n*.59
Balfour, Arthur 82-83, 106-108, 122-124
Beijing Daily News 128
Beijing Government.
 *See* China, Beijing government
Beijing Soviet-Japanese Talks 165-167
Benson, Shepherd 58, 60
Bianco, Lucien 138
Big Three Leaders 2, 8, 29, 69, 77-80, 93, 111, 122
Bliss, Tasker 5, 58, 75, 125, 133*n*.59
Bolsheviks 3, 21, 74, 89, 104, 130, 135-137, 139-140, 142-143, 145-149, 155-158, 160, 164-165, 168, 170, 175-176, 178, 180.
 *Also see* Soviet Russia
Bolshevism 53, 74-75, 90, 142, 150

Boxer Indemnity 22, 34, 94, 96, 102, 143, 157-158
Briand-Kellogg Pact.
 *See* Kellogg-Briang Pact
Bryan, William J. 11, 16
Bullitt, William C. 179

Cai Hesen 146
Changchun Soviet-Japanese Talks 165
Chen Duxiu 22, 103-104, 107, 135-137, 140, 142-147, 150
Chen Gongbo 145-147
Ch'en, Jerome 136-137
Chiang Kai-shek 180
Chicherin, Georgii 168
Chinda, Sutemi 48, 54, 63, 68, 75, 112-113, 119
China
 Beijing government 4, 12, 16-17, 36, 38-39, 43-44, 46, 49, 56, 60, 89, 93-94, 105-107, 118, 122, 130, 131*n*.22, 142, 147, 151, 160, 163-164, 180
 consular jurisdiction.
 *See* extraterriality
 declaration of war against Germany and Austria 22, 24, 29
 delegation to the Paris Peace Conference 2, 5, 7-8, 10-11, 16, 24, 26, 29, 33-36, 39-44, 46-49, 54-55, 60, 63-64, 66, 69, 77-78, 80, 90, 93-94, 96-98, 100, 103, 105-108, 112, 114, 116, 118, 121-

221

222    INDEX

China. delegation to the Paris Peace Conference (*continued*) 122, 125, 128, 130, 135, 140, 142, 155-156, 175
  11 April 1919 communiqué 44
  extraterritoriality 38, 40, 49, 81, 143, 157-158, 162
  March 1919 Memorandum 44, 47
  preservation of sovereignty 7-8, 10, 22, 39, 42, 58, 69, 73, 76, 80, 82, 84-86, 89-90, 94, 98, 100-102, 118, 120, 124, 127, 155, 160, 162-163, 167
  secret Sino-Japanese agreement of 1918.
    *See* Treaties, September 1918 Sino-Japanese Agreements
  Soviet card, playing 160
  War Participation Bureau 34, 62
Chinese Communist Party 1, 4, 22, 103-105, 107, 135-136, 140, 142-151, 163, 175, 180
Chinese Cultural Revolution 180
Chinese Delegation.
  *See* China, delegation to the Paris Peace Conference
Chinese Eastern Railway (C.E.R.) 4, 135, 139, 143, 156-158, 160-161, 163-165, 168, 170, 172*n*.32, 176-178
Chinese Nationalism 127, 138, 149, 163
Chow Tse-tung 105
Chu, Pao-chin 163
Clemenceau, Georges 41, 55, 77-78, 80, 111, 114, 116, 122-123
Communist International (Comintern) 135-136, 140, 142-143, 145-148, 150, 163, 168
Confucius 42, 47, 97, 137
Council of Four 92*n*.42, 125-126
Council of Three 1, 98

Dalian Concession 179-180
Dalian Soviet-Japanese Talks 165
Dang Shaoyi 35
Darwin, Charles 137
Deane, Hugh 150
Degrees of Separation 108, 140
Democratic-Capitalist Model 1
Dickinson, Frederick 86, 127
Direct Restitution 2-3, 5-6, 13-14, 16, 18, 22, 24, 28, 33, 36, 38, 40-43, 46-48, 55, 60, 62, 65-66, 68, 75-76, 78, 82, 89, 93, 96-98, 103, 107-108, 120-123, 139-140, 142-143, 146, 149, 155-156, 160-161, 163-164, 168, 177
Dov Bing 147
Drysdale 104

East Asia 11, 13, 106, 167, 176-177, 179-180
EP-3 "spy plane" 96
Eto, Shinkichi 89
Europe 1, 3, 14-15, 28, 33-34, 42, 44, 46, 48-49, 53, 96, 100, 106, 108, 111, 137, 144, 146, 156, 160
Extraterritoriality.
  *See* China, extraterritoriality

Face
  gaining 48, 75, 108, 140, 149, 171
  losing 5, 28, 46, 48-49, 65-66, 75, 93-94, 96-97, 100, 107-108, 112-113, 118-119, 122, 124, 140, 149, 160-161, 170-171
Fairbank, John King 138, 144, 152*n*.16
Far East 2, 4, 11-16, 27, 40, 53, 55-56, 58, 64, 66, 69, 74-76, 80, 86, 96, 107, 112, 116, 124, 143, 157-158, 171, 176-177, 179
Far Eastern Republic 158
Feigon, Lee 144
Fifield, Russell 36, 86

Fiume, Dispute over  77, 84, 91*n*.37, 111
Floto, Inga  133*n*.59
Fourteen Points.
  *See* Wilson, Woodrow. Fourteen Points
Fujian Province  16,
France  8, 11, 17, 21-22, 24, 27, 29, 34-35, 43, 47-48, 54-56, 58, 64, 73, 77, 80, 84, 88, 94, 97, 111, 113, 118, 122, 157

Geographical propinquity.
  *See* Lansing-Ishii notes
Germany  1-2, 5, 7-8, 10-18, 20-22, 24, 26-29, 33-34, 36, 39-44, 46-48, 53-56, 58-60, 65, 68-69, 73, 75, 78, 80-82, 85-86, 88-89, 93-94, 96-98, 100, 102, 104, 106-108, 112-114, 120, 130, 137-140, 142, 161, 175-177
Godshall, Wilson  130
Goto, Shimpei  24, 27
Great Britain  8, 10-13, 21-22, 24, 27, 29, 34-35, 42, 47, 53-56, 59-60, 64-65, 77, 80, 84, 94, 97, 103, 111, 113, 122-124, 128, 157, 173*n*.55
Gu Weijun.
  *See* Koo, V. K. Wellington
Guangzhou Government  16-17, 35, 74, 96, 104, 116, 145, 148-149, 164
Guomindang.
  *See* Nationalist Party

Han Suyin  144
Hankey, Maurice  123-124
Harding, Warren G.  162
Harriman, Averell  179
He Weide  17, 34-35, 38
Hornbeck, Stanley K.  4, 58-60, 64-65, 67, 75, 82, 85, 97, 112-114, 116, 118-124, 133*n*.59
House, Edward  58, 85, 125, 133*n*.59
Hughes, Charles  88

Ijuin, Hikokichi  54
Indirect Restitution  2, 5-6, 13, 24, 46-48, 65-66, 76, 89, 93, 97-98, 107-108, 121, 140
Inner Mongolia  13, 16, 166-167
International Financial Consortium  161
International Law  33, 49
Israel, John  138
Italy  8, 21-22, 24, 27, 29, 54-56, 58, 64, 77, 84
Iurin, Ignatii  158
Iyenaga, Toyokichi  53, 102
Izvestiia  142

Japan
  delegation at the Paris Peace Conference  2-3, 5, 8, 24, 26, 28-29, 33, 41, 44, 46, 53-54, 62-66, 69, 74-78, 80-82, 84-85, 88, 94, 97-98, 100, 102, 106, 111-112, 114, 121-123, 128, 133*n*.59, 161, 176
  government  4, 11-18, 20-22, 24, 26-29, 34, 36, 38-39, 41, 48-49, 53-56, 60, 62-64, 69, 74, 76-77, 86, 88-89, 93, 100, 102, 122, 130, 160, 165, 167-168, 172*n*.32, 173*n*.55, 176-179
  Kwantung Army  178
  ultimatum to Germany  11, 15, 28-29, 55
Jiang Jieshi.
  *See* Chiang Kai-shek
Jiaozhou  1-2, 7-8, 10-11, 13, 17-18, 20-21, 33, 40-42, 44, 46-48, 55, 58, 62-63, 65-66, 68-69, 78, 80-81, 88-89, 93, 97-98, 102, 113, 120, 122, 161, 175
Jinan  14, 24, 93, 143, 161
Jiujiang  17
Joffe, Adolf  148, 155, 158, 160, 163-164

Karakhan, Lev  135, 138-139, 143-145, 148-149, 151, 155-161, 163-169, 172$n$.32
Kato, Takaaki  11, 13, 15, 175
Kawamura, Noriko  132$n$.38
Kellogg-Briang Pact  178
Kerr, Philip  123
Kiaochow.
  See Jiaozhou
King, Wunsz  43
Konoye  53-54
Koo, V. K. Wellington (Gu Weijun)  3, 5, 33-39, 41-43, 46-47, 49, 55, 62-64, 73, 78, 80, 107, 116, 118, 121, 123, 128, 131$n$.12, 155-156, 160-161, 163-165, 170, 172$n$.18, 176
Korea  7, 13, 113, 135, 145, 166-167, 176
Korean War  180
Kuo, Thomas C.  143

Lansing, Robert  5, 22-24, 26, 36, 38-39, 41, 48, 58, 68-69, 75, 85-86, 88, 92$n$.42, 92$n$.49, 112-116, 118-125, 127, 133$n$.59, 139-141
Lansing-Ishii notes  22-23
League of Nations  44, 54, 70$n$.6, 74-75, 80, 84, 86, 90, 93, 100, 111, 113, 116, 124-128, 130, 170, 173$n$.55
Lenin, Vladimir  136, 143-146, 148-149, 151, 163
Levine, Marilyn  138, 146
Li Da  136
Li Dazhao  107, 135-137, 140, 142-144, 150
Li Zhisui  96, 109$n$.6
Liang Dunyan  12
Liang Qichao  1, 17-18, 22, 27, 43, 49, 89, 105-107, 111
Liao Zhongkai  149
Liaodong Peninsula  10-11, 27-28, 48
Lloyd George, David  41, 55, 75, 77-78, 80, 111, 123

Lodge, Henry Cabot  127
Lu Xun  136
Lu Zhengxiang  34-35, 63, 78, 80, 97-99, 116
Lu Zhongyu  105
Lüshun  10

MacMurray, John V.A.  5
Makino, Nobuaki  41-43, 46, 54-56, 60, 64, 70$n$.6, 77, 81, 100, 102, 118-123
Manchuria  4, 13, 16, 27, 35, 40, 43, 58, 88, 113, 127, 139, 150, 156-157, 164-165, 166-167, 174, 176, 178-180
Mao Zedong  96, 103-104, 107, 109$n$.6, 144, 151
March 1919 Memorandum.
  See China. March 1919 Memorandum
Maring (Henk Sneevliet)  146-148
Marxism  104, 136-137, 139, 142-145, 147, 150, 163
Matsui, Keishiro  54
May Fourth Movement  1, 94, 103-107, 112, 118-119, 135-140, 142-145, 149-151, 175
McCormick, Vance  4, 84, 111, 128-129, 133$n$.59
Meiji Restoration  40
Meisner, Maurice  142
Mencius  42, 97
*Millard's Review*  106, 111
Millard, Thomas F.  111-112
Mongolia  13-14, 21, 43, 88, 178
  Also see Inner Mongolia, Outer Mongolia
Moseley, George  139
Moses, George H.  126-127
Myth of Equality  1, 4, 10, 16, 18, 21-22, 39-40, 44, 85, 88, 93-94, 96, 106, 113, 130, 136, 139-140, 143, 147, 150-151, 155-158, 160-161, 163-165, 170-171, 175-176, 180

Myth of Wilson's Betrayal 1-2, 38, 138, 140, 142, 150-151, 165, 170-171, 180

Nationalist Party 35, 50n.13, 118, 136, 147-150, 163-164, 180
New Culture Movement 136
*New Youth* 138, 142-143
Nine Power Treaty 161, 168, 170
North, Robert C. 138, 144

October Revolution (1917) 4, 18, 136-137, 142-143, 158, 176-177, 179, 181n.4
*Also see* Soviet Russia, Soviet Union
Ojha, Ishwar C. 150
Okuma, Shigenobu 12
Ono, Yeiji 26
Open Door Policy 10, 12-14, 16, 18, 20, 22-23, 30n.20, 89, 98, 113, 130, 162, 177, 179-180
Orlando, Vittorio 41, 55
Outer Mongolia 13-15, 18, 21-22, 163-164, 167, 170, 176

Paikes, Aleksandr 158, 167
Paris Peace Conference 1-8, 11, 18, 22, 24, 26-27, 29, 33-34, 35-36, 38-39, 41-42, 44, 46-48, 53-56, 59, 62-63, 75-77, 84-85, 89-90, 93-94, 98, 100, 102-104, 106-107, 113, 119, 124, 126, 128, 130, 136-138, 142-143, 146, 148-150, 156-157, 160-163, 165-168, 175, 177-178, 180
Peking University 103, 135, 138, 142, 144
Phillips, William 92n.42
Pichon, Stephen-Jean-Marie 55, 131n.12
Polk, Frank L. 160
Portsmouth Peace Treaty 10, 13, 165-168, 176-177
Pugach, Noel H. 138

Qingdao 10-12, 14, 17, 21, 24, 27-28, 53, 59, 63, 65-66, 81-82, 93, 100, 104, 113, 120, 143, 161

Red Army.
*See* Soviet Russia, Red Army
Reinsch, Paul 12, 14-15, 22, 39-40, 62, 74, 86, 103, 114, 119
Rice, Edward E. 144
Russell H. Fifield 36
Russo-Japanese War 10, 27, 177

Saich, Tony 139, 153n.49
Saionji, Kimmochi 54
Schell, Orville 149
Schurmann, Franz 149
Schurman, Jacob Gould 108, 144
Schwartz, Benjamin 145
Scramble for Concessions 8, 14
Secret Agreements, 1918.
*See* Treaties, September 1918 Sino-Japanese Agreements
Shandong Concession 4-5, 8, 10-15, 17-18, 20-22, 24, 26-29, 33-34, 36, 40-41, 43, 46-48, 54, 56, 60, 64-65, 68-69, 75, 81, 86, 89-90, 93-94, 96-98, 100, 107, 112, 124, 130, 142-143, 148, 160, 162, 175, 177
Shandong Peninsula 1, 12, 82, 98, 100, 102
Shandong Question 1-8, 26-29, 38-41, 43, 48-49, 54, 56, 58-59, 64, 68-70, 74-77, 80, 91n.37, 100, 105, 107-108, 111, 116, 128, 132n.38, 136-138, 156-157, 161-162, 164, 170-171, 175, 177, 179-181
Shandong Railway 11-12, 14, 26, 38, 40, 42, 59, 68, 139, 157, 160-164, 172n.32
Shandong Resolution 85, 94, 97-98, 102-103, 105-107, 111, 113-114, 116, 118-119, 122, 124-125, 128, 135-136, 138, 140, 142, 145, 148-150, 155-156, 160, 163, 170

226  INDEX

Sharp, William G. 19, 35
Shen Ruilin 168-169
Shimonoseki, Treaty of.
  *See* Treaties, 1894 Sino-Japanese Treaty of Shimonoseki
Siberia 53, 113, 136, 158, 179
Sino-Japanese War 4, 11, 27, 177
Sino-Soviet Treaties 165, 167, 170
Sneevliet, Henk.
  *See* Maring
Soong, T. V. 180
South Manchurian Railway 157, 168, 176
Soviet Government 130, 135-136, 138-139, 142, 147, 151, 155, 157-158, 162-165, 167-168, 170, 176-180
Soviet Russia 3, 90, 103, 130, 135-140, 142, 145-146, 149, 155-158, 160, 163, 168, 175
  propaganda in China 2, 63, 105, 135-136, 139, 142, 149-150, 157, 165, 168, 179
  Red Army 135, 157
  Red Influence in China 174, 178
Soviet Union 1, 3-6, 96, 136, 139, 148-151, 155-156, 162-165, 167-168, 170-171, 174-180
Spheres of Influence/Interest 1, 4, 10, 13, 31n.41, 38, 112-113, 118, 155, 162, 167-168, 170, 176-177
Stalin, Joseph 179-180
Stead, Wickham 91n.37
Sun Yat-sen 16-17, 34-35, 74, 96, 136, 140, 147-150, 163-164
Sun Zhongshan.
  *See* Sun yat-sen
Sze, Sao-ke Alfred 34-35, 64

Taiwan 16, 50n.13, 118
Teng, Ssu-yu 144
*The Manchester Guardian* 46
Tibet 43
Tokyo Soviet-Japanese Talks 165

Treaties
  1894 Sino-Japanese Treaty of Shimonoseki 27
  5 March 1917 Russo-Japanese Secret Treaty 22
  14 August 1945 Sino-Soviet Treaty of Friendship and Alliance 180
  6 March 1917 Franco-Japanese Secret Treaty 22
  7 June 1915 Sino-Russian-Mongol Tripartite Treaty (1915) 21
  13 April 1941 Soviet-Japanese Non-aggression Pact 177-179
  20 January 1925 Soviet-Japanese Convention 168, 176, 178-179
  24/28 September 1918 Sino-Japanese Agreements 27, 33, 39, 41, 43-44, 62-63
  28 March 1917 Italian-Japanese Secret Treaty 22
  25 May 1915 Sino-Japanese Twenty-one Demands 5, 8, 14-22, 24, 26, 34-35, 43-44, 60, 63, 76-78, 82, 104, 106, 128, 156, 160, 168, 170
  21 February 1917 British-Japanese Secret Treaty 22
Triple Intervention of 23 April 1895 11, 27-28, 48, 53, 68, 108
Trotsky, Leon 5, 144, 157
Truman, Harry 179
Tsarist Russia 2-4, 8, 10-11, 13-18, 21-22, 24, 27-29, 34-35, 47-48, 54, 56, 64, 74, 90, 103, 113, 130, 135-140, 142-143, 145-146, 148-149, 151, 155-158, 160-168, 170, 175-177, 180
Tumulty, Joseph P. 74, 77, 85-87, 135
Twenty-one Demands.
  *See* Treaties, Twenty-one Demands

Uchida, Viscount 102
United Front Policy 136, 147-150, 162-164

INDEX 227

United States Senate Committee on Foreign Relations 122, 125-128, 173*n*.55
United States Government 1-2, 5, 12, 16, 48
United States State Department 5, 35, 38, 56, 58, 88-89, 124

Versailles Peace Treaty 66, 96, 112, 114, 116-117, 121-122, 125, 128, 130, 140, 142, 150
Vilenskii, Vladimir 139, 142, 157, 159
Vladivostok 143
Voitinskii, Gregorii 143-146

Wang, C. T.
 *See* Wang Zhengting
Wang Zhengting 3, 34-35, 62, 64, 116, 118, 155-156, 164-165, 168, 170, 172*n*.32, 177
Washington Conference 7, 22, 160-162, 177
Wei Chenzu 34
Weihaiwei 10
White, Henry 5, 58, 75, 123, 125, 133*n*.59
Whiting, Allen S. 140
Wilbur, C. Martin 149
Williams, Edward T. 4, 58-60, 64-67, 69, 75-76, 82, 85-86, 92*n*.50, 97, 133*n*.59

Wilson, Woodrow 1-6, 8, 12, 17, 19, 22, 24, 28-29, 33, 36-39, 41-42, 49, 54-56, 58-60, 64-66, 68-70, 70*n*.6, 73-78, 80-90, 91*n*.37, 93-94, 96-100, 103-108, 111-116, 118-119, 121, 123-130, 132*n*.38, 133*n*.59, 135-138, 140-141, 144, 146, 148-151, 160, 162-163, 165, 168, 170, 175, 180-181
 Fourteen Points 39, 41, 74, 92*n*.50, 94, 98
Wood. G. Zay 7
World War I 1-2, 4, 11, 13, 21-22, 34, 39-40, 54, 69, 77, 91*n*.37, 105-106, 137, 142, 167, 177, 179
World War II 2, 4, 70*n*.6, 162, 177, 179

Xinjiang 176, 178
Xu, President of China 63, 105, 114, 116, 118

Yakhontoff, Victor A. 145
Yalta Agreement 179-180
Yellow Peril 80
Yoshizawa, Kenkichi 166-167
Yuan Shikai 16-17, 21, 35

Zao Julin 105
Zhang Silin 158
Zhang Yongjin 155, 170
Zhang Zongxiang 24-25, 26-27, 60, 105
Zhang Zuolin 4, 164-165
Zhou Enlai 144

## About the Author

**Bruce A. Elleman** completed a bachelor's degree at the University of California at Berkeley, a master's degree in Russian history at Columbia University, a master's degree in International history at London School of Economics, and a doctorate in Russian and Chinese history at Columbia University. He has also earned certificates from Columbia University's East Asian Institute and Harriman Institute. Dr. Elleman has spent three years in China and Taiwan, one year in Russia, and two years in Japan engaged in research and language study. He is an Associate Professor in the Strategic Research Department, U.S. Naval War College, Newport, R.I.